ACCA

NEW SYLLABUS
PRACTICE & REVISION KIT

Paper 2.1

Information Systems

BPP Publishing
August 2001

First edition August 2001

ISBN 0 7517 0788 0

British Library Cataloguing-in-Publication Data
A catalogue record for this book
is available from the British Library

Published by

BPP Publishing Limited
Aldine House, Aldine Place
London W12 8AW

www.bpp.com

Printed in Great Britain by W M Print
47-47 Frederick Street
Walsall
Wes Midlands
WS2 9NE

We are grateful to the Association of Chartered Certified Accountants for permission to reproduce past examination questions. The answers to past examination questions have been prepared by BPP Publishing Limited.

CONTENTS

BPP
PUBLISHING

Question and answer checklist/index

The headings in this checklist/index indicate the main topics of questions, but questions often cover several different topics.

Preparation questions, listed in italics, provide you with a firm foundation for attempts at exam-standard questions.

Questions preceded by * are **key questions** which we think you must attempt in order to pass the exam. Tick them off on this list as you complete them.

Questions set under the old syllabus *Information Analysis* paper are included because their content is similar to those which will appear in the Paper 2.1 exam.

PART C: EVALUATING INFORMATION SYSTEMS

Implementation and quality issues

Security and legal compliance

PART D: SCENARIO QUESTIONS

Scenarios

MOCK EXAM 1

Questions 55 to 60

MOCK EXAM 2 (PILOT PAPER)

Questions 61 to 66

BPP PUBLISHING

TOPIC INDEX

Listed below are the key Paper 2.1 topics and the numbers of the questions in this Kit covering those topics.

If you need to concentrate your practice and revision on certain topics or if you want to attempt all available questions that refer to a particular subject (be they preparation, exam-standard or case study/scenario-based questions), you will find this index useful.

BPP
PUBLISHING

BPP PUBLISHING

THE EXAM PAPER

The examination is a **three hour paper** divided into **two sections**.

		Number of Marks
Section A:	3 compulsory questions (20 marks each)	60
Section B:	Choice of 2 from 3 questions (20 marks each)	40
		100

Section A is based on a short narrative scenario. This section will have three compulsory questions from across the syllabus linked to the narrative scenario. Each question will be worth 20 marks giving a total of 60 marks for this section.

Section B contains three independent questions, one question from each main area of the syllabus. Each question is worth 20 marks. The candidate must answer two questions giving a total of 40 marks for this section.

Additional information

The examination does not assume any use of any systems development methodology. Practical questions will be set in such a way that they that they can be answered by any methodology. However the following examples of models may be useful:

Syllabus heading	*Example models*
Documenting and modelling user requirements – processes	Data Flow Diagram Flowchart
Documenting and modelling user requirements – static structures	Entity-relationship model Object Class model
Documenting and modelling user requirements – events	Entity Life History State Transition Diagram

Analysis of pilot paper

Section A scenario

Insurance company has developed an unsatisfactory information system
1   Project risk assessment
2   Solving and preventing system problems
3   Quality assurance and testing in systems development

Section B (Two from three questions at 20 marks each)

4   Outsourcing; Legacy systems; Project management software
5   Systems analysis interviews; Event model construction
6   Post-implementation review; Measuring software effectiveness; Controlling change

HOW TO PASS PAPER 2.1

Revising with this Kit

A confidence boost

To boost your morale and to give yourself a bit of confidence, **start** your practice and revision with a topic that you find **straightforward**. The **preparation questions** are either relatively easy, or shorter than those you will face in the exam.

Key questions

Then try as many as possible of the **exam-standard questions**. Obviously the more questions you do, the more likely you are to pass the exam. But at the very least you should attempt the **key questions** that are highlighted in the questions and answer checklist/index at the front of the Kit.

No cheating

Produce **full answers** under **timed conditions**; practising exam technique is just as important as recalling knowledge. Produce answer plans if you are running short of time.

Imagine you're the marker

It's a good idea to actually **mark your answers**. Don't be tempted to give yourself marks for what you meant to put down, or what you would have put down if you had time. And don't get despondent if you didn't do very well. Refer to the **topic index** and try another question that covers the same subject.

Ignore them at your peril

Read the **Tutor's hints** in the questions. They are there to help you. (Other 'Tutor's hints' are included in the answers to explain the approach taken in the suggested solution.)

Trial run for the big day

Then, when you think you can successfully answer questions on the whole syllabus, attempt the **two mock exams** at the end of the Kit. You will get the most benefit by sitting them under strict exam conditions, so that you gain experience of the four vital exam processes.

- Selecting questions
- Deciding on the order in which to attempt them
- Managing your time
- Producing answers

CURRENT ISSUES

Recent articles

The content of relevant articles published before February 2001 is reflected in the BPP Study Text for *Information Systems*. Articles published since then which are of direct relevance to the syllabus are listed below.

'The software package approach to information systems development', Steve Skidmore, *Student Accountant,* March 2001.

'Information systems – the objectives of the new examination', Steve Skidmore, *Student Accountant,* June/July 2001.

USEFUL WEBSITES

The websites below provide additional sources of information of relevance to your studies for *Information Systems*.

- ACCA   www.accaglobal.com
- BPP   www.bpp.com
- Financial Times   www.ft.com
- Project Manager Today   www.projectnet.co.uk
- US based Project Management Institute   www.pmi.org
- Computer and Internet terminology   www.pcwebopaedia.com

SYLLABUS MINDMAP

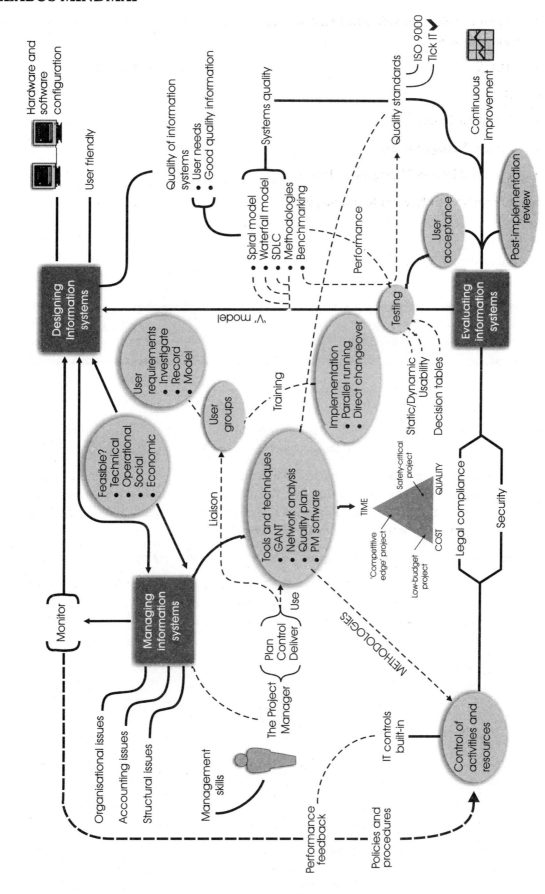

OXFORD BROOKES

The standard required of candidates completing Part 2 is that required in the final year of a UK degree. Students completing Parts 1 and 2 will have satisfied the examination requirement for an honours degree in Applied Accounting, awarded by Oxford Brookes University.

To achieve the degree, you must also submit two pieces of work based on a **Research and Analysis Project.**

- A 5,000 word **Report** on your chosen topic, which demonstrates that you have acquired the necessary research, analytical and IT skills.

- A 1,500 word **Key Skills Statement**, indicating how you have developed your interpersonal and communication skills.

BPP was selected by the ACCA to produce the official text *Success in your Research and Analysis Project* to support students in this task. The book pays particular attention to key skills not covered in the professional examinations.

> AN ORDER FORM FOR THE NEW SYLLABUS MATERIAL, INCLUDING THE OXFORD BROOKES PROJECT TEXT, CAN BE FOUND AT THE END OF THIS KIT.

MBA

Plans for a new joint MBA have been announced by the ACCA and Oxford Brookes University. This new qualification will be available worldwide from 2001.

It follows the existing agreement between ACCA and Oxford Brookes to offer ACCA students the opportunity to qualify for BSc in Applied Accounting. Both institutions have now agreed to strengthen links through the development of a postgraduate qualification designed for ACCA members. Preliminary work has begun on the new MBA.

For further information, please see the ACCA's website: www.accaglobal.com

Questions

> **MANAGING INFORMATION SYSTEMS**
>
> Questions 1 to 14 cover the 'Managing Information Systems' area of the syllabus, the subject of Part A of the BPP Study Text for Paper 2.1.
>
> Further questions on these subject areas are included in the Scenario Questions and the Mock Exams in this Kit – refer to the topic index on pages (vi) – (x).

1   PREPARATION QUESTION: IT AS A STRATEGIC RESOURCE   *27 mins*

The proposition that information technology is now a strategic resource and should be managed as such, tends to revolve around such factors as costs, needs, opportunities, all-pervasiveness, stakeholders and management support systems.

Required

Explain how each of these factors might be used to support such an argument.   **(15 marks)**

2   INFORMATION SYSTEMS STRATEGY   *36 mins*

Many major organisations use formal strategies to identify development priorities for information systems (IS).

Required

(a) Discuss the reason for this.   (10 marks)
(b) What are the major stages in the development of an IS strategy?   (10 marks)

     (20 marks)

3   BUSINESS AND IS/IT STRATEGY ALIGNMENT   *36 mins*

The XF Company Limited manufactures a limited range of domestic electrical products for use in kitchens including washing machines, fridges and cookers. The Board is currently considering expanding activities to produce other electronic entertainment systems such as televisions and DVD players (which are produced by most of the company's main competitors).

The XF Company's mission statement is to '*produce high quality domestic electrical goods at an affordable price*'. The company will need extra funds to finance this expansion and will need to approach the bank for a loan. It appears that a significant investment in IT and plant and machinery will also be needed.

Required

Explain the steps that the Board of XF need to undertake in order to provide a strategic analysis of their Company and produce a gap analysis for the new investment.   **(20 marks)**

Guidance note

Ensure your answer emphasises strategic issues - otherwise you may find you focus on a few of the things that the directors must do, such as approaching the bank, without seeing the 'big picture'. Plan your answer to ensure all stages of the gap analysis are included.

BPP
PUBLISHING

4   PREPARATION QUESTION: IT EXPENDITURE   *27 mins*

Discuss the following propositions.

(a) Information technology in an organisation should be regarded as an investment opportunity rather than an expense.   (6 marks)

(b) Information technology services should be run as a business within a business and managed as a profit centre, using an appropriate chargeout technique.   (9 marks)

(15 marks)

5   PREPARATION QUESTION: DECENTRALISATION AND END-USERS

27 mins

The trends towards distributed data processing and end-user computing can have a significant effect on the structure of information technology in an organisation.

Required

(a) (i)   Analyse the advantages and disadvantages of centralisation and decentralisation of information technology to a large organisation.

(ii)   Suggest some information technology activities which, despite the trend towards decentralisation, might best be carried out centrally.   (8 marks)

(b) (i)   Explain why end-user computing is increasing and suggest examples of activities which end-users might be responsible for.

(ii)   What impact might end-user computing have on the organisation of the information technology function?   (7 marks)

(15 marks)

6   OUTSOURCING; DEPARTMENT STRUCTURE   *36 mins*

A large insurance company is currently reviewing the way its information system are provided. The company has traditionally developed its own systems in-house and the current Information Systems (IS) department has 250 staff and is headed by the IS director.

(a) External consultants have suggested that the company should consider outsourcing technical support, the user help desk and new systems development. The IS department would remain in a smaller form and would mainly maintain established systems.

Required

Explain what is meant by outsourcing, and describe, from the perspective of an outsourcer (such as the insurance company), *four* advantages and *three* disadvantages of outsourcing.   (15 marks)

(b) The IS director, alarmed by the consultants' suggestions, has put forward an alternative proposal. He has suggested that the traditional hierarchical organisation of the department be replaced by a flat structure. Several management posts will be lost in this re-structuring and this will bring immediate cost savings.

Required

Explain what is meant by a 'flat structure' and why a 'flat structure' is particularly appropriate to an IS department.   (5 marks)

(20 marks)

7   CENTRALISED V DECENTRALISED   *36 mins*

AB plc is a national freight distribution company with a head office, five regional offices and a hundred local depots spread throughout the country. It is planning a major computerisation project. The options which are being considered are as follows.

(a)   A central mainframe system with terminals at each depot.
(b)   Distributed minicomputers at each regional office.

Required

Draft a report to the board of AB plc describing the ways in which each of the options would suit the company's structure and explaining the advantages and disadvantages of each.   **(20 marks)**

8   PREPARATION QUESTION: FEASIBILITY   *27 mins*

(a)   Many organisations undertake a feasibility study before taking the decision to commit to a full-scale systems development.

Required

(i)   Describe the main objectives of the study.
(ii)   Explain the different types of feasibility it will consider.   (9 marks)

(b)   A feasibility study will often commence with the terms of reference.

Required

Briefly explain (with examples) *three* elements that are usually defined within the terms of reference.   (6 marks)

                                                                        (15 marks)

9   PREPARATION QUESTION: CRITICAL PATH   *27 mins*

The diagram below shows a project plan for a systems development project. The project plan is shown in both 'activity on node' and 'activity on arrow' conventions.

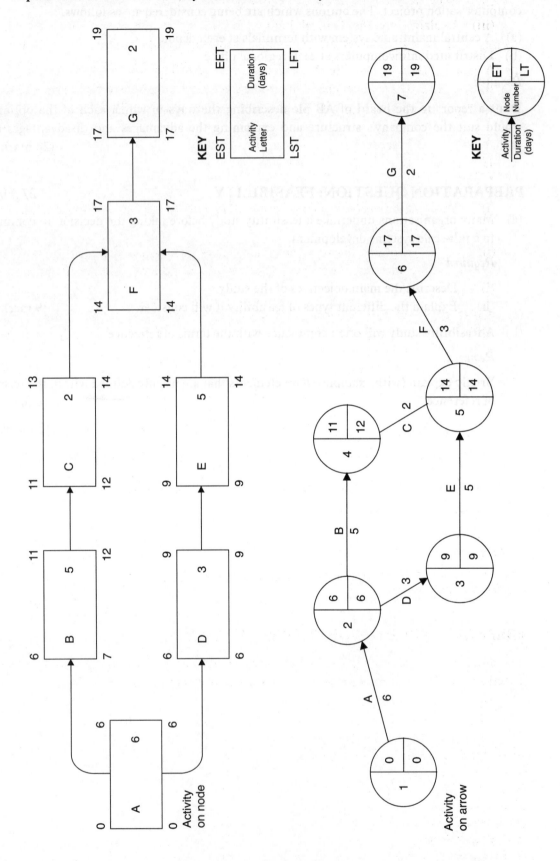

Required

(a) (i) What is the meaning of the term Critical Path?   (2 marks)

     (ii) What activities lie in the Critical Path of this project?   (1 mark)

     (iii) Explain why the Critical Path is significant to the project manager when allocating resources and monitoring the progress of the project.   (2 marks)

(b) A mistake has been found in the original project plan. The precedences for activities A, B, C, D, E, F, G are unchanged but two new activities now have to be added. No other activities are affected by the inclusion of the two new activities. These are:

Activity	Precedence	Duration
H	D	4 days
I	H	8 days

     (i) Re-draw the network (using the notation you are familiar with) amending it to reflect these changes.   (4 marks)

     (ii) In the re-drawn network, how many days (if any) could activity E over-run without affecting the overall duration of the project? Assume that no other activities over-run.   (2 marks)

(c) A manager looks at the network and suggests that B will almost certainly have to be re-worked after the completion of C. He suggests that this fragment of the network should be re-drawn as follows.

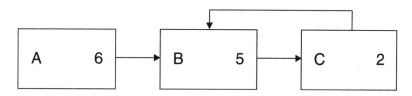

     Explain why this is not acceptable and show how such re-work should be represented in the project network.   (4 marks)

(15 marks)

Guidance note

You may find it helpful to produce a quick plan for the network - to check your logic and to enable you to produce a neat 'final' network.

10   PREPARATION QUESTION: NETWORK CHART   *27 mins*

The following activities, time estimates and precedences have been identified for the selection, purchase and implementation of a software package.

	Activity	Precedence	Estimate (days)
A	Define Project Initiation Document	-	5
B	Define requirements	A	8
C	Define training plan	B	3
D	Issue Invitation to Tender	B	3
E	Select Supplier	D	2
F	Install hardware and software	E	5
G	Training course	C,F	3
H	Enter master file data	G	5
I	Convert operational data	F	9
J	Parallel running	H,I	10

BPP PUBLISHING

Required

(a) (i)   Construct a network chart for this project.   (6 marks)

Based on your network chart:

(ii)   What is the elapsed time of the project (in days)?   (2 marks)

(iii)   What are critical activities (the critical path) of the project?   (2 marks)

(iv)   How many days could activity H overrun without affecting the overall duration of the project? Assume that no other activities overrun.

(2 marks)

(b)   Briefly describe how project management software can assist in developing the initial project plan.   (3 marks)

(15 marks)

11   FEASIBILITY STUDY   *36 mins*

An important step in the implementation of any computer system is the feasibility study. Senior staff in an organisation may be unconvinced of the value of the study.

Required

(a)   Briefly explain what is meant by a computer feasibility study, and what such a study should achieve.   (3 marks)

(b)   Give a justification for each of the main sections which should be contained in the feasibility study report.   (5 marks)

(c)   Identify three members of a 'typical' feasibility study team, and provide a one sentence description of their role.   (3 marks)

(d)   Comment briefly on the suggestion that if a special purpose package is to be purchased, then there is no need for such a study.   (3 marks)

(e)   List four major factors which might justify the introduction of a computer system for production planning and scheduling in a manufacturing company.   (6 marks)

(20 marks)

12   PROJECT COSTS AND BENEFITS   *36 mins*

A project feasibility study presented to senior management must always contain a detailed 'cost justification' for any proposed computer system.

Required

Describe the costs and benefits relevant to this analysis.   **(20 marks)**

Guidance note

Costs can be categorised as one-off or recurring - explain why this distinction is important.

Benefits may be measurable or may be intangible. Explain how a financial value may be placed on benefits.

13   PROJECT INITIATION

36 *mins*

Project management in the ABC company

Dave is the project manager in-charge of a project team installing new software in the ABC Company. The installation is currently three weeks behind schedule, with only seven weeks left before the installation should be complete. Due to the time constraints, Dave has cancelled all project meetings to try and focus his team on meeting the project deadlines. While this action has had some slight improvement in the amount of work being carried out, members of the team have been complaining that they cannot discuss problems easily. Most of the team are professional staff with appropriate project management qualifications.

Over the last week, both of the systems analysts have left to move onto other assignments due to double bookings by the project management company. This did not help the morale of the remaining team members. To try and compensate for the lack of staff, the project manager has asked two other team members with a small amount of systems analysis experience to continue their jobs. To try and impress upon them the seriousness of the situation, Dave also made these members responsible for any mistakes in the analysis documentation.

In the last few days, the working situation in the team has become significantly worse, with many minor quarrels and disagreements breaking out. Dave has chosen to ignore these problems, and simply asked the team to focus on completing the project.

Required

(a)   Identify and explain where the ABC Company project is being poorly managed.

(10 marks)

(b)   Explain how the project manager can help resolve these difficulties.   (10 marks)

(20 marks)

Guidance note

You may find it easier to structure your answer with headings for each problem you identify, and then in two separate paragraphs, answer the two parts of the question. This should ensure that actions to resolve the problem are included in your answer.

14   CRITICAL PATH ANALYSIS

36 *mins*

The Board of the Mutley organisation are considering establishing a web site to sell their products. The Mutley organisation specialises in the selling of garden plants and furniture; none of the Board has any Internet selling experience. However, they have noticed that many organisations now have Internet sites and think that Mutley should follow suit.

Most of the stock information, which will be needed for the on-line ordering section of the Internet site, is already held on a personal computer in the accounts office. However, the package is DOS based any may not be compatible with current Internet database packages. The staff at Mutley are taking a significant interest in the project, and would like to be consulted on the establishment of the Internet site. Based on this information, the Finance Director prepared the following summary of the tasks necessary to establish the Internet site.

Activity	Description	Duration (weeks)	Proceeding activities
A	Agree company vision and objectives for Internet site	3	-
B	Prepare full analysis of existing systems	6	A
C	Prepare and send out ITT document	1	B
D	Obtain additional detail regarding user requirements	6	B
E	Review ITT responses and appoint supplier	1	C
F	Supplier writes web-site	7	D, E
G	Prepare data for transfer	3	D
H	Install new hardware	3	D, E
J	Test web site	2	F
K	Live test	1	G, H, J

Required

(a) Prepare a CPA from the information prepared by the finance director, stating the critical path. (14 marks)

(b) Briefly explain one other techniques that can be used to monitor the *progress* of a project. (6 marks)

(20 marks)

Guidance note

This is a fairly standard question on critical path analysis. Remember the need for dummy activities to join what appear to be difficult gaps in the network. In part (b), note the emphasis on the word *monitor*, it is this area that you need to think about and discuss in your answer.

DESIGNING INFORMATION SYSTEMS

Questions 15 to 33 cover the 'Designing Information Systems' area of the syllabus, the subject of Part B of the BPP Study Text for Paper 2.1.

Further questions on these subject areas are included in the Scenario Questions and the Mock Exams in this Kit – refer to the topic index on pages (vi) – (x).

15   SYSTEMS INVESTIGATION   *36 mins*

Investigating and documenting the current business system is one of the stages of the systems development life cycle.

Required

(a) Briefly explain three reasons why it is important that the analyst should investigate and document the current business system.   (8 marks)

(b) Briefly describe four methods or models used in investigating and documenting the current business system.   (12 marks)

                                                                          (20 marks)

Guidance note

This question asks for specific numbers of areas to be discussed in each section. Spend roughly equal amounts of time on each item - to ensure you pick-up the 'easier' marks available for each area.

16   NEW SYSTEM IMPLEMENTATION   *36 mins*

A new company is to be formed by the merger of two existing organisations to set up a national chain of cash and carry retail shops for cut-price furniture and kitchen units. A characteristic of the company policy is to be centralised stock control, with small local stocks and twice-weekly deliveries to each store. As management accountant you have been nominated as a member of a feasibility study team being formed to evaluate the proposals from different manufacturers for the supply of computer hardware and software to implement the required information system.

Required

(a) State who you would expect to see as the other members of a feasibility study team of five.   (2 marks)

(b) Identify the major information requirements of the system.   (4 marks)

(c) Describe the principal stages involved in the implementation of the proposed system in the 100 shops already open for business which, at present, operate rather different systems.   (10 marks)

(d) Explain the criteria used to evaluate the choice of system.   (4 marks)

                                                                          (20 marks)

17   STAGES OF A SYSTEMS DEVELOPMENT PROJECT   *36 mins*

Required

Identify and briefly describe the major stages in a computer systems development project.

                                                                          (20 marks)

11

18   SYSTEMS DEVELOPMENT LIFECYCLE   *36 mins*

WRF Inc trades in a dynamic environment where it is essential that information is presented quickly and clearly to its staff. The information can come from the company's database or from other staff members. Significant processing of the information is also required on each individual's Personal Computer (PC) before effective decisions can be made.

WRF Inc intends to upgrade its computer system to improve speed and clarity of information. Each member of staff will have a PC linked to a Local Area Network (LAN). Each PC will run *Windows 98* and a word processor and spreadsheet on its local hard disk. The network will be used for centralised backup, access to a central database, and storage of data files. The LAN will also be used for communication within the office by E-mail.

The system analyst in charge of the project thinks that users will require a Pentium processor running at 75 megahertz with 16 megabytes of RAM. The network will incorporate a central file server and run at a low baud rate. He is pleased that the system will cost only $US 1,500 per user (about £1,000). The systems analyst is on a fixed term contract which terminates when the system installation is complete.

Users have broadly welcomed the move although they have not been formally told of the system change. The requisitioning department of WRF Inc has now questioned the order for the computer hardware and software because of lack of authorisation from the Board.

Required

Write a report to the Board that briefly explains the Systems Development Life Cycle (SDLC) and explains why the SDLC would be preferred to the situation outlined above as a means of providing a system changeover for WRF Inc.   **(20 marks)**

19   PREPARATION QUESTION: CASE TOOLS   *27 mins*

Required

(a)   Explain what a CASE tool is.   (3 marks)

(b)   The following issues are important in systems development.

- Producing and maintaining documentation
- Adhering to development standards
- Maintaining a logical data dictionary
- Prototyping

With reference to the four issues above, explain what advantages a CASE tool offers the systems developer compared to systems development using manually produced and maintained diagrams, standards and documents.   (12 marks)

(15 marks)

20   STRUCTURED APPROACH/CASE TOOLS   *36 mins*

Required

(a)   Most large organisations use a 'structured' approach in the development of information systems. Describe the main stages in such an approach.   (12 marks)

(b)   Define 'CASE tool', and explain what contributions can a CASE tool make to the development of information systems?   (8 marks)

(20 marks)

21   WATERFALL MODEL
36 mins

The Niagara Organisation specialises in the production of trainers and similar sports shoes. The organisation has grown rapidly in terms of turnover and complexity of manufacturing systems during the past three years, and is currently updating or replacing many of its computer systems. This update is only partly complete, and will continue for the next two years.

The accounting system within the organisation is nine years old and is about to be replaced. The existing system runs off a central mainframe with four terminals. The proposed system will have a central database with ten on-line PC's all connected to the same LAN.

The directors have agreed that to save system development time, a model of software development based on the waterfall approach, will be used. Consequently, the new software will have similar functionality to the current system. However, it is known that a new manufacturing system will be available before the new accounting system is complete. Unfortunately, the accounting system will already have been specified at this time, and so it will not be amended to take account of the new requirements.

The accounts staff are also very busy, and will only have time to discuss system design towards the end of each month when the previous months' processing of accounting data and report production is complete.

Required

Explain the limitations of the use of the Waterfall model of software development within the Niagara Organisation, briefly suggesting alternative approaches that will remove these limitations.   **(20 marks)**

Guidance note

Check the question requirement carefully – you must focus on the **limitations** of the waterfall model, not simply explain the model. You should be able to come up with ideas regarding what is needed to make systems development in this situation more appropriate.

22   PREPARATION QUESTION: ENTITY RELATIONSHIP MODEL: ENTITY LIFE HISTORY
27 mins

The following two models may appear in a structured systems lifecycle:

- Entity Relationship Model (or Logical Data Structure)
- Entity Life History

Required

(a) Briefly describe the purpose and notation of each of these models.   (10 marks)

(b) What benefits would there be if the two models were created and maintained with a CASE tool?   (5 marks)

(15 marks)

23   PREPARATION QUESTION: ENTITY RELATIONSHIP MODEL   *27 mins*

A normalised entity-relationship model (logical data model) has been produced for a structured walkthrough (Figure 1). The model consists of an entity-relationship diagram (logical data structure) and a set of normalised tables that define the entity types and their relationships.

The walkthrough is concerned with agreeing the business rules of the application before the system is designed and developed. You have been asked to attend this walkthrough to help establish whether the model does correctly represent the business requirements of the organisation.

Figure 1 Normalised entity-relationship model (logical data structure)

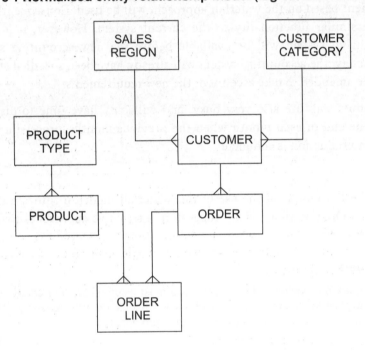

Normalised tables	
PRODUCT TYPE:	**Product-type-code**, product-type-description
PRODUCT:	**Product-code**, price, product-description
ORDER LINE:	**Product-code, order-no**, order-quantity, *customer-no
ORDER:	**Order-no**, order-date, *customer-no
CUSTOMER:	**Customer-no**, name, address, *region-code, *customer-category-code
SALES REGION:	**Region-code**, region-description
CUSTOMER CATEGORY:	**Customer-category-code**, customer-category-description
Key:	
ENTITY TYPE NAME:	**Keyfield**, *foreign-key-field, other-fields

Required

(a) Briefly explain the notation of the entity-relationship model (logical data structure).

(5 marks)

(b) Prior to the walkthrough you have spotted two errors in the model. The first is in the PRODUCT entity and the second in the ORDER LINE entity.

Identify each error and explain how it should be corrected.   (4 marks)

(c) At the walkthrough one of the users asked the following question.

'We are constantly re-categorising our customers. Will it be possible to show a history for each customer showing what category they are in now and what categories they used to be in with the date they changed category and a brief explanation of why that category change was made?' The user provides an example of her requirement.

Customer-no	Customer Category Code	Effective date	Reason for change
13245	A	12/12/2000	New account
	B	03/04/2001	Increased sales
	C	14/09/2001	Increased sales - better margins
	B	17/11/2001	Reduced sales
15675	A	13/01/2001	New account
	B	06/07/2001	Target account

Explain why the entity-relationship model (Figure 1) does not support this requirement and explain what changes would have to be made to accommodate this business requirement.   (6 marks)

(15 marks)

24 **MODELLING TECHNIQUES**   *36 mins*

Required

(a) Explain the place of

- Process models
- Static Structure models, and
- Events models

In the design of information systems, using an example of each type of model to support comments made in your answer.

Note. You do not have to draw any model.   (14 marks)

(b) Briefly explain the techniques that can be used to ensure that process models accurately reflect user requirements.   (6 marks)

(20 marks)

Guidance note

The Information Systems syllabus includes three different models that are used in the development of information systems. This question is designed to check your understanding of these models. Note the requirement not to draw any model; you just limit your answer to a verbal explanation!

For part (b), try and think how information systems can be checked prior to the physical system being developed; this should give you some ideas for your answer.

25   EVENT MODEL (ENTITY LIFE HISTORY)   *36 mins*

The ROG company manufacturers a wide range of electronic goods with parts being supplied by over 600 different suppliers. New suppliers are added to the authorised suppliers list after a check is made on the quality of goods to be supplied.

Goods are received on a daily basis with payments being made at the end of each month. A few suppliers also purchase electronic equipment from ROG and settle their accounts net of any sales value due to ROG.

Purchases from specific suppliers ceases either when the quality of goods falls or when the product range of ROG changes meaning that parts from that supplier are no longer required.

Required

(a) Explain the difference between the logical and physical design of information systems, briefly explaining the steps involved in physical system design.   (8 marks)

(b) Prepare an event model for supplier accounts in the ROG company.   (7 marks)

(c) Explain the reasons for using an event model in designing information systems.

(5 marks)

(20 marks)

Guidance note

In part (a), remember the distinction between logical and physical models; the logical is the theory and the physical how this theory is actually put into practice.

If you are not sure what an event model is (part (b), then check out the question information. The detail appears to be split over three areas, which indicates that a life history model may be appropriate. Finally for part (c), you can include specific comments about ELH's as well as more general comments on the use of diagrams.

26   PREPARATION QUESTION: DATA FLOW DIAGRAM   *27 mins*

An analyst has recorded the following information at an interview.

Interview 1

Orders are received directly from customers. The order details are checked to ensure that the product and payment-type are valid values. Rejected orders are sent back to the customer. Accepted order details are stored on an order file. At the end of the day, despatch notes are raised for all orders received that day. A copy of the despatch note is sent to the customer and a second copy is sent to the warehouse. The despatch-date is noted on the order file. At the end of the week an invoice is raised and sent to the customer. The invoice-date is noted on the order file.

The analyst has documented this information in the following data flow diagram.

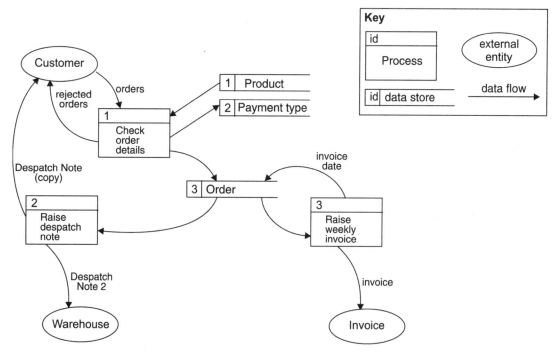

Required

(a)   Identify *three* errors in the diagram and explain how each error should be corrected.

(6 marks)

The analyst undertakes a second interview and records the following information.

Interview 2

The check on product was not understood correctly at the first interview. Only part of the order details check is concerned with ensuring that the product is a valid value. The check also looks to see if there is sufficient of the product in stock to fulfil the order. If not, the whole order is put on hold and an explanatory letter is sent to the customer. These 'on-hold' orders are fulfilled as soon as sufficient stock has been received to fulfil the whole of the order. A goods received note is raised for each delivery of stock from a supplier. Once all the order has been despatched then the 'on-hold' order is converted into an ordinary order.

(b)   Re-draw the data flow diagram to reflect this new information as well as the corrections to the errors in the original diagram.   (9 marks)

(15 marks)

Guidance note

In part (a), read through the narrative and compare this with the DFD as drawn; this should help you find the errors. Re-drawing the DFD should be straightforward – producing a rough plan of the DFD first will help you produce a neat diagram.

27   PREPARATION QUESTION: ENTITY RELATIONSHIP MODEL   *27 mins*

A systems analyst has noted the following points in an interview with a user.

Orders are received from customers.

Orders may be received by post from trade customers or through e-mails from appointed agents. Each agent is responsible for many domestic customer accounts.

For example

Agent **Cullum** is responsible for forty domestic accounts including **J Haq**.

Each individual order is received from only one customer. For example order no. **107** was received from customer: **J Haq**.

Customers place many orders in the year. For example **J Haq** placed four orders in 2001 – order Nos. **53, 107, 125,** and **567**.

Orders are usually for multiple products. For example order no. **107** requested 14 copies of product no. **1435**, 23 copies of product no. **5342** and 1 copy of product no. **8474**.

Orders may be modified until the invoice is raised. Order modifications are usually due to changes in order quantities.

At the end of the week an invoice is raised. This lists the orders placed in that week and produces a detailed price breakdown and invoice total for all the orders placed in the week. The invoice is sent to the customer.

Customer payments are recorded in a spreadsheet. Some customers send cheques that cover many invoices. On some occasions a customer part-pays the invoice because there is a dispute over some of the products billed in the invoice.

Orders are deleted after seven years or if the customer goes into liquidation.

Required

(a) Construct an entity-relationship diagram (logical data structure) from the information recorded in the interview. Clearly state any assumptions you have made.   (10 marks)

(b) The following information recorded in the interview cannot be easily represented on an entity-relationship model.

- Orders may be received by post from trade customers or through e-mails from appointed agents.

- Orders may be modified until the invoice is raised. Order modifications are usually due to changes in order quantities.

- Orders are deleted after seven years, or if the customer goes into liquidation.

Briefly describe an alternative model for documenting and analysing such information and explain why it is more appropriate than the entity-relationship model (logical data structure) for modelling this information.   (5 marks)

(15 marks)

28   PREPARATION QUESTION: DATA FLOW DIAGRAM   *27 mins*

Required

Convert the following information for a child vaccination and immunisation system from its textual format into a data flow diagram (DFD).

'There is a legal obligation upon local health authorities to provide facilities for vaccinating people against disease. Treatment normally commences when a child is one month old and registration of each child for their course of vaccinations is initiated by the birth of the child.

'The system operated by Mediserve Health Centre requires information from which it can produce a program of vaccination notification for the parents and the health centre staff. This information is obtained from the birth registration form. A consent form is completed by the health visitor and signed by the parent or guardian when visiting the child around the tenth day after birth. Protection is available against a variety of disease and parents may agree to all, none or some of the scheduled immunisations and vaccinations. If all are accepted, separate courses will be scheduled between one month and 16 years.

'A diary appointment system must be maintained which notifies families at the appropriate time and checks that parents are not notified if treatment has already taken place or, more distressingly, if the child has died. The system must provide facilities for adding and deleting children to and from the vaccination program if they have transferred in or out of the health centre's area (or if they have died) and provide a record of completed appointments.

'Doctors are paid for immunisations and the system facilitates automatic payment.'

(15 marks)

29   PREPARATION QUESTION: OUTPUT/SCREEN DESIGN   *27 mins*

(a) Describe *five* objectives that should be kept in mind when designing output.   (5 marks)

(b) Identify *five* guidelines which should be observed in order to ensure the design of useful input documents.   (5 marks)

(c) What factors should be taken into account for effective screen design?   (5 marks)

(15 marks)

30   PREPARATION QUESTION: SOFTWARE DESIGN   *27 mins*

ACCA Learning-aids Ltd. sells study and revision aids for the ACCA examinations. These aids include study texts, revision booklets, self-study packs, cassette tapes, CDs and instructional videos. They publish a catalogue listing the product code, product description and price of their goods. The catalogue also includes an Order Form. A completed Order Form is reprinted below.

ACCA learning-aids ltd.

ORDER FORM

Mr / Mrs / Miss/ Mr: _HR_

First Name: _STEPHEN_

Surname: _MOORE_

Address: _4121 MILLBANK_

HALIFAX

YORKSHIRE

Tel. no. _0197120_

Subject	Product Code	Product Description	Quantity	Price	Total price
Inf Analysis	6121VO	Teach Yourself Video	1	17.99	17.99
Inf Analysis	5211RC	Revision Study Kit	2	15.00	30.00
Audit Gude	5512RC	Revision Study Kit	1	15.00	15.00

Postage and Packing

UK	2.50
Europe	5.00
Rest of the World	7.50

Total _65.49_

A new computer system is being developed for entering and storing order details. As part of this system it is essential that the information provided on the Order Form can be entered quickly and accurately into the system. It has also been stressed that the system should be easy to use.

Required

Briefly describe five features that the system could include to assist the quick, accurate and easy entry of the order from details. **(15 marks)**

31 **PREPARATION QUESTION: END-USER DEVELOPMENT** *27 mins*

The senior management of an organisation wish to encourage end-user computing in an attempt to reduce the backlog of computer applications awaiting implementation, and to make information more freely and speedily available to management.

Required

(a) What contribution might each of the following make towards reducing the applications backlog and encouraging the spread of end-user computing?

    (i) Fourth Generation Languages

    (ii) Information centres   **(8 marks)**

(b) What problems would you envisage arising as a result of the widespread introduction of small computer systems and end-user computing, and how might such problems be avoided? **(7 marks)**

(15 marks)

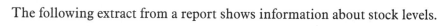

32   OUTPUT DESIGN   *36 mins*

The following extract from a report shows information about stock levels.

The report has two main purposes.

- To highlight products that are below their re-order level.

- To compare the total 'value at re-order level' with the total 'stock value'. The organisation requires that total 'stock value' should not exceed total 'value at re-order level' by more than 10%.

Report extract

Stock level report   Page 14

Product code	Cost per unit	Units in stock	Stock value	Re-order level	Below re-order level	Value at re-order level
98765	30	20	600	15		450
98766	60	7	420	5		300
98767	59	30	1770	40	********	2360
98768	45	21	945	23	********	1035
98769	23	53	1219	70	********	1610
98770	40	112	4480	110		4400
98771	30	67	2010	50		1500
98772	10	9	90	5		50
98773	40	7	280	5		200
98774	30	23	690	25	********	750
98775	25	45	1125	50	********	2250
98776	45	32	1440	30		1350
98777	12	10	120	10		120
98778	15	15	225	10		150
98779	45	45	2025	50	********	2250
98780	10	30	300	25		250
98781	45	67	3015	50		2250
98782	23	54	1242	50		1150
98783	80	20	1600	10		800
98784	12	78	936	15		180
98785	56	58	3248	50		2800
98786	12	12	144	10		120
98787	6	90	540	100	********	600
98788	50	2	100	5	********	250
98789	78	1	78	5	********	390
Total	881	908	28642			27565

Required

(a) Most organisations have standards for the layout of such reports. For example, the standards may require that each report should have a title (as in stock level report).

List *seven* further standard items that might apply to any system generated report. These standards may or may not have been adhered to by the stock level report extract.

(7 marks)

(b) Briefly describe four ways in which the usability of the stock level report might be improved taking into account the main purposes of the report. (Credit will not be given for standards issues already listed in part (a) of this question.)   (8 marks)

(c)   The accurate data entry of stock information is essential. It has been suggested that the product code should have a check digit attached to it to assist in accurate data entry. Explain what is meant by a check digit and identify what types of input error it should prevent.   (5 marks)

(20 marks)

33   PREPARATION QUESTION: ITT   *27 mins*

A manufacturing company has issued an Invitation to Tender requesting proposals for a replacement to its current inventory control software. The hardware is not being replaced. Three proposals have been received offering competing software package solutions. The manufacturing company wishes to compare the three solutions to decide which (if any) they should buy.

Required

(a)   Describe five issues that will have to be considered in evaluating each proposal. Briefly explain why each issue is relevant and must be included in the evaluation.   (10 marks)

(b)   Initial evaluation suggests that none of the proposals provides the perfect solution. What methods can the company use to assess the strengths and weaknesses of each proposal and hence choose the most effective solution?   (5 marks)

(15 marks)

> **EVALUATING INFORMATION SYSTEMS**
>
> Questions 34 to 44 cover the 'Evaluating Information Systems' area of the syllabus, the subject of Part C of the BPP Study Text for Paper 2.1.
>
> Further questions on these subject areas are included in the Scenario Questions and the Mock Exams in this Kit – refer to the topic index on pages (vi) – (x).

34   PREPARATION QUESTION: SOFTWARE TESTING   *27 mins*

(a)   Two stages of computer software testing are:

- Systems testing
- User acceptance testing

Required

Briefly describe each of these two stages.   (10 marks)

(b)   Certain deliverables in the development life cycle cannot be easily tested because they are in the form of written documentation. This is particularly true of deliverables in the analysis stage, such as data flow diagrams and entity-relationship models (logical data structures).

Required

Explain how the correctness and quality of these deliverables can be checked. (5 marks)

(15 marks)

35   PREPARATION QUESTION: MAINTENANCE AND REVIEW   *27 mins*

(a)   A manufacturing company is about to implement a bespoke inventory control system. The implementation team is keen to collect data that measures the quality of the delivered system. A HELP desk has been set up to support the users of the software.

Required

Define and show the differences between corrective and adaptive maintenance.

(6 marks)

(b)   The implementation team wishes to monitor the user-friendliness and frequency of use of the system. They want to ensure that users find the software easy to use and that managers extensively use the enquiry and reporting facilities.

Required

Suggest a total of three appropriate measures of user-friendliness and frequency of use and describe how such data might be collected, interpreted and acted upon.   (9 marks)

(15 marks)

36   PREPARATION QUESTION: USER OPPOSITION   *27 mins*

Identify and explain common sources of user opposition to system development. Suggest ways in which this opposition could be minimised.

(15 marks)

Guidance note

Think about senior management attitudes as well as those of staff. Identify the fears that people may have.

37 TESTING: DECISION TABLE

36 mins

Programmers and users are testing the order section of the CLP Company's new software. The software is designed to run on a networked computer system, with multi-user access.

The following details relate to the testing of the field to capture the customer account code.

- All customer account codes are six digits in length.
- Each digit is a number.
- A valid code is needed for each order.

Following the checking of the software by the programmers, the entire module will be acceptance tested by users.

Part of the initial specification for this module included the following requirements:

- Ability to process 5,000 orders each hour
- Screen design will mimic the current manual order form
- Processing of one order will take no more than 5 seconds
- Order information will be automatically transferred to the production module

The manager of the ordering department has just been given the latest version of the software on a single user computer. User acceptance testing of the ordering module is scheduled to last two days.

Required

(a) Prepare a decision table to show the amendments required to the customer account code field so that it will meet the field conditions stated above. (8 marks)

(b) (i) Explain the purpose of user acceptance testing (5 marks)

    (ii) Explain the importance of the points made in the initial specification for this module and discuss the actions to be taken if user testing indicates that the specification will not be met. (7 marks)

(20 marks)

Guidance note

The use of a decision table in this context (testing) is specified within the syllabus. The main difference between decision tables used in this context and those relating to other topics is likely to be the increased number of actions in the action entry stub.

38 PREPARATION QUESTION: CONTROLS

27 mins

You have been given responsibility for the control aspects of FT Ltd's computer system. The company has two sites. There are no computer links between the sites.

Head office has 24 PCs linked on a Local Area Network. Each PC has its own processing ability, and is linked via the LAN to central printers, disk storage, file server and tape streamer devices. The LAN is self-contained; there are no modems or other similar external devices attached to it. The subsidiary office has 6 stand-alone PCs, each with its own printer.

Required

Draft a report to the Managing Director of FT Ltd describing the following types of system control and explaining their relevance to each site.

(a) Physical access and security controls.
(b) System software controls.
(c) Application controls. **(15 marks)**

24

39   INPUT CHECKS

36 mins

A user enters examination results into a computer system from information provided on a form compiled by the examiner. The following data is on the manual form.

(a)   Candidate number
(b)   Centre number
(c)   Desk number
(d)   Examination number
(e)   Marker number
(f)   Questions answered
(g)   Marks for each question
(h)   Total mark for the examination

Required

(a)   Briefly describe *five* different types of check that can be used in examination mark data entry to improve the accuracy of the entered data. For each different type of check explain what entry errors it is trying to detect and give an example of its application in the examination mark data entry system.   (15 marks)

(b)   Explain *two* other general design principle that the developer could use to facilitate the speedy and accurate input of the examination mark data.   (5 marks)

(20 marks)

40   PREPARATION QUESTION: PHYSICAL CONTROLS

27 mins

The information systems (IS) department of a country's Department of Tax Collection is currently located in several cities. The government now wishes to centralise the computer systems at one location and is looking for a suitable site.

The committee organising the re-location of the department has identified the following two problems concerning the location of the installation. These will have to be taken into consideration when selecting the site. The problems are:

• Preventing and recovering from physical attack by groups opposed to tax collection.

• Guaranteeing the continuity of the supply and maintenance of essential services to the site.

Required

Briefly describe what measures might be taken to address each of these problems.

(15 marks)

41   PHYSICAL THREATS

36 mins

SCP Ltd is an engineering company which is about to implement a new production planning and control system. Following a strategic level review of the business, the board have decided that one of the company's critical success factors is the production of up-to-date and accurate information on internal (eg customer orders) and external (eg raw materials availability) factors, so that the company can respond quickly to changes in demand and other external circumstances. The new system will enable a rapid response to such information and will provide output for a range of production operations including machine loading, control of raw materials, production set-up, batch control, planned downtime and machine utilisation.

The system is seen as a 'mission-critical' one and the company is setting up a new computer centre, which will take responsibility for this system and also take over existing systems currently under the auspices of the finance, sales and personnel departments.

You have been asked to advise the company on the security aspects of the new computer centre.

Required

(a) What potential physical threats would you make your client aware of, what precautionary measures would you suggest, and what techniques would you propose be implemented to control access to the computer centre?   (10 marks)

(b) A contingency plan is to be devised outlining measures that should enable operations to continue in adverse conditions.

Explain to the client the purpose of such a plan, how it might be developed, and the standby options which are available.   (10 marks)

(20 marks)

42   PROCESSING CONTROLS   *36 mins*

A government department is responsible for awarding grants to a large number of applicants. The award of grants is based on detailed information supplied by the applicant. There is some cross-checking of the accuracy of the information supplied.

The old system

The work was done by local offices. Forms were completed by applicants and sent to their local office, which would process claim forms and, where necessary, interview applicants to clarify information supplied, and inspect forms and other documents. The application would be either approved or rejected, the applicant informed, and payment made if the application was successful.

The new system

A very large central processing department, using a new computer system, has been established, which has taken over the work of all the local offices, which have now closed. The new system has moved completely from a largely paper form-based system to a unified database system. In this system, all claims and details are received by post or telephone and entered on to the database.

Required

(a) Explain what general control procedures management should be reviewing to ensure an acceptable level of accuracy and service in any large information processing department, whether using paper-based forms or a computer database.   (8 marks)

(b) Explain what systems of internal control and internal check can be applied to database systems with real-time processing.   (12 marks)

(20 marks)

43   PREPARATION QUESTION: DATA SECURITY   *27 mins*

(a)   What are the main threats that an organisation holding sensitive data on computer storage must guard against?   (4 marks)

(b)   To protect such data, a logical access system is essential.

What is a logical access system, and how might it work?   (5 marks)

(c)   Explain the significance of the following terms in the context of data security:

- Encryption
- Hacking
- Computer viruses   (6 marks)

(15 marks)

44   SECURITY   *36 mins*

MN plc is a supplier of fruit, vegetable and flower seeds to the public. Seeds are grown in specialist nurseries in the south of the country MN operates in, and then checked, packaged and despatched from a central warehouse located in a rural area close to the nurseries. The organisation employs about 250 staff in jobs ranging from office administration, tending and watering plants through to truck drivers and web-site designers.

Staff in the organisation are allowed unlimited Internet access in terms of both on-line time and the types of site that can be visited. To make the system easy to use for staff, passwords are based on user name and are changed monthly; the password being user-name with a suffix of two numbers denoting the month (eg January is 01 and July 07).

MN plc's first web site was established three months ago with the aim of selling seeds on-line to a wider customer base. However, as the site was seen as an experiment, full encryption and anti-virus software was not purchased.

(a)   Explain the need for encryption and anti-virus software in MN plc.   (6 marks)

(b)   Evaluate the effectiveness of the password procedures at MN plc and explain the actions that need to be taken to remove any weaknesses that have been identified.

(8 marks)

(c)   Explain the relevance of the UK Computer Misuse Act to limiting the spread of computer viruses.   (6 marks)

(20 marks)

Guidance note

Remember to relate your comments back to the situation in MN plc.

BPP PUBLISHING

PART D: SCENARIO QUESTIONS

Questions 45 to 54 are scenario questions – 60 marks worth of questions per scenario. These questions are designed to help you prepare for the compulsory questions that will appear in Section A of the examination.

---

45   WRAY CASTLE

108 mins

Wray Castle is an engineering company which is about to implement a new production planning and control system. Much of the work in the factory is batch production. The company needs to be able to respond quickly to changes in demand and other external circumstances. This means that up-to-date, accurate information is required from internal and external sources.

The new system will have to cope with a range of operations, including machine loading, materials control, batch-size calculation and machine utilisation. Bar coding and machine readable badges will be used for on-line entry. The system will be a sophisticated one which will have to be capable of assessing the effect on production of events within and beyond the factory gates.

There is at the same time a lot of pressure from the marketing department, which wishes to invest in a computerised market planning and research system, which would be 'owned' by them rather than by the computer centre. The marketing director was told, when the company's sales order processing system was developed, that this would meet her needs for the provision of suitably analysed information, but it does not do so.

The sales order processing system functions well, but is not without its problems. It was delivered late and documentation is poor. The lack of documentation has been particularly problematic, for example where systems breakdowns have occurred, where enhancements have been requested and where new users have needed to be trained. All this has resulted in slow, drawn-out maintenance and redevelopment work and in staff costs which have been well in excess of original estimates, both for programming and for training.

The company plans to continue to follow the traditional systems development cycle for all its systems development.

Required

(a)   Critically assess the role which the company's steering committee might play in determining priorities for computerisation.   (15 marks)

(b)   Write a memorandum to the managing director setting out what you consider to be the major weaknesses of the systems development cycle and explaining how systems prototyping might help.   (15 marks)

(c)   How could the features of a structured systems methodology be applied to overcome the problems previously experienced by Wray Castle?   (15 marks)

(d)   Describe the different methods which a systems analyst might use to assess the information requirements of the marketing department, noting briefly any shortcomings of the methods.   (15 marks)

(60 marks)

46 ISEC

108 mins

Introduction

Four years ago the government introduced a Certificate of Proficiency in Information Systems. All information systems staff with over five years practical experience are eligible to sit for certification. Candidates have to take three examination papers and pass all three at one sitting. Successful candidates are allowed to call themselves Certified Information Systems Practitioners. Examinations are set in April and November and are conducted in centres all over the world.

The task of organising the certificate was given to a new organisation called ISEC (Information Systems Examination Centre).

ISEC

- Publishes and maintains the examination syllabus
- Appoints examiners, markers and invigilators
- Processes scripts and results
- Publishes statistical analyses of examination results

ISEC is set up as an independent trading company and it has to record a profit.

It was originally forecast that ISEC would have to deal with about 3,000 candidates per annum.

However, the success of the scheme, particularly abroad, has meant that over 11,000 scripts had to be processed in the last sitting of the papers.

ISEC has a chief executive who has three department heads reporting to her. The departments are as follows.

Administration department

The administration department has seven staff. They are responsible for:

- Storing and acknowledging applicants for the examination

- Sending examination instructions to candidates

- Receiving examination scripts from the examination centres and distributing these to examination markers

- Receiving marked scripts back from the markers and recording the results

- Sending examination marks to candidates and publishing statistical analyses of the results.

The head of section has produced a simple single-user spreadsheet for recording applicants, receipt of examinations and final results. The spreadsheet records:

- Applicant registration number and the date of application

- The date the examination instructions were sent to the candidate

- The date the candidate's completed examination script was received from the examination centre

- The date the examination script was sent to the marker and the name of the marker

- The date the marked examination script was received back from the marker

- A record of the marks for each question for the candidate

- The date marks were sent to the candidate

- Simple statistical analyses of results, by paper, marker and question

Copies of application forms have to be passed to finance and administration who raise an invoice for the examination fee. Details of successful candidates are passed to education department who produce a certificate and add the candidate to the Member's Register. The spreadsheet automatically produces a total of the number of scripts marked by each marker. These details are also passed to finance and administration.

Education department

The education department has five staff and is responsible for:

- Defining and publishing the examination syllabus
- Scheduling and organising examination centres and organising invigilators
- Appointment of external examiners
- Checking that examinations set by the external examiners are of the required standard
- Auditing examinations to ensure that examination marking has been fair and consistent
- Producing membership certificates and maintaining a Membership Register

There are three stand-alone personal computers (PCs) in this department used for word processing. Details of the examination schedule and examination centres are passed to the administration department. External examiner details are passed to finance and administration who pay the examiners an annual fee.

Finance and administration

The finance and administration department has three staff. It is responsible for:

- Payment of external examiners and markers
- Receipt of payments from candidates
- Payment of full-time staff
- Maintenance of the accounts ledger

The department has a single user personal computer running standard purchase, sales and nominal ledgers together with payroll.

Although each department is computerised there is no link between any of the PCs either within or between departments.

ISEC are currently considering a project to integrate the three departments of the company. A software house specialising in examination systems has suggested a solution based on a local area network with a dedicated file server based in the administration department. It is proposed that this will support three personal computers (PCs) in the education department, three PCs in finance and administration and a further four PCs in the administration department. The software might be a standard package or a system specially written by the software house for ISEC.

ISEC are considering the costs and benefits of such integration.

Required

(a) (i)   Describe three benefits that are likely to arise at ISEC from integrating the current systems.   (10 marks)

    (ii) Describe four types or categories of cost (actual values are not required) that will be incurred if the current systems are integrated using the solution suggested by the software house.   (10 marks)

(b) In examining the economic feasibility of the project the organisation will have to consider methods for evaluating costs and benefits of the application. The chief executive is not familiar with these methods.

(i)   Describe what is meant by each of the following two methods and give *two* advantages and *one* disadvantage of each.

(1)   Payback period or time to payback   (5 marks)

(2)   Discounted cash flow (net present value and internal rate of return)

(6 marks)

(ii)   Briefly comment on the difficulties associated with applying such methods in assessing the economic feasibility of an information systems project.   (3 marks)

(c) In looking at the technical feasibility of the system it has been agreed that the accurate, fast and cheap collection of data for examination scripts is essential. For each examination script the system needs to record:

- The candidate who has written that examination script
- The marker of that examination script
- Which paper that examination script is for
- The centre the candidate sat the examination paper at
- The questions they attempted in their script
- The marks given for each question by the marker
- The total marks for each examination script

(i)   Given that 99% of all candidates registered attend and sit the examination, what information could almost certainly be pre-recorded on an examination answer book? Identify any problems associated with pre-recording such information.

(8 marks)

(ii)   The following data collection methods have been suggested for the examination system:

(1)   Optical mark recognition
(2)   Optical character recognition
(3)   Bar coding

Briefly describe *one* of the data collection methods given above.   (3 marks)

(iii) For the method that you have selected in part (ii), describe its potential application in the examination system, highlighting where it would be particularly appropriate and where it would not.   (5 marks)

(d) A feasibility study should consider the operational feasibility of a project.

(i)   Describe *three* issues that should be examined in determining the operational feasibility of a project.   (6 marks)

(ii)   Suggest and briefly explain what operational issues might arise at ISEC.

(4 marks)

(60 marks)

47   AMALCAR   *108 mins*

Amalcar Staffing Ltd is a company specialising in the supply of temporary staff on short-term contracts to several industrial sectors. Staff are employed (full-time or part-time) by Amalcar and then hired out to client companies. The clients are invoiced weekly for the hours worked by the contract staff. The staff are either paid weekly or monthly directly by Amalcar. Employee taxes and staff welfare are the responsibility of Amalcar.

The need to produce client invoices quickly and accurately led to the company developing a bespoke client billing system. This was written and installed two years ago by a software house specialising in staffing and recruitment systems. The system operates on a local area network (LAN) supporting four users in the billing office. Staff on contract return their weekly timesheets to the billing office, whose staff enter the time details into the billing system which produces client invoices.

Amalcar's rapid expansion led to the decision to sub-contract (or outsource) staff payroll processing to a computer bureau. Copies of the weekly timesheets are sent to this bureau which produces the payroll details and payslips for Amalcar. The contract with the payroll bureau is negotiated on an annual basis and is due for renewal in two months' time.

Six months ago the management of Amalcar decided to recommence payroll processing within the company and to discontinue the bureau contract. There were two main reasons for this decision.

(a)   To improve access to information. Amalcar's managers increasingly require access to cost and income data to help them evaluate current contracts and bid for new ones.

(b)   To reduce costs. The bureau has indicated that charges for the next contract will be 'substantially' larger than the current contract.

A small team was set up and an appropriate package selected and purchased. The selected package is well established with over 1,000 users in the country. There is an active independent user group which has a specialist payroll sub-group.

The task of implementing this package within the company is the responsibility of the billing office manager. The software will be installed on the LAN in the billing office and the system expanded to support six users. The number of staff employed in the office will also increase from four to six to cope with the new responsibilities. The billing office manager has attended the three day standard course to learn how to use and install the package. This course runs once per month at the software company's headquarters and costs £750 per delegate.

It is currently envisaged that details of hours worked will be entered separately into the billing (for invoicing) and payroll systems. A link between the two may be developed in the future, but it is not part of the current project.

The billing office manager has broken the implementation of the payroll package down into the following main activities.

(a)   Produce project plan and terms of reference
(b)   Attend training course (billing office manager only)
(c)   Install payroll software
(d)   Recruit two new employees
(e)   Upgrade hardware
(f)   Agree training objectives
(g)   Agree training material
(h)   Attend training courses (other staff)
(i)   Prepare user documentation
(j)   Create master files
(k)   Prepare test plan
(l)   User tests

The activities (a) and (b) have already been completed.

Required

(a) The billing office manager is considering two system implementation options:

- Parallel running
- Direct changeover

(i) Explain what is meant by *parallel running* and *direct changeover* and give two advantages of each.   (12 marks)

(ii) Which option would you recommend for Amalcar? Briefly explain why you believe that your recommendation is the better approach to implementation.

(3 marks)

(b) Training is an essential part of successful implementation. The billing office manager has included some elements of training in her initial project breakdown, but she would welcome your views on the training requirements of the new system and how they could be fulfilled. Four options are currently being considered. She points out that the usual everyday work of the billing office will have to continue during this training period.

The four options being considered are as follows.

- Sending each employee on the standard three-day training course at the software company's headquarters.

- Running the standard three-day course at Amalcar's offices and putting all employees on this course. The software company has quoted a price of £2,000 per course for a three-day course attended by up to 12 delegates.

- Using the billing office manager to teach employees individually, so spreading her knowledge through the organisation.

- Buying a CBT (computer based training) package available from an independent training company. This CBT package costs £40 for a single user licence and covers the facilities and installation of the payroll package.

(i) Choose three of these training options. For each option chosen, give *three* advantages and *three* disadvantages.

(18 marks)

(ii) Recommend *one* of these training options, justifying your choice.   (3 marks)

(c) The suppliers of the payroll software have sent the billing office manager details of a support (or maintenance) contract which they recommend should be taken out for their payroll software.

(i) Explain what a support (or maintenance) contract is and what facilities and services should be included in such a contract.   (7 marks)

(ii) Explain why it is essential for Amalcar to subscribe to this contract.   (3 marks)

(iii) The billing office manager has also received information from an independent user group inviting Amalcar to subscribe to its payroll sub-group. Explain what is meant by a user group and what benefits there are for Amalcar in becoming a member.   (5 marks)

(d) The project breakdown produced by the billing office manager represents her initial view of the constituent parts of the project. A colleague has suggested that these should be represented on a network diagram so that network analysis can be used to determine the critical path and the elapsed time of the project.

(i)   Identify what further information would need to be recorded about the activities before this network diagram could be drawn.   (4 marks)

(ii)   Explain the term 'the critical path' and explain why it is essential that the billing office manager knows which activities lie on the critical path.   (5 marks)

(60 marks)

48   ELEX   *108 mins*

Introduction

Elex is a supplier of electrical products. It is a private limited company. Elex has an in-house Information Systems (IS) department consisting of an IS Manager and eight development staff. The department is primarily concerned with supporting and maintaining accounts and payroll applications. These applications operate on a mainframe computer and are written in COBOL. The IS manager reports directly to the financial director. Ten years ago the IS department wrote a simple order processing system (again in COBOL) and until six months ago this had been operating on the mainframe supporting ten terminals in the operations department.

A year ago the operations director decided to replace the order processing system. He argued that the system written ten years ago no longer supported the procedures and volumes of his department. Furthermore, he wanted a more modern flexible system using personal computers (PCs) and operating in the Windows environment. Users would also have access to spreadsheet, word processing and management reporting software which would allow them to use their PCs to improve their overall effectiveness and efficiency.

The IS manager suggested that the replacement order processing system should be developed in-house but the timescale she suggested reflected the lack of Windows and PC knowledge amongst her staff and this led to this option being rejected by the operations director. However, it was agreed that the IS department would purchase, install and support the personal computers and a new member of staff was taken on with this responsibility. The new member of staff was also given the task of training users in spreadsheet and wordprocessing software.

Software selection

The company decided to buy a software package to fulfil its requirements. A Steering Committee of the IS manager, the warehouse manager and the operations director was formed to select the most appropriate package. At its first meeting the IS manager suggested that a formal requirements specification should be developed using a structured methodology and this should be the basis of package selection. The other two members disagreed with her selection. The warehouse manager said, 'We know what we want. We want the facilities of the old system plus a few new requirements and a different user interface. We will know which package we want when we see it.' The operations director and warehouse manager agreed that they knew 'intuitively' what they wanted and asked the IS manager to restrict her input to technical rather than business issues. No other employees were involved in the software package selection.

After this meeting the IS manager resigned from the Steering Committee to be replaced by the sales manager. The new Steering Committee selected three companies and invited each company to demonstrate its product to the Steering Committee. It specified that each demonstration should take no longer than half a day. Only two of the invited companies attended. The first company was rejected on price and so the other company, a small software supplier (HR-SOFT) with a relatively new product, was selected. HR-SOFT provided a reference site (another customer who used the software) and the operations director telephoned the site to ask a few questions about HR-SOFT. The reference site (a dairy) confirmed that the software fulfilled their requirements and that generally it was reliable ('although we have not yet used all its facilities'). Some concern was expressed about the training organised by HR-SOFT. 'That's OK', said the operations director, 'It costs too much. We are going to do our own training anyway'.

Software implementation

Six months ago the system was implemented on a twenty-user computer (PC) network in the operations department. The PCs were bought directly from a manufacturer. HR-SOFT recommended a minimum configuration of the PCs but was not involved in hardware purchase and installation.

Unfortunately the software has not been successful or popular. In fact software problems during implementation caused the IS manager to telephone the reference site again. During that telephone call it emerged that the dairy was actually a different version of the software product operating on a mainframe computer. In fact, as HR-SOFT later admitted, the Elex system was only the second implementation of the PC version of the software. This system had been re-written in a relatively new programming language and some difficulties had been experienced. At the time of the presentation to the Elex Steering Committee, the first user of the PC version was experiencing reliability problems with the software and hence had not be used as a reference site.

Post implementation review

Eventually the increasing problems and discontent with the software caused the managing director to organise a post-implementation review undertaken by external consultants. On receipt of their report the operations director resigned. A new operations director was than appointed.

The post-implementation review undertaken by the consultants specifically identified three main problem areas.

Functional shortcomings

The software package does not appear to support the procedures and requirements of the organisation. It is estimated that the package fulfils about 80% of the organisation's actual requirements. Furthermore it also has facilities and features that are not required by the company. These cause confusion to the users of the system.

Performance

The company receives 60% of its orders over the telephone. Entry of these orders is often affected by slow response times (confirming customer account details and product availability) and this leads to frustration, poor customer service and inefficient use of the telephone sales staff. This requirement had not been identified by the Steering Committee and no attempt had been made to assess system performance prior to implementation.

System down-time

There appears to be a significant amount of system 'down-time' when orders cannot be entered into the system. HR-SOFT accepts that there are some problems with the product (which will be fixed in a new version due in three months) but believes that a large number of problems are due to unreliable hardware and operational errors made by the telephone sales staff.

The consultants also undertook a user-satisfaction survey. It showed that many users have a low confidence in the system because of its error rates and the fact that it does not support their operational procedures. One of the telephone sales staff commented, 'It just does not work in the same way we do'. The survey also revealed that the planned training had not taken place. Instead users were expected to learn the software from the user manual. Twenty copies of the manual had been bought so that a copy could be placed nest to each personal computer. However, as one user commented, 'It (the manual) is too large and too technical and it is impossible to relate its contents to our business procedures'.

Finally, the consultants commented on the lack of project management procedures and standards at Elex. They suggested that no employee had been made project manager for the project and hence responsibilities had become blurred and confused. In the end 'everybody thought that someone else was doing the work'.

Required

(a) The post-implementation review identified three specific problem areas:

    (i)   Functional shortcomings
    (ii)   Performance
    (iii) System down-time

For each of these problem areas discuss the likely reasons for the problems identified by the consultants, and describe what advice you would give to reduce the chance of making similar mistakes in future projects. (18 marks)

(b) Three suggestions have been made for addressing the current problems with the software.

    (i)   To purchase the source code of the software package from HR-SOFT and to bring future development in-house. The in-house team would make the changes required, remove unwanted features and support and develop the system in the future.

    (ii)   To replace the software with a bespoke system developed in-house in COBOL. This would run on the mainframe system using dumb terminals.

    (iii) To commission HR-SOFT to make the changes required and to investigate the performance problems of the system and to recommend improvements.

Give *one* advantage and *one* disadvantage of each suggestion. (17 marks)

(c) The managing director of Elex has decided to establish a formal project to recommend the future direction and development of the order processing system. The project team will make their recommendations in six months' time. In the meantime, the managing director has asked whether there is anything that can be done in the short-term to improve the situation.

Suggest, with reasons, short-term actions that you feel the managing director should consider while waiting for the project team to make its recommendations.

(10 marks)

(d) The new operations director is the project manager of the team set up to recommend the future direction and development of the order processing system. The operations director has asked for a brief description of the responsibilities of the project manager so that he understands his role before he takes on the project manager's job.

Describe the responsibilities of a project manager in the areas of:

- Producing the project quality plan
- Scheduling and monitoring
- Communication (15 marks)

(60 marks)

49 CAET TEXTILES   *108 mins*

Caet Textiles is a large multinational clothing company. It is organised into six business units. These units are supported by internal information systems (IS) department currently employing 30 staff.

There have been increasing internal criticism of the performance of the IS department. One of the business unit managers believes that the company should concentrate on its core business (clothing) and outsource the information systems function. 'We are not a software house. We just need a limited number of staff to commission, purchase and support the systems. We should outsource the rest to a specialist computer company to take responsibility for operating, managing and controlling the information systems function.'

A management consultancy has been appointed to examine the IS function. Its report has identified *four* shortcomings. These are described below.

Extract from management consultancy report:

Four shortcomings have been identified in the information systems function.

1 Problems of operational understanding

Some applications have been difficult to use. Such problems were particularly severe in the order processing system implemented one year ago.

The business unit manager commented that: 'The problem was that the system just did not reflect the way we worked. It looked all right on paper – but when we tried to use the system it was just unusable. The sequence of data entry did not match the manual order form, the menu structures were inappropriate and the error messages incomprehensible. Order entry was slow and error-prone so the operators soon had little confidence in the system.'

The IS project manager for this system reacted angrily when we put these points to him. 'The problem was that the users had not read the documentation. We showed them the sequence of the order entry with a simple flowchart. They just could not be bothered to read it. Then, when they got the system, they complained.'

2 Fulfilling user requirements

The functional correctness of some software projects has been an issue. A recent software project for the manufacturing business unit is a good example.

The business unit manager commented that: 'The manufacturing project was yet another example where the IS department, after continual delay and requests for more time, still failed to deliver a system that fulfilled the business requirements.'

In contrast the project manager responsible for the project asserted that: 'The users did not know what they wanted. Every time we thought we had got it right they changed their minds again. The only thing they never changed their minds about was the project deadline date!'

3 Lack of user ownership

User departments are reluctant to sign-off project deliverables, particularly those in the earlier stages of the project. There is a tendency to hope that it will come right in the end.

One of the business units responded to this criticism by commenting that: 'There appears to be very little visible progress in the earlier stages of the project (except for lots of meetings). There is nothing tangible to assess and sign-off.'

The IS staff agreed with this observation. One felt that users were quick to criticise but were less prepared to commit to requirements. 'There appears to be a climate of fear. They worry that if they sign-off requirements which are later shown to be wrong or incomplete then they will be reprimanded by their manager.'

4   **Little control over the costs of development**

The costs of the Information Systems department are currently divided equally between the six business units. There is no attempt to apportion the cost of IS resources to their use in each business unit.

The business units believe that: 'We have to pay the salaries of information systems staff whether they are working or not. So they might as well get on with something useful.'

In contrast the IS department felt that: 'The business units do not understand the costs of responding to their requirements. There is no accountability; no attempt to justify the costs of systems development against the benefits that the system will bring to the organisation.'

Required

(a) One of the business unit managers has suggested that the information systems function should be outsourced to external suppliers.

Describe four advantages to Caet Textiles of outsourcing the information systems function.   (20 marks)

(b) The IS department at Caet Textiles does not currently use structured software development techniques. The IS manager believes that the shortcomings identified by the management consultancy would be resolved by introducing a combination of structured techniques supported by CASE (Computer Aided Software Engineering) tools and prototyping with Fourth Generation Languages.

Briefly explain what is meant by:

(i)   Structured techniques supported by CASE tools.   (7 marks)
(ii)   Prototyping with Fourth Generation Languages.   (8 marks)

(c) Explain how the combination of structured techniques and prototyping would address the specific shortcomings of:

(i)   Problems of operational understanding.   (5 marks)
(ii)   Fulfilling user requirements.   (5 marks)
(iii) Lack of user ownership.   (5 marks)

identified in the management consultancy's report.

(d) Describe solutions to tackle the other shortcoming, *little* control over the costs of development, identified in the management consultancy's report. Comment on any issues your solutions would raise.   (10 marks)

(60 marks)

50   BARNES PLC

108 mins

Barnes plc is a large manufacturing company. It has traditionally developed many of its information systems in-house and the data processing (DP) department currently employs about 100 staff.

The following main applications are currently supported.

Application	Package/Bespoke	Development language
Process control	Bespoke	FORTRAN
Integrated accounts	Package	
Payroll	Package	
Order processing	Bespoke	COBOL
Quality control	Bespoke	COBOL
Marketing information	Bespoke	4GL

There are approximately 20 smaller applications developed in-house to respond to the needs of individual departments. However, the DP department does not have a good reputation. User departments frequently complain about missed deadlines, poor quality software and lack of functionality.

A new IT director has recently been appointed. He believes that most of the problems have been caused by the organisation's emphasis on building bespoke solutions.

His view is that 'Packages are the way forward. We can no longer afford the luxury of building our own systems.'

He is also critical of the systems development life cycle in place at Barnes.

He claims that 'We have made the mistake of forcing all our system developments - whether they are bespoke systems, application packages or small one-off systems through a standard systems development life cycle (SDLC). This SDLC (listed below) has led to unnecessarily long elapsed times on projects.'

Stage 1	Feasibility study
Stage 2	Systems specification
Stage 3	Programming and unit testing
Stage 4	Systems testing
Stage 5	User-acceptance testing
Stage 6	Implementation

The new IT director proposes that all future systems will be implemented using standard application software packages. He claims that:

'Standard packages offer cost and time savings as well as guaranteed quality. We will be looking for packages that fit 80% or more of our business requirements. We will not be commissioning any changes to the functionality of the package. If the package does not exactly fit the business than the business must change to fit the package. We have already successfully implemented packages for accounts and payroll. We must now repeat that success in other areas of the business.'

The IT director has agreed that staffing will be kept at the current level for the foreseeable future. He states that: 'We obviously need staff to implement our package policy, although I will be looking for a significant contribution from the user areas.'

BPP
PUBLISHING

Required

(a) (i) Explain what is meant by a:

- Software package   (3 marks)
- Bespoke solution   (3 marks)

  (ii) The IT director identifies three benefits of adopting the application software package approach.

  'Standard packages offer cost and time savings as well as guaranteed quality.'

  Explain how the software package approach can offer each of these three benefits to Barnes plc.

- Cost savings   (4 marks)
- Time savings   (3 marks)
- Guaranteed quality   (4 marks)

(b) The managing director of Barnes plc is concerned about the IT director's new approach. Before he agrees to the approach he asks you to:

  (i) Identify and explain _three_ risks of adopting the software package approach suggested by the IT director compared with the internal bespoke systems development approach traditionally used in the company.   (9 marks)

  (ii) For each risk identified in part (i) suggest solutions to reduce or remove its possible effect.   (12 marks)

(c) The Systems Development Life Cycle (SDLC) adopted by the department for bespoke systems development is described in the case study scenario.

  (i) Briefly describe each stage in the SDLC.   (10 marks)

  (ii) Explain how each stage might be changed (if at all) by the adoption of the application software package approach suggested by the IT director.   (6 marks)

(d) The IT director's view is that the business should change its processes to fit the software. Briefly outline your argument either in support of, or against, the IT director's view.   (5 marks)

(60 marks)

51 **X COMPANY**   _108 mins_

Background

The X Company is being established to sell insurance on the Internet. The company will provide a website with basic insurance information; customers will then telephone the company to discuss their specific insurance requirements with a trained sales representative.

Details of the proposed sales system

Full details of the proposed system are given below.

1 After visiting the website, the customer telephones the X Company.

2 The representative obtains some initial customer information including name and address and checks the X Company database to find out if customer has any previous insurance purchases from the company.

3 If the customer has previous purchases, then the telephone call is transferred to the Existing accounts section.

4   Full details of the new customers are obtained and entered into the customer database.

5   Details of the precise insurance products are discussed, with the representative making reference to the customer details file and the insurance products file, both held on specialised databases.

6   After these discussions, the customer is provided with a quote for their insurance requirements. The quote is sent to the customer via e-mail with a copy being placed on a quote database with a link back to the customer database for easy retrieval.

7   After receiving the quote, the customer may decide to telephone the X Company again to purchase the insurance.

8   On receipt of the telephone call, the representative accesses the quotes master file and checks the quotes details again with the customer.

9   Any amendments to the quote are agreed.

10   The customer pays for the insurance using a credit card, which is validated with reference to an on-line database of credit cards.

11   The final quote is sent back to the customer via e-mail with a copy to the accounts department for filing.

Information to be stored on the customer master file will include:

- Name
- Address
- Opinion regarding insurance risk (from talking to the customer)
- Age
- Racial origin
- Health of the customer
- Previous insurance history

Software development process

Software will be written by providing an initial specification for the whole information system. This logical design will then be translated into a physical design by producing specifications for each module of the system. An experienced project manager will supervise the whole design process, because only a limited time and cost budget is available for the detailed testing of the software.

Development of this particular software package will be outsourced, although other software programs have been written in-house. The new software will be require to integrate will the existing accounting software; however, time for testing will be limited because this software is used for at least 20 hours each day.

Required

(a)   Prepare a process model of the system to record and prepare insurance quotes for new customers. (20 marks)

(b)   (i)   Explain the main aims of the Data Protection Act 1998 and the rights of data subjects under that Act. (10 marks)

      (ii)   Explain the actions that the X Company must carry out in relation to the Data Protection Act 1998. (10 marks)

(c)   (i)   Explain the 'V' model of software testing, showing how this can be used to provide appropriate control of software development in the company. (14 marks)

      (ii)   Explain any weaknesses in the model in respect to the situation in the X Company. (6 marks)

(60 marks)

Guidance note

For part (a), note that a Data Flow Diagram is one example of a process model (a flowchart is another example).

In part (b), there are 'clues' within the scenario regarding the data being held on the system, and therefore the actions that the X Company must take. In part (c), remember that the "V" model has links 'across the V" to provide control during software development.

52   HB MANUFACTURING

108 mins

HB is a manufacturing company based in one country. It has four factories, each located in a different city, and a head office in the country's capital. Each factory manufactures different products, so there is no need to transfer raw materials or finished goods between the different locations.

IT systems have been developed independently to meet the specific requirements of each factory and head office. The precise IT configuration in each location therefore reflects the required use in that location. For example, factory A has a LAN with a shared database while factory B has mainly stand-alone computers with access to the Internet via dial up telephone connections from each PC. Allowing each location to establish its own IT system has provided few problems for the Board of HB. Control of IT expenditure has remained with managers at each factory, so the managers have been motivated to ensure that IT systems are efficient and meet their specific needs.

However, the Board of HB would like to implement a WAN to link all the factories to each other and to Head Office. This will enable data to be shared between the different sites and provide some of the necessary infrastructure to sell all products from a single website. The website is currently under development, but is unlikely to be available for another 12 months. Prior to these decisions, the IT strategy of HB had been limited to delegating individual budgets to the four factories.

The Board of HB has recently appointed an IT director. At her first Board meeting, the director noted that an IT strategy was required. She also made an outline proposal for a new IT system including:

- A WAN to link the four factories and Head Office

- A LAN within each location to share data on stock levels, production, accounting and other information using the client server computing model

- All accounting operations to be centralised at Head Office with Information transfer over the WAN

- WAN access to be provided by time-share on a Virtual Private Network run by the national rail company

- A database administrator to be responsible for implementing and maintaining the hardware and software

The project has a significant budget representing 4% of the turnover of the organisation.

Initial reaction from users to the idea of a revised system has been mixed. While the upgrading of some IT systems is seen as a positive step, lack of involvement in drawing up the outline proposal and fear of loss of control over system development are concerns that will need to be addressed.

Required

(a) Write a memo to the Board of HB explaining the need for an IT strategy, providing relevant examples from the situation in HB where possible.   (20 marks)

(b) (i)   Explain the terms:

•   Local Area Network

•   Wide Area Network and

•   Client – Server

in the context of HB's computer system.   (12 marks)

(ii) Discuss the advantages for HB of centralising its accounting system at Head Office.   (8 marks)

(c) (i)   Discuss how the user-interface for the new accounting system can be made more user-friendly.   (10 marks)

(ii) Discuss the importance of structured walk-throughs in obtaining user involvement in systems change projects.   (6 marks)

(iii) Briefly explain one other method of helping users understand the layout of the system.   (4 marks)

(60 marks)

Guidance note

In part (a), focus your answer on the need for an IT strategy, rather than on details of the information systems that may be implemented as a result of this strategy.

(b)(ii) – there are only 8 marks on offer, so don't spend too much time making a long list of advantages. Instead, focus on a few key points that are relevant to HB and explain these.

(c)(i) - as with (b)(ii), it is possible to include a long list of points in your answer. However, given that there 10 marks on offer, try and include 5 points with **brief** explanation.

In part (c)(iii), explain what a prototype is, and how it could help users understand the layout of the new system.

 53 M-E-QUIP   *108 mins*

Introduction

M-E-Quip Ltd is a distributor of motor parts and spares. The company purchases parts for most major types of motor vehicle from the manufacturer, and then sells these on to individual garages where motor vehicles are repaired and serviced.

M-E-Quip Ltd has 46 branches and one Head Office within the country it operates in. The branches are normally located within major cities, close to the garages where repairs are made. All accounting and stock control information is processed at Head Office, with each branch being linked to this location using a Wide Area Network (WAN).

The WAN was implemented two years ago, with current network traffic being about 50% higher than initially budgeted for. The WAN supplier provides a relatively poor service, although it is cheap. One query that M-E-Quip had at the time concerned the lack of external e-mail capability using the WAN, although the supplier suggested this was not an important issue for M-E-Quip.

Ordering and sales system

Customers normally telephone M-E-Quip with their orders. The stock levels are checked on computer and where items are in stock they are despatched using M-E-Quip's vans within two hours. 90% of orders can be fulfilled in this way. For the remaining 10% of orders, stock is obtained either from another branch of M-E-Quip or directly from the manufacturer. Stock levels at other branches are normally checked by telephoning stock controllers at the individual branch, the computer system does not allow access to the stock records of other branches, even though these are held centrally. Delivery is made on the next working day.

In order to provide this level of service to garages, M-E-Quip maintains a high stock level. This is an expensive option in terms of working capital management, but necessary to provide good customer service.

Computer systems development

The Board of M-E-Quip tend to operate in an autocratic style; decisions are made for the company without always fully appreciating the impact of those decisions (or computer systems) on the staff working for M-E-Quip.

Backup arrangements for the system include a tape streamer at Head Office, with the copy tapes being stored in an off-site location. No backup is carried out at the individual branches because no transaction data is stored at these locations.

Problems noted with the existing computer configuration

Disruptions to the WAN, resulting in stock levels not being available at individual branches for up to four hours on some days. These disruptions have been caused by a lack of bandwidth on the network provider from which M-E-Quip rents its WAN communications infrastructure. M-E-Quip commenced a five-year agreement for the provision of WAN services two years ago with this provider, although the service has been consistently below standard.

The managers in individual branches would like to provide specific promotional offers to their customers based on the purchase history. However, detailed purchase information is only available off-line at Head Office, while the computer systems at the branch do not easily allow for and appropriate word processing software is not available at the branch level.

Errors in the stock information, resulting from lack of processing controls at Head Office. For example, stock transactions have been processed twice, and in a few cases; stock movements from one branch have been allocated against the master files for a different branch.

Some managers are leaving M-E-Quip because they were dis-satisfied concerning their ability to amend the computer systems to meet their own requirements.

Required

(a) (i)   Explain the concept of distributed processing.   (3 marks)

     (ii) Discuss the advantages of distributed processing within M-E-Quip Ltd.
                                                                                   (12 marks)

     (iii) Describe the backup procedures available to M-E-Quip using distributed processing and the WAN.   (5 marks)

(b) (i)   Discuss the disadvantages of M-E-Quip's existing outsourcing contract with the WAN telecommunications provider, noting the actions that can be taken to try and remove those disadvantages.   (8 marks)

(ii)   As far as the information allows, discuss the costs involved in implementing the distributed processing system.   (12 marks)

The development of the revised IT system is being put out to Tender. The Directors of M-E-Quip are uncertain whether they will continue with the existing WAN supplier, and are seeking alternative suppliers for their new systems project.

(c) (i)   Explain the purpose of an Invitation to Tender.   (3 marks)

(ii)   List the contents of an Invitation to Tender and explain the relevance of each point to the situation in M-E-Quip.   (12 marks)

(iii) Explain how the Board of M-E-Quip can choose a supplier from the proposals submitted by suppliers in response to the Invitation to Tender.   (5 marks)

(60 marks)

Guidance note

Part (a) investigates the change from centralised to decentralised processing. The case study information contains reasons for this change, you should explain them in the context of the question.

The problems of outsourcing are examined in part (b). Use your knowledge of general problems with outsourcing as a starting point, then relate this knowledge to the case study.

In part (c), the directors appear to be at the end of their tether with their existing outsourcing company, and have issued an Invitation to Tender to attract alternative suppliers. You need to understand the contents of a typical ITT to answer this question.

54   MALTOVIA

108 mins

System overview

The Government of Maltovia, a country with 35 million people, obtains and stores data on each citizen. The data obtained ranges from name, address and place of birth through to criminal convictions and known memberships of political or similar societies.

Information is stored in the central information building, which is located in a remote rural area, over 15 kilometres from the nearest major town. The data comprises a central database and some paper-based records. A staff of 250 people work in this building, all of whom have to obtain security clearance from the government's secret service prior to commencing employment. From individual computer terminals, passwords provide the main access control to data on the computer system. Passwords are changed each week, although staff are allowed to choose their own password.

Revised system

A new data retrieval software system (on the existing hardware) will be implemented into the information storage building within the next 12 months. User requirements have already been obtained, although due to the relatively secret nature of the information systems, the analyst in-charge of the project is uncertain whether or not those requirements have been correctly documented. Staff have also been too busy to provide full details of their work and do not have the time to imagine what a new computer system can provide for them. Documentation so far has been limited to Data Flow Diagrams and narrative system notes.

Before programming of the new software commences, the analyst has decided to produce some prototypes of the new system.

Required

(a) (i)   Explain the aim of physical access controls over a computer system.   (3 marks)

   (ii)   Discuss the controls that can be used to ensure only authorised personnel can gain access to the Maltovia central information building.   (10 marks)

  (iii)   Explain the risks of using password controls as the main access control within the central information building. Briefly suggest a method of overcoming these risks.   (7 marks)

(b) (i)   Explain, with the aid of a suitable diagram, the steps in producing and agreeing a prototype.   (10 marks)

   (ii)   Discuss the disadvantages of prototyping for the Maltovia information centre.   (10 marks)

(c) (i)   Suggest and explain a framework that can be used to ensure that project objectives are agreed between the analyst and users prior to a project being undertaken. As far as the case study allows, explain any problems that the analyst will face when trying to apply your criteria to a project.   (10 marks)

   (ii)   Explain how the users in the information centre can be encouraged to become more involved with the systems project.   (10 marks)

(60 marks)

Guidance note

For part (a), imagine yourself entering a high security building; this should help identify many of the controls in use. Remember though that controls have to be cost-effective and practical.

In part (b), remember that prototyping in this situation is no different to any other situation. The only difficulty is that the prototype may be less 'correct' than in other situations.

Finally, in part (c), the basic problem is that staff do not appear to want to be involved with the project. This will pose problems for the analyst, as well as the staff if the final system does not meet their requirements.

Answers

1   PREPARATION QUESTION: IT AS A STRATEGIC RESOURCE

Costs

In most organisations the **spending** on IT is sufficiently high that **decisions** about the spending should be taken at a **strategic level** - both because of the impact on the cash resources of the organisation and because of the amounts involved. Much expenditure is at the 'leading edge' of technologies, for example on expert systems or on computer integrated manufacturing, rather than on traditional data processing activities. Many recent surveys published in national newspapers and journals suggest that organisations believe that **much IT expenditure is wasted**, largely because investment does not follow an organisational strategy. The capital costs involved mean that IT cannot be treated as an operating cost, but must be evaluated and controlled as capital expenditure.

Needs

The **needs** of the organisation must be **balanced** against each other in terms of **competing for resources** and in terms of their impact on factors such as **costs** and the **effectiveness** of the organisation. This consideration of needs must be done at a strategic level to allow for **all relevant factors** to be taken into account. In the early days of computing, IT was seen as a **support** activity, geared primarily towards accounting for and processing business transactions which had already taken place. This is still true in many businesses, but **IT has become increasingly critical** to the provision of services or manufacture of goods. In the financial sector, for example, IT is now core to the ongoing operation of many organisations.

Opportunities

IT both provides direct and indirect opportunities (in **internal systems** as well as potentially **revenue generating external systems**) as well as opportunities in terms of **reduced costs** and impacts in other **intangible areas** such as **morale and quality of management**. These opportunities are often of such importance that they should form part of the strategic direction of the organisation.

In the financial sector again, IT can be used to **create new businesses** (Reuters created an electronic marketplace where businesses could trade via Reuters Terminals) or to **gain a competitive advantage** by improving the customer interface (eg Internet-based banking). In other businesses, **computer aided design** and **computer aided manufacture** can be used to improve productivity and performance.

Changes in the **economic context** mean that IT must be the subject of an organisational strategy. The impact on businesses of privatisation or deregulation (for instance in telecommunications and broadcasting) is massive and must be addressed at strategic level. The impact of such developments in the UK has led to major changes in the way many organisations do business; because IT is at the heart of their operations, they need to develop a strategic view to remain competitive.

All-pervasiveness

IT is now an activity which **impacts on most areas** of most organisations. As a result it should be considered in such a light, and considered at a strategic level when planning for its use and expenditure on it. Initially it was a 'specialist' activity but **schoolchildren** are now invariably using PCs at school and those who were unable to, now in middle or senior management, are under pressure to familiarise themselves with the new technology. This means that **increasing numbers** of staff in any organisation are **familiar with** the medium and as a result **expecting to use IT** in their work. Pressure for end-user computing facilities is increasing, and **customers** expect their suppliers to use modern technology.

Stakeholders

Because of the nature of IT and the investment required to start and maintain an adequate IT function, **stakeholders** will often be involved in some of the deliberations regarding its **specification and procurement**. This involvement will imply that the profile of IT is raised to the strategic level.

Governments are increasingly affecting IT development and practice. In the UK, the **Data Protection Act,** the **Computer Misuse Act** and the (forthcoming) **Freedom of Information Act** affect many organisations.

As noted above, **customer pressures** will also be important (eg retail chains and standardisation of documentation for EDI).

Employees may also be able to affect developments.

Management support systems

Since one of the primary reasons for many IT functions is to **provide management support,** by its very nature it becomes a strategic tool, and will need to be considered as such. Management may use **expert systems, spreadsheets** for sensitivity analysis, **teleconferencing** for meetings, **decision support** systems and **executive information systems**.

2   INFORMATION SYSTEMS STRATEGY

(a) Reasons for having a formal IS strategy

Information is now regarded by many organisations as something more than a useful by-product of commercial data processing. Instead, it is seen as a **resource** of an organisation, like the organisation's pool of human skills, fixed assets, goodwill and so forth. **Planning** in all these areas is widely regarded as desirable, so that an organisation can adapt to a changing environment.

As information is so critical to an organisation's success, then the provision of information must be an important organisational activity. Just as many organisations have a long-term plan covering sales and markets, production and so forth, so too **a long-term plan** is needed for **information provision**.

An organisation's **financial investment** in information technology is also **substantial,** especially with the proliferation of computing power around different departments. Moreover, information technology **spans** areas of management which previously would have been distinct: high volume data processing; telecommunications and office administration. Many organisations report dissatisfaction with the outcomes of their investments. Some **overall direction** is therefore required.

A **strategy** is a long-term plan, concentrating on the overall performance of the system, stating long-term objectives and goals, and outlining the measures to achieve them. Strategies are articulated **differently** in different organisations. In some circumstances, the organisation's very **survival** in a hostile economic climate is the long-term goal. The strategy contains the measures to achieve it. In other organisations the goal might be **growth** in market share.

Because information technology is pervasive throughout the business, and can significantly affect the relationship an organisation has with its customers, the **IT strategy** should be developed **within the overall corporate plan**. IT has to **compete with other investments** (eg other fixed assets) or expenditure programs for resources, and **implementing IT can be very disruptive**. Moreover, with the growth of **end-user computing**, it is important that there is at least **some central direction** to ensure that the IT resources are used to the best advantage of the organisation. This will not be the case if the organisation is plagued with **incompatible** hardware and/or software.

A **strategy for information systems** will therefore be **part of the overall organisational strategy** and will be geared to meeting organisational objectives. Equally significantly, it **demonstrates the importance of IT** to senior management and their commitment to it. Finally, it has the function of laying down the **plan for managing IT** in terms of **technical standards** and **organisational responsibilities**.

(b) **Developing an IS strategy**

Each organisation goes about the task of developing an information systems strategy in a different way. It may be carried out by a **corporate strategy department**. On the other hand, it may be carried out by a special team selected from **user departments** and the organisation's **computing professionals**. **Management consultants** may be involved, especially if the organisation lacks management time or expertise.

Making IT strategy part of the strategic plan for the organisation as a whole might involve a **culture change** for some organisations, especially those with long-established corporate strategy departments.

However, **all** strategy developments are likely to conform in some respects to the model outlined below.

A model

(i) Personnel devising the strategy are given **terms of reference**. The brief may be very broad, or quite narrowly defined. The terms of reference may be developed from the overall organisational strategy.

(ii) A **plan** is made for the strategy development exercise. This means defining in more detail what exactly is the subject of the study, from considerations of potential competitive advantage to purely technical decisions which need to be decided at strategic level. The plan would detail the timetable, required resources, and specify the outputs of the planning process.

(iii) **Strategy definition**. Three types of document are written.

   (1) The **information systems** strategy. This details the long-term information plan to support business strategies or to create new strategic options.

   (2) The **information technology** strategy seeks to provide a framework for the analysis and design of the organisation's technical infrastructure (eg communications, computing hardware, open vs proprietary systems).

   (3) The **information management** strategy refers to the management of information systems, in terms of necessary resources, authorisation procedures for systems development projects, cost control, and management of the technology (eg security policy).

(iv) **Strategy implementation**. The strategy is then set to work. To be successful, the exercise should have a **high profile** within the organisation and there should be suitable **commitment** to it from senior management. This means that any demarcation problems should be sorted out.

(v) **Review**. The success of the strategy should be reviewed on a rolling basis.

3   BUSINESS AND IS/IT STRATEGY ALIGNMENT

1   **Mission statement**

The first stage in any strategic analysis is to produce or revise the company's mission statement. The mission statement provides a reasons for the business existing and explains what the organisation actually does.

In this situation, the current mission statement states that XF will be producing *domestic* goods. The move into entertainment systems will therefore entail an amendment to the mission statement as a wider range of goods will be produced.

An appropriate statement may be:

To '*produce high quality electrical goods at an affordable price*'; dropping the word domestic provides the company with the opportunity to produce any electrical goods, including therefore entertainment systems.

2   **Interpret the mission to the company's stakeholders**

The major stakeholders who will need to be convinced about the change in strategy include the shareholders and the bank.

The need for change must be presented to shareholders in a positive way, with the need to expand the product range to provide increased returns and more effective competition being mentioned. If shareholders can see some benefit for themselves, they are more likely to retain their shareholding, or even increase this if profit and dividend forecasts are favourable.

The directors have already recognised the need for a loan to finance the expansion. The bank will expect to see cash flow and sales / profit forecasts to justify the request for a loan. The directors will need to stress again the improved competitiveness that expanding the product range will provide, and possibly explain the problem of not expanding the range. Any existing loan may be in jeopardy if the XF company does not remain competitive and provide a suitably large product range to compete effectively.

3   **Set objectives**

Objectives explain how the mission statement can be achieved. They are very similar and in many places used synonymously with the terms goals. The objectives will normally be measurable to help provide some success criteria. Checking that the objectives have been met will show the success, or otherwise, of the organisation.

Objectives that can be used in this situation include:

(i)   Profitability - overall and by product line to show precisely the additional benefit of manufacturing the new product lines

(ii)   Return on capital employed to monitor investment in any new IT equipment and other plant and machinery

(iii)   Dividend paid to show the increase in returns to the shareholders

4   **Environmental analysis**

An environmental analysis will help to identify the specific threats to the company as well as the benefits of making the investment decision. Various techniques including PEST and SWOT analysis can be used to try and ensure completeness of the analysis.

In this situation, the main threat appears to be the lack of a complete product range in the marketplace. This presumably limits the effectiveness of XF's sales strategy. Threats may also include whether the company can continue as a going concern without the investment.

Opportunities will include being able to compete effectively, and hopefully using existing knowledge of domestic goods to decrease the research and development time of entertainment goods.

5   **Position analysis**

Position analysis provides more detail that the initial environmental analysis. This analysis starts to ensure that the company has sufficient resources to undertake the expansion as well as checking other areas are in place such as the supply chain and overall value chain.

6   **Corporate appraisal**

A corporate appraisal completes follows steps 4 and 5, making the directors to make the decision to commit to the new investment. Results from the environmental and position analysis are reviewed before the final decision to commit to the project is made.

7   **Gap analysis**

The gap analysis compares the outcome of step 6 (that is what will be done) with the objectives in step 3. This is a check between where we are now with where we want to be. Any gaps identified, such as lack of money, IT, plant and machinery etc will be noted and formal plans and budgets prepared to obtain the resources.

4   PREPARATION QUESTION: IT EXPENDITURE

(a)   **Investment or expense?**

IT expenditure is a major item in the budgets of many organisations. In some organisations there is a clear perception that today's IT expenditure should be made as a part of an **overall organisational strategy** and that it may bring benefits for years to come, for example by conferring **competitive advantage**.

If a business by its nature either does not require IT or cannot make use of IT then IT should not be introduced. However, once a particular sector of a business **needs** to use IT then it is most constructive to see the situation as an investment opportunity.

Relevant factors to consider include the following.

(i)   What **resources** are needed for the development and operation of the particular system.

(ii)   The **investment appraisal method(s)** to be used.

(iii)   The **risk analysis** approach to be adopted.

(iv)   What **funding** is available, and at what cost; and how this fits in with the overall strategy.

(v)   Whether any of the IT functions are run as **external** bureaux facilities with direct income.

(vi)   How **quickly** the expenditure **benefits** will accrue.

(vii)   How the expenditure will **impact on other activity**

(viii) How the **benefit returns** from the system will be **monitored**

(ix)   How costs will be **allocated** across different systems.

(x)   How **expenditure** will be monitored.

(xi)   How **standards** will be maintained in the event of decentralised purchasing.

In general, it will be necessary for IT projects to **compete with other types of projects** for funding. If unlimited funds are available, then all positive NPV projects can be undertaken; if funds are limited, then IT projects may not be undertaken at all.

It should be remembered that treating any area of an operation which **does not produce direct revenue** as an investment opportunity is difficult, and monitoring the costs while successfully managing productivity is also very difficult, as in any large construction activity.

(b) **Charges** can be established for all activities in an operation, and charging for services can be applied across the organisation. The IT area is often a prime candidate for this type of approach. Factors which might influence the decision adopted for charging include the following.

    (i)   A need to **apportion** the costs of the IT function accurately to the areas requiring it.

    (ii)   A need to **establish the true cost** of the IT operation.

    (iii)   A need to establish **areas of waste** in the IT function.

    (iv)   A need to analyse the **case for decentralisation**.

    (v)   Whether parts of the IT function could be used to **generate external income**.

    (vi)   What **internal and external rates** should be charged for IT services.

    (vii)   Whether the amounts which would be charged warrant the **cost of the charging mechanism**.

    (viii)   Whether any bookkeeping system is available to **control** the charging.

    (ix)   Whether there would be undue **negative impact** from cross-charging, either on the **operation** of the organisation or on the **morale** of personnel.

    (x)   Whether **compensation** would be due in the event of the IT department's failure to perform or deliver.

The **focus** of the IT function is also important to the decision to run it as a profit centre. Factors here include the following.

    (i)   Whether the emphasis is on **service** levels, **expenditure** or **both**.

    (ii)   Whether the IT (and other functions) are to be run as **business centres**.

    (iii)   Where the IT **funding** is to come from.

    (iv)   How **independent** the IT function should be allowed to become.

    (v)   Whether other departments in the organisation could then **source** their IT activity from **other** IT providers.

Techniques by which user departments pay for IT services incurred by central departments are known as **chargeout techniques**, but are sometimes referred to, perhaps imprecisely, as **transfer pricing** techniques. There are three broad possibilities.

    (i)   Information technology can be treated as **a corporate overhead**. Under this system IT is treated as a general administrative expense, and is not allocated to user departments. In other words, user departments do not have to 'pay' for IT services out of their budgets.

    (ii)   A **cost-based chargeout** means that users are charged a proportion of the costs of the IS department according to some measure. However, simply splitting the IS department costs on a percentage measure at the beginning of the budget period is inappropriate as it may not reflect **actual use**. Cost-based chargeout systems should motivate users to employ computer resources efficiently. It is felt that pricing computer services will achieve two results.

(1) It will allocate scarce computing resources according to **economic efficiency**.

(2) It will **regulate overall demand** for computing services within an organisation.

(iii) **Market-based chargeout methods** are used where the IS department sets its own prices and charges for its services to make a profit. This is only workable in a situation where there is an external market for the same services.

5 PREPARATION QUESTION: DECENTRALISATION AND END-USERS

(a) (i) Many large organisations are currently either divesting control of their central IT function or downsizing the operations onto PCs. The downsizing often results in a sharp move from a large IT function to just network management and PC support functions.

Benefits of centralisation

(1) **Enhanced control** over both processing and data. With the function contained, senior management should be able to exercise fairly strict control over the software side of the organisation, the day to day processing of the data and the security of the raw and processed data. For example, standard reporting formats and procedures can be introduced throughout the organisation.

(2) Ease of producing **consolidated results**. With the data in a central location the production of reports relating to the whole organisation should be easier than if the data had to be collected from a number of sites.

(3) There may be **economies of scale** from the operation of one (larger) computer at a single location, rather than the use of a number of processors in different locations. However, the **costs** involved (the equipment, the specialised staff needed and the **infrastructure** required to support larger computer installations) form a persuasive argument in **favour** of **moving away** from a **central** facility. In addition the specialist staff involved often have no role which is directly related to the organisation's objectives - they are employed solely as **a necessary overhead** because of the use of the central facility.

(4) Centralisation may allow the organisation to employ **fewer systems professionals**. However, centralised staff are often too remote from an organisation's actual operations to be able to address actual operating requirements properly.

Advantages of decentralisation

(1) **Savings on staff** can be substantial - specialist staff requirements can often be reduced to one or two; instead, higher technical skills will be demanded of line management.

(2) **Savings on communications equipment and infrastructure** can also be large. In addition a large degree of resilience is obtained from using larger numbers of smaller machines, any one of which can normally be replaced without impacting on the others.

(3) Enhanced standards of **report presentation**. Software on smaller machines often leads that on larger machines in terms of its presentation capabilities.

(4) **Focus at a local level**. Because the staff involved at each location would be close to the operation they would know the details, be able to respond to them quickly and could also be encouraged to 'own' both the problems and the solutions. Solutions could be produced using very standard software such as small database programs, spreadsheets and word processors.

(ii) **Central activities**

Activities which might be best left in a central function might include:

(1) **Personnel** management
(2) **Support** and **network management**
(3) **Standard setting** (eg corporate style) and **monitoring**
(4) **Communications equipment** specification and procurement
(5) Overall information technology and information systems **strategy**
(6) Central **purchasing**

(b) **End-users**

(i) End-user computing is increasing for two main reasons.

(1) The first is that the **cost of end-user processing** continually **reduces** (software prices remain static or fall gradually; hardware prices are on a general downward trend) while the facilities and ease of use of the tools have improved. As mentioned above, databases make only simple or minimal programming demands, while spreadsheets and other packages often provide all the processing required, at a superior level of presentation.

(2) The second is that the **cost of central solutions continues to increase** while the delays in obtaining specific relevant solutions from central facilities (the applications backlog) are often considerable.

(ii) End-user computing has much the same impact on the central IT function as decentralisation does.

(1) The first result of the shift will be a **reduction in the staffing requirements** in the IT area. Some IT staff may be transferred to larger or more important decentralised sites.

(2) Secondly the **staff** who remain will be required to **adopt a new role** - of central **support to the new 'user-IT' staff**. IT staff may not previously have been mindful of any need to encourage users to learn about IT and use their services, and the new supportive role will require a distinct change of approach.

(3) Some organisations respond to the pattern of decentralisation by setting up an **information centre**. An information centre is a small unit of staff with a good technical awareness of computer systems, whose task is to provide a **support function** to computer users within the organisation. The information centre staff would act as a go-between or bridge between computer users and the organisation's DP department, or external hardware and software suppliers. An information centre would be expected to **provide aid and support** to people who use computer systems and to **help users to tailor applications** to their specific requirements. They are particularly useful in organisations which use distributed processing systems or PCs quite heavily, and so have many 'non-technical' people in charge of hardware, files and software scattered throughout the organisation.

6   OUTSOURCING; DEPARTMENT STRUCTURE

> **Tutor's hint**. It is possible to answer this question reasonably well with little reference to the case study – but to score very highly you should relate the points you make to the situation faced by the insurance company. Be careful in part (b)(ii) to apply your knowledge of flat structures to the IS department.
>
> In part (a)(i) we have included more advantages and disadvantages to show a broader range of answers.

(a)   **Outsourcing** means that some of the activities that were performed by staff employed within an organisation are now carried out by staff employed by a third party.

In the question, a **contract** would be agreed between the organisation and a third party, and technical support, user help and systems development would then be run by the **third party** rather than the organisation itself. The third party provides the services to the organisation and **employs the staff**, including payment of employment taxes, training, etc, for a fee and the organisation is **relieved of the management** of those particular areas.

(i)   **Advantages of outsourcing**

The advantages of outsourcing, from the point of view of the outsourcer will include the following.

- **Cost control**

  An outsourcing contract normally provides for a **fixed price** contract for specified services. Where this contract extends over two or three years the organisation will find that **budgets** are easier to set and costs **easier to monitor** because they are specified in the outsourcing contract.

- **Economies of scale**

  Because the Facilities Management (FM) company is employed by a number of organisations, will be able to obtain **economies** in some areas that would not be available to individual organisations. For example, **specialist staff** will be available on a part-time basis; product development **costs can be shared** between the clients of the FM company.

- **Employees skills and knowledge**

  Many small to medium sized organisations cannot offer their IT staff a well-defined career path. The result of this is that many staff will tend to stay for a short period of time to gain some experience and then move to new jobs. The organisation therefore loses the skill and knowledge of those individuals. However, an outsourcing company can **offer more staff development** through the different organisations it services. Skills and knowledge of individual staff will be available to organisations when required.

- **Specialist staff more easily available**

  Staff with **specialist skills can be shared** between a number of organisations. An individual organisation may not be able to afford a programmer with specific skills (eg HTML programming). The organisation may have to hire contract staff to obtain these skills. However, the FM company can provide these staff as required, and their knowledge is retained in the FM company for later use if required.

- **More resources are available on demand**

  If the organisation requires more staff for a particular project, eg a systems changeover, then these can be obtained from the outsourcing company. The benefit to the contracting organisation is that more staff are available, almost on demand, so the whole process of job interviews and selection is avoided.

(ii)   **Disadvantages of outsourcing**

- **Information provision is too important to contract out**

  All organisations rely on the information produced by their IT systems to **run a successful business**. It may not therefore be appropriate to sub-contract the provision of this information or any part of the IT systems to a third party. **Information provision**, unlike cleaning or catering and other commonly outsourced services, is **essential to the organisation** and should therefore be retained in-house.

- **Increase in risk**

  If IT systems are outsourced, then more **confidential information** will be available to people who are not employed by the organisation. This will increase the risk of **accidental or deliberate disclosure** of that information to third parties. Retaining IT systems in-house allows the organisation to exercise more control over who is allowed to view confidential information, which in turn decreases the risk of disclosure.

- **Competitive advantage**

  The organisation may miss opportunities to gain some competitive advantage because the FM company **does not fully understand the organisation's business**. Similarly, there is no onus on internal management to **keep up with new ideas** because the FM company should be doing this. Opportunities may again be missed because both internal managers and the FM company miss some new ideas. Retaining control of IT systems should hopefully avoid these problems because staff will be **looking for new ways** to enhance the system for their own or their clients' benefit.

- **'Lock in'**

  When a contract is awarded to an FM company, it can be very **difficult to reverse** that decision in the future. Should the organisation wish to retake control of IT systems again in the future, it will find this difficult due to a **lack of in-house knowledge**. A lot of planning (and considerable cost) would therefore be needed to re-establish the IT department in-house.

- **Lack of cost focus**

  Using an outsourcing company means that managers do not always obtain a proper **awareness of the costs and benefits of IT**. The FM company is paid a monthly fee, and this may be **difficult to relate** to the service being provided. Retaining IT development in-house would provide managers with a clearer cost of IT because any IT requests are likely to be paid for from their own **department budgets** rather than be an apportionment of **company overheads**.

(b)   A **flat structure** means that there are **fewer levels** of management. Diagrams showing
typical Tall and Flat organisations follow.

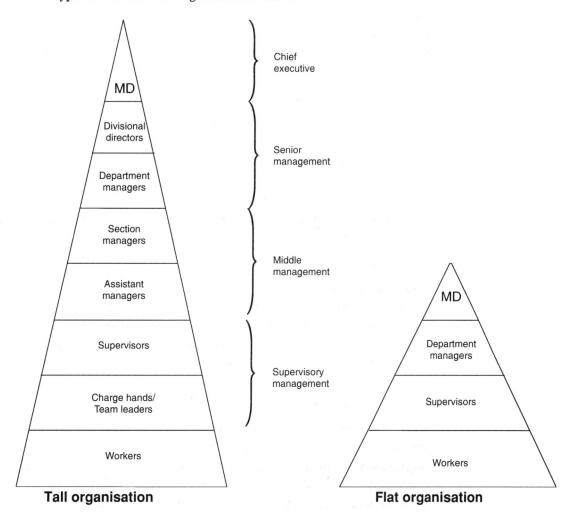

Tall organisation   **Flat organisation**

A **flat structure** can be appropriate to an IS department because it **reflects the project
based nature** of the IS department's work.

A large amount of the work of the IS department is project based rather than role
based. This means that **traditional role-based structures will be inappropriate** for the
department. A project manager may find that there are no projects to manage one-week
and then 4 projects the week after. Similarly programmers may have three programmes
one week and none the week after. Retaining normal functional roles means that a lot
of the time of important individuals can be wasted.

However, using a flat management structure implies that individuals are **drawn from a
'pool' of resources** for individual projects, **as they are needed.** Staff may have to
perform slightly different roles at different times. In some situations, one large project
may need only one 'project manager'. Other project managers will therefore be found
roles managing sections of the project, rather than the overall project. This may create
some friction but staff are kept **fully employed** and hopefully **more motivated** by this
arrangement. Changing the **remuneration structure** of the organisation to reflect the
role rather than an individual job will ease the introduction of this method of working.

7   **CENTRALISED V DECENTRALISED**

REPORT

To: The Directors, AB plc
From: A Consultancy
Date: 30 March 20X1
Subject: Configuration options for the new computer systems

Terms of reference and executive summary

Further to your letter of instruction of 28 January 20X1, we were asked to produce a report for the half year board meeting specifying the reasons for and against using different computer systems. The current manual system was documented, and a number of options discussed with management. This report summarises the results.

The two options being actively considered are the following.

(a) A central mainframe with terminals at each depot (the 'centralised system').

(b) Minicomputers such as IBM AS/400s at each regional depot connected together over a network (the 'distributed system').

The second option, using a network of minicomputers, is better suited to the organisation's requirements. We recommend that this option be actively considered.

Centralised system

This will involve setting up a room at head office or a central location in which to run the mainframe-based system. This room will have to have good environmental control, together with security. In addition you should consider establishing a back-up computer facility which could be used in the advent of a breakdown on the main machine.

The centralised system will be linked to the depots by leased telephone lines. These will be expensive to run, but in the case of the larger depots will provide voice facilities, allowing you to save on the current voice phone charges.

The system will require specialised staff to run it. This will impose a new department on the organisation, and will result in an additional headcount of approximately fifteen. There will be a small loss of jobs at the regional level.

Advantages of the centralised system

(a) Having a central up-to-date set of data which will be accessible by all depots.

(b) Maintaining a single set of data, which will eliminate inconsistencies in data used for different purposes.

(c) Providing the head office with the centralised control which the current system lacks, as freight can be tracked from one depot to another.

(d) Setting up of a centralised and specialised DP team with expert knowledge focused in one department.

Disadvantages of a centralised system

(a) Capital costs. The back-up system and the high cost of the main computer are both major factors.

(b) Operating costs, for example, high telecommunications costs.

(c) The problem of being entirely dependent on one machine. Computers do fail, and the impact on the business of the central machine failing would be great.

Distributed system

This would involve installing a minicomputer at each region, and another at the head office. Although space would have to be found for each, they can be installed in standard office environments. Staff would have to be trained at each site, and these staff could provide back up in the event of others being on leave or sick.

Advantages

(a) Keeping the responsibility for the system with the regions. This would encourage the regions to 'own the system' and would also encourage them to keep the data accurate.

(b) In the event of any single machine failing it would be reasonably easy to acquire another on a short-term basis.

(c) Lower communication costs, as most line usage will be within individual regions.

(d) Speed of processing is improved and local priorities can be better satisfied.

Disadvantages

(a) Control would require on-going monitoring and effort. A supervisor at each region would have to be designated as the person responsible for ensuring procedures were adhered to.

(b) Installation of, and training on, new versions of software would take more time and cost more. In addition, the logistics of installing later releases of software would require careful monitoring.

(c) Capital costs, involving acquisition of six minicomputers, will be high, although with phased regional implementation this can be spread more easily than a single mainframe purchase.

(d) Operating costs, particularly staff costs, will be high as it will be necessary to maintain a certain level of expertise at each regional office, resulting in some duplication.

8   PREPARATION QUESTION: FEASIBILITY

> **Tutor's hint**. Your answer should identify the main objectives of the feasibility study. Ensure you don't confuse the contents of a feasibility study report with the terms of reference.
>
> In part (b) we have given you several more alternatives than the question required.

(a)   (i)   **Objectives**

A feasibility study is a formal study to decide **what type of system** can be developed which **meets the needs** of the organisation. The main **objective** of a feasibility study is to ensure that a project can be carried out, literally is the project *feasible*? This will be considered in terms of whether the technical and operational **performance** required can be achieved using **existing technology** for an acceptable **cost**. Subsidiary objectives will be defined in each of these areas, as explained in part (b).

(ii)   **Types of feasibility**

(1)   **Technical feasibility**

The requirements of a project must be technically achievable. Any solution must be able to be implemented using **existing or proposed hardware, software and any other equipment**. Some of the criteria that the equipment may have to meet include:

- Processing a given **volume** of transactions
- Meeting a requirement to **store** files of a given size
- Guaranteeing **response times**
- Supporting of a given **number of users**

The project will be checked to ensure that the exact criteria can be met.

(2) **Operational feasibility**

The proposed solution or system must fit into the **existing operational structure** of the organisation. If the solution conflicts with the way that organisation operates, for example if it **changes** management responsibilities or reporting structures, or it involves unacceptably high **costs** or **redundancies,** the solution may not be acceptable. A project must fit into the existing operations of an organisation to gain acceptance. A project that does not meet this aim is likely to fail due to **lack of management support** or **lack of understanding** of how the new system works in the overall context of the organisation.

(3) **Social feasibility**

Social feasibility means looking at whether the project fits in with the existing **social structures** in the organisation or checking to see which of these need amending. The areas that will he investigated to ensure compatibility in this section will include:

- **Personnel policies**

- **Job specifications** and whether these need to be amended

- Possible **industrial disputes** due to changed responsibilities or work practices

- Changes in **skills requirements**

- **Motivation** of employees both before, during and after the project

(4) **Economic feasibility**

Even though a project may meet the feasibility criteria above, it must still prove to be **economically feasible**. This means that it should be the 'best' computerised solution that is **affordable** from those under consideration.

Costs that will be considered include **capital** costs (hardware and software) and **revenue** costs (support, maintenance), and **one-off** costs such as training. **Benefits** are generally less tangible, but may include **speed** of processing, **savings** in staff costs, and a higher **quality**, more **competitive** product or service.

Also, the project should be judged in terms of **opportunity cost,** or what else the organisation can do with the money to be invested in the project. Just because the project passes the other feasibility criteria and will make a positive return does not mean that it should go ahead. Precedence may still be given to **other projects** (eg a new fleet of delivery vans) if this is more important to the company at the time a decision needs to be made on the project.

(b)

> **Tutor's hint.** Your answer might have expanded upon any of the following possible terms of reference.
>
> (a)   To **investigate** and report on an **existing system**, its procedures and costs.
> (b)   To define the **systems requirements**.
> (c)   To establish whether these requirements are being met by the **existing** system.
> (d)   To establish whether they could be met by an **alternative** system.
> (e)   To specify **performance criteria** for the system.
> (f)   To recommend the **most suitable system** to meet the system's objectives.
> (g)   To prepare a detailed **cost budget**, within a specified budget limit.
> (h)   To prepare a draft **plan for implementation** within a specified timescale.
> (i)   To establish whether the hoped-for **benefits** could be realised.
> (j)   To establish a detailed design, implementation and operating **budget**.
> (k)   To **compare** the detailed budget with the costs of the current system.
> (l)   To set the **date** by which the study group must **report back**.
> (m)   To decide which **operational managers** should be approached by the study group.

Terms of reference

The terms of reference for a feasibility study are normally set out by the steering committee. The terms **explain the objectives** of the feasibility study and will normally include the following.

(i)   **Objectives**

The objectives of the feasibility study including the deliverables – that is **what the feasibility study should produce** when it has been completed.

Many feasibility studies conclude with a series of **alternatives**, for example, recommendations on whether to continue with the project, and if so, **what further actions** are required to continue.

(ii)   **Definition of system and system requirements**

The **requirements** of any revised system will be stated in the terms of reference, and the **system itself** needs to be clearly identified (eg the sales order processing system might include sales order processing only, or it might be inextricably linked to stock and production systems).

This information is needed to help identify **what information is already produced** by existing systems. The amount of work required to implement a revised system will be tailored to take into account what is already available in an organisation.

(iii)   **System recommendation**

The study will investigate a small **number of possible solutions** and recommend the **most appropriate** to the organisation being studied.

The study will need to take into account the specific **standards** and **operations** that already exist in an organisation. Different solutions will therefore be required in different situations. Care will have to be taken to ensure that any solution **really does match** the specific situation of the organisation.

(iv)   **Costs and resources**

The terms of reference will need to set out the **funds and resources available** to undertake the study. For instance a team of ten systems analysts can clearly conduct a more extensive study than one analyst working alone, but will cost considerable more. and will need more equipment (PCs, analysis tools).

(v) **Reporting deadline**

This is the date when the feasibility report is due from the steering committee.

The reporting deadline is necessary so that the Board can **set a date to make a decision** regarding the recommendations from feasibility study. The format of the report will also be defined so that it can read and assimilated quickly when it is finally produced.

9   PREPARATION QUESTION: CRITICAL PATH

(a) (i)   In a network diagram, the critical path is the sequence of activities that will take the longest time to complete. If there is a delay to any of these activities then this will result in a delay to the overall duration of the project.

(ii)   Activities on the critical path are: A. D, E, F and G.

(iii)   As noted in (i), a delay in any of the activities on the critical path will result in delay in the overall project. Identifying the critical path is useful for the project manager because it indicates those activities that must be monitored closely. Other activities not on the critical path can be allowed to over-run their time by the amount of float (the difference between the earliest finish time and the latest finish time). To ensure that the project is completed on time, experienced resources will be allocated to the critical activities so that these are not delayed. Similarly, if two activities are falling behind schedule, then additional resources are added to the critical activities first to ensure that the total project time is not increased.

(b) (i)

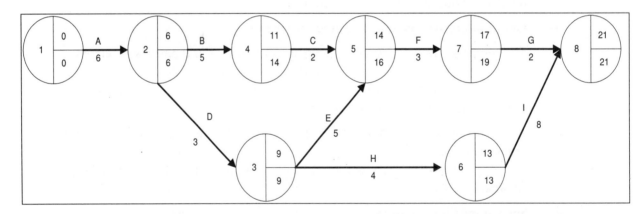

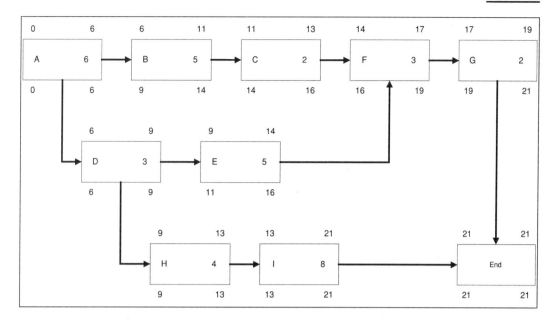

(ii)   Activity E can overrun by up to 2 days.

(c)   A network shows a series of activities progressing through time. This means that loops are not allowed in the network, as this would effectively mean repeating sections of the project which is not possible given the linear flow of the network diagram.

In the example, C cannot start until B is complete, but similarly, B cannot start until C is complete, making the network unworkable; B can never start.

As an alternative, the network can be re-drawn with a new activity in place of the re-work of B. This content of this new activity will be defined and a new letter allocated to it, as shown below.

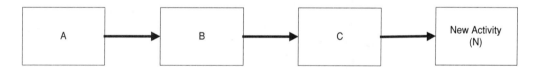

10   PREPARATION QUESTION: NETWORK CHART

(a)   (i)   See next page.

(ii)   The elapsed time of the project in days is 42.

(iii)   The critical activities on the critical path are: A, B, D, E, F, I and J.

(iv)   The number of days that activity H could overrun, with all other activities meeting their budgeted times is 1 day. Activity H must start on either day 26 or 27 to meet the deadline of day 32.

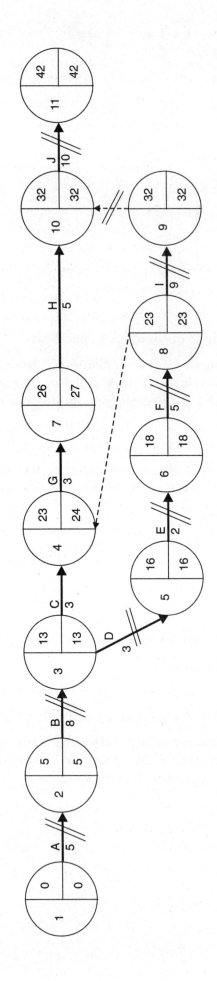

**Network Analysis
Software Implementation**

(b) Project management software can assist with the development of the initial plan in a number of ways.

Automating production of the project plan

Project management software will accept details of the various activities in a project. This information can then be used by the software to **produce appropriate documentation** such as network and GANTT charts, saving a considerable amount of manual development time.

Amending resources

With all the links and dependencies built into a model, the planner can amend the resource constraints to see overall effect on the project. The effect of increasing the amount of overtime to be worked can be **quickly and easily seen**, with changes in the project being summarised by the software.

Resource constraints

Many network charts assume that **time** is the main constraint within a project. However, there **may be other constraints** such as workers available or amount of supply of a specialist material. Entering these constraints into the software may produce amendments to the plan, such as activities running in parallel being run separately, due to lack of appropriate resources.

11   FEASIBILITY STUDY

(a) A computer feasibility study is intended to evaluate the appropriateness of computerising an application which had been accomplished manually or by using another system. It is intended to accomplish three things.

(i)   Assess the information processing requirements found in an application.

(ii)   Identify and investigate various alternatives which could satisfy the requirements identified.

(iii)   Inform management about the options and the costs, benefits, technology, risks, labour implications etc of each.

(b) **Each of the three sections or stages in a feasibility study may be justified.**

The assessment of needs provides the foundation for all other analysis. Here one identifies what tasks are to be computerised and quantifies the requirements in terms of volume, speed, accuracy, security etc. Without this understanding of what the system will need to do it is most unlikely that an effective or economical system will be obtained. This phase looks primarily at the **functions to be performed** and the required performance standards.

Given the required tasks and performance standards a **variety of alternatives** may be reviewed and compared. The objective here is to keep an open mind and consider a full range of options. Several options might satisfy all performance criteria and then be referred to management for a final decision, perhaps with a recommendation for one.

The information provided to management on costs, benefits, etc allows them to consider any systems acquisition, development or upgrade. This information allows systems to be **compared more effectively**.

(c) The study would normally be carried out by a **feasibility study team**. This team would include:

   (i) Someone from the **software house** having a detailed knowledge of computers and systems design

   (ii) One or two **senior managers** having a detailed knowledge of the workings and staff of the departments affected

   (iii) An **accountant** to carry out cost-benefit analyses of the proposed system, and prepare a detailed budget for installing it

(d) The best solution for the organisation is best identified through a thorough **investigation,** as would be provided by the feasibility study. The understanding gained by studying an existing system and formalising its operation **will aid in designing** a new system, or in **developing a specification** for one. Any purchase of a package without first developing **a sound specification** is likely to leave the company with a system unsuited to their needs.

(e) Four factors which would justify **introducing a new computer system** for production planning and scheduling would be these.

   (i) **Better control over the handling of customer orders** so that these are dealt with more expeditiously.

   (ii) **Improved production planning** to allow the company to fill orders more effectively and deliver production in a more timely fashion.

   (iii) **Inventories will be more closely monitored** and improved production planning will reduce the amount of work in progress. These reductions will reduce the company's need for working capital to yield a direct improvement in cash flow.

   (iv) By improving its production scheduling it will find that **better use of both equipment and labour will result**. This will improve profits, perhaps significantly.

12   PROJECT COSTS AND BENEFITS

A proposed system may be in **competition for resources** with other projects in a company. A **monetary evaluation** provides at least a **common scale** by which different projects can be measured.

A distinction can be made between **one-off costs** and **recurring** costs.

One-off costs can be of a 'capital' or 'revenue' nature.

On the **capital** side, this may include the cost of **equipment, software** (if purchased outright rather than leased), and any new **buildings** or office installations.

'One-off' **revenue** items may include a variety of **systems development** costs. These include the cost of **management time,** the **salaries** of the systems analysts and a great deal of time spent in **implementation**. Other one-off expenditure will include **recruitment** of appropriate staff, training, and possible **redundancy** costs.

The distinction between 'capital' and 'revenue' is an important one. The project is likely to be justified in '**cash**' terms, whereas the costs most likely to appear in the company's profit and loss account relating to capital expenditure will be the **depreciation** of fixed assets over a number of years. Depreciation is not a cash flow at all, and so the effect on 'profit' will not bear an immediate relationship with the initial cash outflow. One-off revenue expenditure, however, is likely to be charged immediately to the profit and loss account. The decision to buy a new system will be made on the basis of '**cash flows**' (ie does the company have enough money?) rather than '**profits**'.

Recurring costs, apart from the non-cash items mentioned above, include:

- **Sa**laries for operational staff
- Data **transmission** costs
- Consumable **supplies** (paper, disks)
- **Power**
- **Rental**
- Hardware **maintenance**
- Software and hardware **support**
- **Leasing** charges for hardware and software if held under licence
- **Disaster recovery** arrangements
- **Training**

Benefits

The benefits from a proposed new system must also be evaluated wherever possible. These ought to consist of the following.

(a) **Savings** because the old system will no longer be operated, including:

   (i) Savings in **staff costs.**

   (ii) Savings in **other operating costs,** such as consumable materials.

(b) **Extra savings** or revenue benefits because of the **improvements** or enhancements that the new system should bring eg:

   (i) Possibly **more sales revenue** and so additional contribution.

   (ii) Better **control**: for example with a new stock control system, fewer stock losses from obsolescence and deterioration.

   (iii) Further savings in staff time resulting perhaps in **reduced future staff growth**.

(c) Possibly, some one-off revenue benefits from **sale of equipment** which the existing system uses, but which will no longer be required. Second-hand computer equipment does not have a high value, however. It is also possible that the new system will use **less office space,** and so there will be benefits from selling or renting the space accommodation.

In addition, computerisation might produce a one-off benefit by making the company's operations **more efficient**. The information provided may allow more control over the detail of the company's operation, which will mean that the company's resources will have less chance of being wasted.

The relevance of NPV

These costs and benefits will normally be given a monetary value which in many cases may be the most appropriate way of treating them. An organisation might employ **discounted cash flow techniques** to estimate the **future costs or benefit**.

However, discounted cash flow techniques cannot accurately account for the **non-quantifiable costs and benefits** of any installation. As computer systems become more sophisticated, their applications in management become much more generalised. It is hard to put a value on the number of **improved decisions** a manager is able to make using a decision support system, for example.

13 PROJECT INITIATION

Leadership style

(a) The leadership style of the manager is tending to be autocratic; that is team members are being told what to do without the opportunity to discuss the decisions being made. This leadership style tends to be appropriate for staff who need a lot of guidance through a project.

(b) In this situation, most of the staff have professional qualifications, indicating that they are able to think though problems for themselves and monitor their own work effectively. A more appropriate management style would be participative. Dave could discuss the work to be done and then let staff carry out this work. This approach would benefit staff by providing them with more responsibility and benefit Dave by freeing up more time to monitor the overall progress of the project.

Lack of communication

(a) The cancelling of project meetings can have an adverse effect on morale, as well as making communication between the team members more difficult. While it appears that more work will be carried out on the project, if staff feel that they are not being communicated to, or that they cannot discuss problems, then overall work efficiently is likely to suffer.

(b) This problem is easy to resolve; Dave should re-introduce the team meetings and apologise for making the mistake of cancelling them in the first place. This will provide an appropriate channel of communication and help team members realise it was not their fault that the meetings were cancelled.

Lack of project updates

(a) The other problem with cancelling team meetings is that project team members will not be aware of how the project is progressing overall. Team members may not feel motivated to work harder if they perceive that other members are not "pulling their weight". The possibility of conflicts within the team suggest that morale and trust may be low, and so motivation may be an issue.

(b) Re-introducing the team meetings will assist communication and help all team members to see how the project is progressing. When all team members can see that everyone is working hard, then this will have a positive impact on morale and the overall amount of work being done.

Accountability for errors

(a) Making team members accountable for errors is acceptable, where those members made mistakes in the first place. However, in this situation, the "trainee" systems analysts were not responsible for a large percentage of the analysis work as this was carried out by the previous analysts.

(b) Dave should really be grateful that these two team members are attempting to continue this important work, and not place hindrances in their way. An appropriate way of maintaining motivation would be to simply ask for explanation of any errors found; accountability for those errors can be decided later, if necessary.

Conflicts within the team

(a) The number of small disputes within the team indicate that working relationships are not good. These problems will tend to affect overall communication and working efficiently within the team, as members will not feel that they can discuss problems with each other.

(b) In this situation, Dave is wrong to ignore the problem; his team is already behind schedule and trying to hide the problem is more likely to make it worse. Dave must attempt to resolve the conflicts in some way, preferably by meeting and discussing with the team members why the conflicts are arising.

If the problems cannot be resolved, the project will continue to fall behind schedule. The conflicts and the lack of trained analysts may indicate that the project deadlines need to be moved, or the project cancelled until a full working team with good relationships can be used.

14   CRITICAL PATH ANALYSIS

(a)

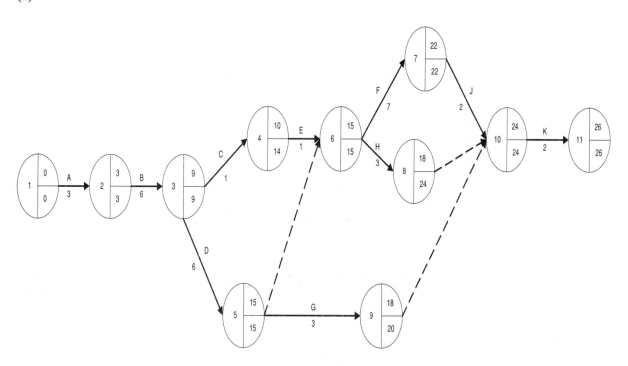

The critical path is A, B, D, F, J, K.

(b) One of the potential failings of a network diagram is, although it shows the expected timings for a project, it does not easily show the actual time taken. Monitoring a project using the diagram is therefore difficult.

There are alternatives to using a network diagram.

A GANTT chart is similar to a horizontal bar chart. The different activities in a project are listed on the left of the diagram, and the timescale placed on the X axis. When the budgeted start and finish times for each activity are known, these can be plotted on the chart. The timescale is used to show the activities relate to each other over the duration of the project; potential clashes are therefore identified.

As the project progress, the actual time for each activity can also be plotted on the GANTT chart. The actual time is normally identified using a bar of a different colour placed under the budgeted activity. Identifying the actual time assists control of the project because over-runs on specific activities can be seen, and the knock-on effect to subsequent activities noted.

15   SYSTEM INVESTIGATION

(a)   The reasons why an analyst should **investigate and document** the current business system can be summarised as outlined below.

To obtain user input

It is important that users are involved in the systems project because they will be able to provide valuable information concerning how the system works. In any systems project, it is easy for users to be 'left out' of the systems development; this may lead to rejection of any final system as well as providing lack of confidence in the systems analysts and their team. Involving users in data collection will involve them in the project as well as helping to ensure that the systems documentation is as complete as possible.

To understand the problems with the current system

Any new system will be designed, not only to meet new design specifications, but also to **alleviate problems with the current system**. If information about the current system is not obtained, then any problems in the systems will not be identified and so the new system will not be written to remove those problems. Areas that may be improved by this analysis include introducing better controls, easier to follow work methods and clearer systems design and documentation.

Decrease new development work

Many of the features that are in the current system will be used in the new system. Providing documentation of the system will **help the analyst to understand** how the old system works. Having obtained this information, the analyst can decide whether or not to use the functionality of the current system or to write new software. If the current system information is not obtained then this decision cannot be made and software development work for the new system may take longer.

(b)   Methods and models that can be used in investigating and documenting the current business system will include:

Questionnaires

Using a questionnaire means that the same set of questions can be sent to a large number of staff **quickly and cheaply**. The questionnaire can be tested prior to distribution to ensure that the questions are complete and accurate, while the large sample size can attempt to obtain a good representation of the target audience. However, the response rate from questionnaires can be quite low (typically 30%), and it is not always possible to remove ambiguity in the questions asked or ask additional questions to expand on the comments made.

Interviews

Interviews tend to provide better information than questionnaires because the interview is an **interactive** process. The interviewer can asked additional questions to check the understanding of the interviewee, while the interviewee can check understanding of questions being asked to avoid any ambiguity. The interviewee may also be able to provide additional insights into the current system, which will not have been provided in a questionnaire. However, interviews can take a long time to organise and carry out which may limit their use.

Flowcharting

A flowchart is a **pictorial representation** of the document flows in a system. This can be very useful for checking the accuracy of information collected about the current system because the user will be able to see document and the departments that the documents move through on the flowchart itself. Flowcharts do, however, take a long time to produce and can be difficult to modify should they be incorrect. Also, although they show document flows clearly, they may not show exactly what information is needed to complete a document or where pure data flows (as opposed to document flows) are in the system. Other techniques may therefore be required to provide a complete picture of the current system.

Decision tables

A decision table will help the analyst show in **tabular format,** all the different outputs that can be obtained from a set of inputs. For example, customers may be awarded discounts based on the product purchased, the value of transactions made during the year and even the day of the week that the product is purchased on. A decision table can be constructed to show the **different combinations of factors** ('conditions' in the table) that will result in specific discount amounts ('actions'). This table can be validated by discussions with users to provide the analyst with confidence that all appropriate discount rates have been accounted for. The decision table assists programming work by making potentially difficult decisions easier to understand.

16   NEW SYSTEM IMPLEMENTATION

(a)   The other members of the feasibility study team must bring their own particular knowledge and expertise to the study. There must be **operational expertise,** and this might be provided by three managers:

(i)   The central stores manager
(ii)   The distribution manager
(iii)   The manager of a store or group of stores in the chain

The management accountant should have an understanding of the costs and financial aspects, and some IS knowledge too, but it would also be sensible to include the IS manager in the team (assuming of course that the organisation has an IS manager).

(b)   Major **information requirements** of the system are as follows.

(i)   Current amounts of stock held centrally and locally, for each item, in physical quantities and value.

(ii)   Stock-outs in the central stores, and locally, and their duration.

(iii)   Periodic sales for each item, analysed by store and in total.

(iv)   Stock delivery requirements (each half-week) for each store - ie stock orders for each store and in total.

(v)   Delivery loads and schedules for each vehicle - ie delivery schedules.

(c)   The **principal stages in the implementation of the proposed** system are as follows.

(i)   **Select the hardware and software** required, as a result of the feasibility study. Order the hardware and software, with agreed delivery dates. Arrangements for back-up and maintenance should be made.

(ii)   **Install the equipment** centrally and in the shops. If there is to be a staged implementation of the new system, equipment might only be installed in a few selected shops at first.

(iii)   There must be **staff training,** ideally provided by the supplier or dealer. If training is made to coincide with the delivery of the hardware and software, the staff can carry on training by practising on the company's own equipment after the training course has ended.

73

One or two 'experts' in the system should be appointed. These would deal with queries from other operators of the system, and act as the link with the supplier's back up and maintenance service.

(iv)   **Testing**. Ideally, the new system should first of all be tested on 'dummy' data. The testing process could be used both to iron out operational snags with the new system and to continue the process of staff training.

(v)   **File creation**. Files for the new system must be created before the system can be operational. This can be a long and tedious process.

(vi)   **Changeover to the new system**. The changeover to the new system should be planned carefully. To start with, a few stores and head office could begin to operate the new system in a pilot run. Lessons could be learned from the pilot run and applied to the subsequent introduction of all the other stores to the system. (The option of parallel running would probably not be practicable for retailing operations, where stores staff might only have time to record sales once, using whatever point-of-sale hardware is introduced for the new system.)

(vii)   **Review and evaluation**. The new system should be reviewed and evaluated, once it has settled down, to determine whether or not it is achieving its intended objectives.

(d)   **Criteria to evaluate the choice of system**

(i)   **Reliability**. The reliability of the software and hardware should be checked, eg by following up references from other users of similar systems.

(ii)   **Costs and benefits**. The benefits of the system should outweigh the costs. The costs would include software and hardware purchase costs and running costs such as maintenance and the rental of any data communication links that might be used etc.

The benefits might be difficult to evaluate but include:

(1)   Lower stockholding costs
(2)   Fewer stockouts and so more sales and profits
(3)   Possibly, fewer staff costs

The **expected operational life** of the system would also be relevant to the comparison of costs and benefits.

(iii)   **Better management information**. The quality of the management information will be a factor in the choice of system, although the benefits of a better MIS (apart from those listed above) would be virtually impossible to evaluate in financial terms.

(iv)   The **flexibility of the system**. Will it allow the user to expand and modify the use of the system as operational requirements change over time?

17   STAGES OF A SYSTEMS DEVELOPMENT PROJECT

The stages involved from the 'initial proposal' to the new system becoming fully operational may comprise the following.

(a)   Initial study/project identification
(b)   Setting up of the steering committee
(c)   Feasibility study
(d)   Evaluation of the proposals
(e)   System design and development

(f)   Installation and implementation

(g)   Post-implementation review

Each of these stages is described briefly in the paragraphs following.

The initial study

This may or may not involve trained systems analysts. It may be carried out by a team (if necessary) of departmental representatives headed by an experienced manager (for example, the chief accountant). The purpose of the initial study is to clarify the problems the change is intended to solve and to outline the managerial requirements. This stage is essential so that senior management will be able to direct those involved in the detailed feasibility study. The study, sometimes called a job specification, should quantify the disadvantages of the existing system so that a true comparison of costs and benefits can be made with the proposed solution.

The steering committee

The steering committee will normally include representatives of top management from each department affected by the project. Its function is to appoint and control the feasibility study group and it will bear the responsibility of evaluating results of the feasibility study and of making the final recommendation to the board of directors. In a small organisation the feasibility study team or systems analyst may be directly responsible to the board of directors.

The feasibility study

The steering committee, must establish the terms of reference within which the systems analyst and his team will work in carrying out the feasibility study. The aim of such a study is to assess the data processing and information requirements of the organisation, to investigate and recommend possible solutions and to provide management with information on which a decision can be based. This information should include the advantages and disadvantages of each suggestion from the technical, economic, organisational and social points of view. A plan should be made for the development, implementation and control of the recommended scheme.

When defining the new system the analyst must consider any legal, accounting and auditing requirements, especially the level of systems control. He should also produce a new cost/benefit analysis study of the proposed system, as part of the complete feasibility study report.

The evaluation of proposals

Once the feasibility study is completed the steering committee has the task of evaluating the proposals in the report and submitting final recommendations to the board of directors.

The steering committee, or board of directors, must relate the feasibility study proposals to the original objectives laid down. If these objectives are met, and the acquisition of a computer is approved, then the more specific details in the proposal should be considered and approved.

System design and development

Once the feasibility report's recommendations for the computerisation of an application have been accepted, it is the task of the systems analyst(s) to design and then to develop and implement the new system. To design and develop a larger system may require a number of analysts and programmers. The analysts should work closely with user department representatives and representatives from internal audit.

Once the system has been accepted by management the development team will produce a full systems specification. This is a complete documentation of the whole system and must always be properly maintained (ie kept up to date) as parts of the system are changed or added to. The specification is the analysts' means of communicating with management, programmers, operations staff, user departments and auditors. and the documentation should cover reports to management on each part of the system. specifications to programmers. instructions to users (re inputs/outputs). instructions to computer staff.

Programmers will have to develop, and test the specified programs prior to the system becoming operational. Standard programs may be adapted to the proposed system. All work has to be fully documented.

Installation and implementation

This involves planning all the stages of design, installation and implementation (eg by the use of network analysis, critical path analysis, Gantt charts, etc). Once there is some idea of the equipment that will be used the installation planning involves the selection of site for the computer and peripherals, and other data processing department offices. Then comes the preparation of the site (eg air conditioning, strengthened flooring, electricity supplies, fire protection etc). and finally, the installation of all equipment and delivery of tapes, disks etc.

Implementation of the new system involves planning in detail the change-over procedures, the detailed testing of new computer files from the old systems files (with detailed checks on this file conversion). When every detail appears to be satisfactorily covered and tested, the staff have the considerable task of carrying out the actual change-over (direct, parallel or pilot operations - as decided by the systems analyst).

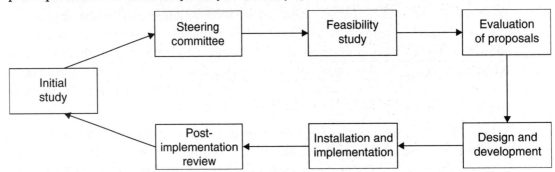

The post-implementation review

In appraising the operation of the new system after the change-over, comparison should be made between actual and predicted performance. This will include (amongst other items) consideration of throughput speed (time between input and output), use of computer storage (both internal and external), the number and type of errors/queries, the cost of processing (data capture, preparation, storage and output media, etc). It is important that the system should be reviewed periodically so that any unforeseen problems may be solved and to confirm that it is achieving and will continue to achieve the desired results. Indeed in most systems there is a constant need to maintain and improve applications and to keep up to date with technological advances and changing user requirements.

18   SYSTEMS DEVELOPMENT LIFECYCLE

REPORT

To: The Board
From: Management accountant
Date: 14 May 20X1
Subject: Computer systems upgrade

This report urges the Board to adopt a **more formal approach** to the proposed systems upgrade than seems to have been envisaged up until now. The approach recommended is The Systems Development Life Cycle (SDLC), which is described in the next section of this report.

No action should be taken regarding the purchase of computer hardware and software until the **needs of the business** have been considered in more detail.

The Systems Development Life Cycle (SDLC)

The SDLC is a **disciplined approach to systems upgrades** intended to reduce the possibility of an end result that **does not meet the needs** of the organisation and **wastes time and money**.

There are six stages, although in practice the stages may overlap.

Feasibility study	Briefly review the existing system
	Identify possible alternative solutions
Systems investigation	Obtain details of current requirements such as data volumes, processing cycles and timescales
	Identify current problems and restrictions
Systems analysis	Consider why current methods are used and identify better alternatives
Systems design	Determine what inputs, processing and storage facilities are necessary to produce the outputs required
	Matters such as program design, file design and security need to be considered
	The end result is a detailed specification of the new system.
Systems implementation	Write or acquire software, test it, convert files, install hardware and start running the new system
Review and maintenance	Ensure that the new system meets current objectives, and that it continues to do so

The cycle **begins again** when a review suggests that it is becoming difficult for an installed system to continue to meet current objectives through routine maintenance.

Why WRF Inc should follow this approach

Arguably WRF has not even reached the end of the **first** of these stages, yet a purchase recommendation has been made for a highly standard system using hardware and software that is **already outdated** in terms of the fast-moving world of IT.

(a) A **systems investigation** is needed so that account is taken of the **specific requirements of users**. At present, users only know of a proposed change through the grapevine: they do not appear to have been formally consulted. This is particularly regrettable since they seem to be enthusiastic about change and would no doubt **have a good deal to contribute** to the specification of an ideal system for their needs.

(b) More **systems analysis** is required to determine what are the problems with the existing system. The upgrade is intended to improve the **speed** and **clarity** of information, but we have no details of how the design of the proposed new system will do this. The following points may be made.

   (i) Windows 98 is **hungry for hard disk space, processing power** and **memory**. The hardware proposed (basic Pentium PCs with running at only 75MHz) is **not adequate** to run Windows 98 versions of applications such as Microsoft Office.

   (ii) Is there a real **need for a LAN and e-mail**? Perhaps there is, or perhaps stand-alone PCs and conventional methods of communication would serve just as well, or perhaps a larger network would be more appropriate. **Other options** do **not** appear to have been **considered**.

   (iii) Information in the company's **existing database** is likely to have to be **converted** in some way to make it compatible with the new system. What will this entail? Will data have to be entirely restructured and if so how. Will all the data have to be re-input, or is there software available to ease the task. Again the **full issues** do **not** appear to have been **considered**.

(c) Account must be taken of the **future needs** of the business. We trade in a dynamic environment and our information needs may well be significantly different in future years. Will the proposed system be able to cope with change and growth? Much of the proprietary software now being released (and no doubt being used by our competitors) is designed for a Windows 95/98 or Windows NT environment and requires a Pentium PC with around 64Mb of RAM and a large hard disk.

(d) The recommended system is reckoned to **cost** about $1,500 per user. Presumably this also includes a **shared element** for the network and communications infrastructure, for all the software and licences needed, and for peripherals such as printers.

   However, we have **not actually been told what the figure includes**: we need a **detailed breakdown** of the **initial cost** and also of **ongoing costs** over the life of the proposed system. We should have similar details for alternatives within budget limits set by the Board.

(e) Arrangements need to be made for the **implementation** of the system. Even in the short term the analyst's contract ends at the installation stage: does this mean that we will be **without his support** during the early days of the system going live, when it would be unusual for there to be no teething problems?

Recommendation

The systems analyst should be asked to satisfy us on all of the above points, and modify his proposals as appropriate.

19 PREPARATION QUESTION: CASE TOOLS

(a) **Computer aided software engineering (CASE) tools**

A CASE tool is a piece of software that produces **documentation** to help with the construction and maintenance of models of logical systems (often following the rules and relationships peculiar to a particular methodology, such as SSADM). They may also facilitate **generation of program code** and **prototyping**.

(b) **CASE tools and systems development**

Systems design is similar to a building project in that it requires detailed plans and blueprints: commonly used methodologies such as SSADM make extensive use of documentation throughout the development process.

(i) CASE tools can **create design diagrams** (for example DFDs) on screen. High quality **documentation** can be produced in a manner similar to most graphics packages, and updating and maintenance of complex models such as DFDs and entity-relationship models is made easy, quite the opposite of the manual approach.

(ii) They can check **adherence** to the design and development **standards** that set out how development will be carried out. A CASE tool will not allow designers to break rules (such as not linking one data store directly to another) that they could easily break accidentally if working manually.

(iii) They can create a logical **data dictionary** from the items identified. Entries are made for entities, data flows, data stores, processes, external entities and individual data items and the dictionary can be easily maintained, checked for consistency, cross-referenced and analysed. This means that it is easy to extract a **list of each occurrence** of, say a particular external entity or **trace the links** between the entities of an entity relationship diagram to the data stores of a DFD.

The complexity of all but the smallest systems would make **manual** maintenance of a data dictionary an extremely **time-consuming and error-prone** task, and manual analysis of relationships between items within a reasonable time-scale would be impossible.

(iv) **Prototyping** is supported by CASE tools in a number of ways.

(1) **Code-generation facilities** automate the production of code in a high level language. **Diagnostic aids** enable subroutines to be tested independently of other programs, and a library of often-repeated procedures which can be incorporated into programs is provided. This means that the **software can be built extremely quickly** and potential users can experiment with it very soon after they have described what they want to the systems developer.

(2) They can show potential users a **demonstration** of a proposed new system, since they make it possible to show how the contents of the data dictionary will appear on display screens (linked together using, say, a series of menus).

20   STRUCTURED APPROACH/CASE TOOLS

(a)   **Structured analysis** is a term used to describe an approach to systems analysis and design which:

(i)   Emphasises the **logical design** of a system (eg types of data, data relationships, what processing operations) over the actual hardware and software.

(ii)   **Proceeds from the general to the particular** (so the system as a whole is designed before individual applications or programs).

(iii)   Is **heavily documented** in a standard way, with evidenced user involvement.

This approach has led to the formation of a number of systems development methodologies. A structured analysis methodology follows the principles outlined above, and organises the design project in a number of defined stages. One such methodology is **SSADM (Structured Systems Analysis and Design Methodology)**. The stages in a SSADM development project are outlined below.

(i)   The **feasibility study** is carried out to examine the 'case' for undertaking a particular project in terms of its **feasibility** (financial, technical, social and ethical) and its **costs and benefits**.

(ii)   **Investigation of current environment.** In this stage the current system is investigated, described and analysed using the techniques of **observation, questionnaires, document description forms** and so forth. A major requirement of this phase is that the current system is properly documented, for example, using **data flow diagrams,** and the **logical data structure** is described. A further product from this stage is a **problems/requirements list** or requirements catalogue.

(iii)   **Business system options.** This involves the specification of the requirements of the new system, where **what users actually require** is laid down in detail. Any solution offered must satisfy these requirements. Options are suggested, from which a shortlist is created. A cost/benefit analysis (in brief) and an assessment of the impact of the proposed system will be prepared, and a choice made.

(iv)   **Requirements specification.** The team takes the results of the previous stage, and arrives at a **requirements specification,** in which detailed DFDs etc are drawn up and specifications for **input** and **output** from the chosen system are prepared.

(v)   **Technical system options.** At this point users are asked to make choices concerning **hardware** configurations and **software**.

(vi)   **Logical design.** In this stage, the **data and file structures** for the new system are designed. This stage also includes the development of output formats, and specifying the type of **dialogue** that users will have with the system, to ensure that it is consistent with what has been prepared so far.

(vii)   **Physical design.** Physical design involves obtaining the design rules from the chosen system, and applying them to the logical data design drawn up in the previous stages. Requirements for audit, security and control are considered.

(b)   **CASE** stands for **computer aided software engineering**. CASE techniques aim to automate the document production process, and to ensure automation of some of the design operation. There are two types of CASE tool.

(i)   **Analysts' workbenches** are software which perform several analysis tasks.

   (1)   **Create** design **diagrams** (eg DFDs) on screen.

   (2)   Check **adherence** to **design standards**.

   (3)   Verify that **diagrams are consistent** with each other and that the relationships are correct.

   (4)   Help generate **specimen input and output documentation** (ie from the data flows identified in the diagrams).

   (5)   Create a **data dictionary** from the data items identified.

(ii)   **Programmers' workbenches** provide similar features to ensure consistency of coding during the later stages of the design cycle.

   (1)   There is usually a **code-generator** facility to automate the production of code in a high level language from, say, Structured English or pseudocode.

   (2)   **Diagnostic aids** enable subroutines to be **tested independently** of other programs.

   (3)   A **library of subroutines** is also provided. These are often-repeated procedures which can be incorporated into programs.

A CASE tool could contribute to the development of an information system in the following ways.

(i)   **Document preparation** and re-drawing of diagrams is made easier.

(ii)   **The accuracy of diagrams is improved**. Diagrammers can ensure consistency of terminology and maintain certain standards of documentation.

(iii)   **Prototyping** is made easier, as re-design can be effected very quickly.

(iv)   **Blocks of code can be re-used**. Many applications incorporate similar functions and processes; if pieces of software are retained in a library they can be used (or modified) as appropriate.

21   WATERFALL MODEL

The Waterfall model of software development breaks the systems development process into sequential stages, with the output from a stage forming the input to the following stage. This process works very well where the user and system requirements are known in advance of development. However, its use becomes more limited where requirements are changing or there are significant time constraints on development. Some of the important limitations of the model are explained in the sections below.

(a)   **Lack of significant design changes**

   The waterfall model **does provide a relatively efficient means of computerising existing** systems, especially where the new system is modelled on an existing manual or computerised system. However, while the system may gain in terms of efficiency of design and delivery, it tends to **lack the use of innovative techniques** or major design changes. The new system will therefore tend to reflect the existing system.

   This **may not be helpful in the case of Niagara,** where the current accounting package is nine years old. Given that the organisation has grown significantly during this time, there may be additional features that are required within the accounting system. Using the Waterfall approach may preclude implementing these features. Use of another model, which starts from a "clean sheet" of paper rather than building on an existing system, may provide a more realistic and user-friendly system.

(b) **Sequential model structure**

The sequential model structure **tends to be restrictive** in **terms of amending specifications** due to changes in requirements part way through system development. Where amendments are made to the specification, then these tend to be difficult and expensive.

In the case of Niagara, it is known that a significant system change will be required part way through the development process. To incorporate this change, the specification for the new accounting system could be delayed. However, if this is not possible, then the use of the waterfall model may preclude any significant change taking place during the system development process. Use of a spiral model may be more appropriate, as the change in the manufacturing system can be incorporated into one of the prototypes during the overall system development.

(c) **Time overruns**

Any sequential model is prone to time overruns, as the start of each stage of the model is dependent on the completion of the previous stage. While this does help to ensure that the entire development process is followed, it does mean that activities that could have been carried out concurrently will not be allowed.

The sequential nature of the approach will not assist the Niagara Organisation. Accounts staff will only be available at a specific time each month; the timing of user input will be critical. If one "window" of time input is missed, then it is possible that the project will be delayed by up to one month awaiting the next slot of free time in this department. There will be an increased risk of poor system design where incorrect assumptions are made concerning user requirements. Similarly, blame may be attached to the developers for delays, where the real reason for the delays is not known. This will not make working conditions easy for the system developers.

This situation is not easy to resolve, although providing more user input time from the accounts staff would be useful. Use of an alternative development approach, which allows some development to continue whilst user input is obtain will help to manage time delays to some extent.

(d) **Review and maintenance**

Review and maintenance are treated as an activity with a definite start and finish. However, for most computer software, **maintenance is continuous and modifications are made on a regular basis.**

By "completing" the maintenance part of the development, amendments for new user requests, or new system requirements will not be possible. Given that Niagara Organisation will be continuing to update systems for the next two years, this implies that the accounting system will soon be out-of-date again, because amended requirements from other systems will not be incorporated into it.

Use of an alternative approach which views maintenance as an ongoing process, such as the spiral model or the "b" model, will help ensure that the accounting software is kept up-to-date.

22 PREPARATION QUESTION: ENTITY RELATIONSHIP MODEL: ENTITY LIFE HISTORY

> **Tutor's hint**. This question is taken from an 'old syllabus' examination. The material is still useful under the new syllabus, although future questions are likely to be able to be answered using a range of modelling techniques.
>
> The syllabus classifies models as Process, Static Structures and Events. Two examples of each are named in the syllabus.
>
> **Process models** – Data Flow Diagram, Flowchart.
>
> **Static structure models** – Entity-relationship model, Object Class Model.
>
> **Events models** – Entity Life History, State Transition Diagram.
>
> The ACCA has stated that future questions will be able to be answered using either one of the two examples provided for each type of model.
>
> Our answer to this question is probably longer than you could produce under examination conditions, to show the relevant points that could be made.

(a) **Entity relationship models**

Purpose of entity relationship models

The main purpose of entity-relationship models is to show a business system in a diagrammatic format. The diagram is then used to talk users through amendments to a system, or a completely new system, so they can start to understand how that system will work.

If the system is accepted, then the model will then be used as a basis for a more detailed design of the system where items such as detailed file specifications will be produced.

Notation of entity relationship models

An entity relationship model is designed to show the how different parts of a system are linked together. The two main parts of the system are:

- **Entities**

  An entity is an object or item within a system. Specific examples will include objects like people, places, files of sales invoices or stocks of raw materials. One entity may occur may times within an entity-relationship model so each is given a unique identifying number to avoid confusion.

  An entity is shown on an entity-relationship model by a rectangle with the name of the entity placed inside it.

- **Relationships**

  The links between different entities are called relationships. In an entity relationship diagram, drawing a line between the linked entities shows the link.

  There are three types of relationship:

  One-to-one, where one entity is linked to one other entity. An example could be one despatch note causes one unique invoice to be raised. This relationship is shown be a straight line joining the two entities.

  One to many, where one entity is linked to many other entities. An example could be one particular component is used in the manufacture of many different products. A single line departing from one entity but branching into three before it reaches the second entity shows this relationship. All three lines join the second entity showing the 'many' relationship.

Many to many, where many entities are linked to many other entities. An example could be many different customers purchase many different products. The line between each entity in this situation is branched at both ends showing the many to many relationship.

Entity life history

Purpose

The purpose of an entity life history is to show, for each individual entity, how that entity is created, what modifies the entity, and finally how that entity is deleted from a system.

Producing a diagram in this format allows an analyst to concentrate attention on one particular entity. This enables a detailed check to be carried out on that entity to ensure that all create, modify and delete activities have been identified. Situations may also be found where these activities no longer occur and so they can be removed from the history.

When the analyst and user have validated the history, it will be used in subsequent system design activities such as object-orientated design where activities are defined within an object.

Notation

The main format of an Entity Life History is a series of rectangles arranged in an hierarchical manner. The first level contains one rectangle which contains the name of the entity being described, such as sales invoice or despatch note.

The **second level** contains three rectangles, which are all linked to the first level rectangle. These rectangles **describe the creation, amendment and deletion** of the entity. If there is only one event that can give rise to each action, such as a despatch note resulting in a sales invoice being produced, then this event is stated in the appropriate rectangle. If there is more than one event, then these are described in the third level of the Entity Life History.

The third level of the Entity Life History is used where there is **more than one event for the creation, amendment or deletion of an entity**. The different events are linked to the appropriate second level rectangle. Where the events are optional, that is either event will result in the appropriate action occurring, then a small circle is placed in the event rectangle. Where an event can occur more than once, such as a customer address changing, then an asterisk is placed in the event rectangle.

(b) Using a CASE tool to create and maintain these models may provide some or all of the following benefits.

Maintenance of central data dictionary

Information about all entities can be maintained in a central dictionary. Keeping all this information in one place makes it easier to maintain and update.

Easier to produce appropriate diagrams

Some CASE tools provide programs to produce diagrams of file and data structures from the entity information held in the central database. Using these tools will make it quicker to produce the appropriate entity diagrams.

Clarity of diagrams

Having the computer produce the diagrams means that the diagrams are likely to be neater and more professional looking.

Update of diagrams

Manual update of diagrams, either using pen and paper or a drawing tool on a computer can be time consuming. If data for either model changes, a new diagram can be printed out quickly and easily using the CASE tool.

Cross-referencing of information

Where both entity relationship models and entity life histories are used, the CASE database can maintain information about the links between these models. In effect, the entities in the relationship model will provide an overview of that entity, with the main detail being maintained in the entity life history.

23   PREPARATION QUESTION: ENTITY RELATIONSHIP MODEL

(a)   **The Entity-Relationship model is designed to show the entities within a particular process and the relationship between those entities.** Each entity is shown as a rectangular box, with the entity itself being an item referred to during the overall process such as a person (eg CUSTOMER), an object (eg PRODUCT) or a document (eg ORDER).

Entities are included in the model because the organisation needs to hold information on them. The information being held is shown in the normalised table below the model. For example, the entity PRODUCT-TYPE is maintained with the data **product-type-code** and **product-type-description,** that is specific detail, or data fields, about the entity. The *product-type-code* provides a unique reference to that product while the *product-type-description* is a description of that particular product.

The lines on the model show the relationship between the different entities. All of the relationships in this diagram are termed 'one-to-many' relationships. For example, one sales region can have many customers, but each customer only belongs to one sales region. The relationship is shown by the branching of the line at the end of the 'many' relationship.

On the normalised table, the link between the entities is shown in the key field. The CUSTOMER entity is related to the SALES REGION by the region-code appearing in the customer table.

(b)   The PRODUCT entity is related on the entity relationship model to the PRODUCT-TYPE. However, in the normalised table, the field PRODUCT-TYPE does not appear as a foreign key in the PRODUCT entity. In the normalised table there is no link between these two entities.

The error can be corrected by adding the PRODUCT-TYPE field to the to the PRODUCT entity type and marking this as the foreign-key. There will now be the required link between these two entities.

The ORDER-LINE entity type includes the field *customer-no* as a foreign key. However, on the model, there is no relationship shown between these two entities. The error is resolved by removing the *customer-no* field from the ORDER-LINE entity in the normalised table.

The link between the ORDER-LINE and the CUSTOMER is established by two other links; one from ORDER-LINE to ORDER (by the foreign key *order number*) and secondly from ORDER to CUSTOMER (using the foreign key *customer number*). The direct link between ORDER-LINE and CUSTOMER is therefore not required.

(c)   **The Entity Relationship model does not support the new requirement because it does not include attributes for** *effective date* **and** *reason-for-change*. These new attributes could be included in the CUSTOMER CATEGORY entity, but this would create a many-to-many relationship in the model; that is one category will relate to many customers, but also each customer can relate to many different categories. This relationship is difficult to support in the model. To resolve this problem, a new entity called CUSTOMER HISTORY can be established to link the CUSTOMER and CUSTOMER CATEGORY entities. The two new attributes can be placed in this entity allowing a *customer-number* to be associated with more than one *customer-category-code*.

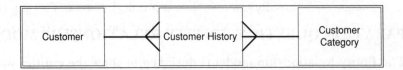

24   MODELLING TECHNIQUES

(a)   There are three different types of models that are used to represent systems; Process, Static Structures and Events.

Process models show the way that data is processed within a system. They concentrate on showing how the data moves around a system rather than providing any explanation of the hardware, software or other physical elements of that system. The aim of the diagram is to provide a basic understanding of how the system works without being distracted by the physical requirements of that system.

One of the main types of process models are Data Flow Diagrams (DFDs). These diagrams show the flow of data through a system. Three basic constructs are used to explain the data flow:

- An external entity identifies where data is input into a system from an outside source (such as another department or a customer or supplier)

- A data store shows where data is kept either temporarily or permanently, and

- A process shows the actions that take place on that data.

The constructs are joined by data flow lines, which show the route taken by the data through the system. DFDs can be used to explain data flows in an existing system, or as a planning tool for a new system to show the data flows that will be required. Because DFDs focus on the data flows, they do not mention the physical configuration of the system.

Static Structure models show the relationship between the different entities within a system. In this situation, an entity can include a person (eg a customer), a document (eg a sales order) or a physical item (eg a product). These entities interact with each other, and the model attempts to show that interaction. The term "static" indicates that the relationships between the different entities can be determined, and that these relationships do not change within that specific system. The aim of the static structure model is to show how entities need to be linked so that a physical system can be designed to meet those requirements.

An Entity Relationship Model (ERM) is an example of a static structure model. The ERM notation includes a box for each entity, with flowlines showing relationships between those entities. A single line joining two entities shows a one-to-one relationship; that is the entities are linked directly (eg a company has one managing director). More complicated relationships are expressed by the flowline branching at the entity to show one-to-many and many-to-many relationships. The former indicate that many entities can be linked to one single entity (eg a customer can place many orders). Many-to-many relationships are not usually allowed within database constructs and will be broken down to give a number of one-to-many relationships.

Events models are designed to show the changes that can take place to a specific entity or data item within a system. There are three main events that occur to an entity; namely **creation** of the entity, **amendment** of the entity and finally the **death or removal** of an entity from a system. The modelling of these events is important because it shows the processing that must take place within a system. As with other models discussed in this answer, the events model does not show how the amendments to the entity will actually take place in a physical system. The aim of the model is to show what changes are required so that these can be incorporated into the physical system design.

An Entity Life History (ELH) is an example of an event model. It shows the three main processes that happen to each entity, with examples of each process. Additional detail is provided to show whether update events are recurring or not. Again, provision of this information will help provide a correct physical representation of the logical system.

(b) **Techniques that can be used to ensure that process models meet the user requirements**

Structured walk-throughs are used to present a design of a system to the users. The system is explained to users by way of diagrams and other documentation, and the users can check completeness of their requirements from this information. Links may also be made to the initial requirements specification to ensure that all user requirements are met within the system. At the end of the walk-through, the system may be signed-off to show agreement with the specification.

A prototype (or mock up) of the system can be constructed to **show the logical processing that will take place within a system.** Reviewing the prototype and amendments made to the final system design will identify any omissions from user requirements. Prototyping is normally identified with checking the user-interface, although it is also useful for agreeing completeness of data to be input or displayed.

25   EVENT MODEL (ENTITY LIFE HISTORY)

(a) The logical design of an information system focuses on how the different entities within a system need to relate to each other. This design is provided independently of the system's organisation and processes and includes establishing the requirement for the data and file structures to be used.

The physical design provides the necessary detail on how the system will actually process data. The logical design is used to produce an initial physical design, which shows in overview how the physical system will operate.

Physical design involves:

- Producing an initial physical design based on the logical design for the new system

- Defining any further processing required to produce the required outputs in the new system

- Creating the program specifications for the system

- Assessing program specifications for performance

- Finalising the data and file structures
- Production of user documentation

(b) Entity Life History – Supplier Account

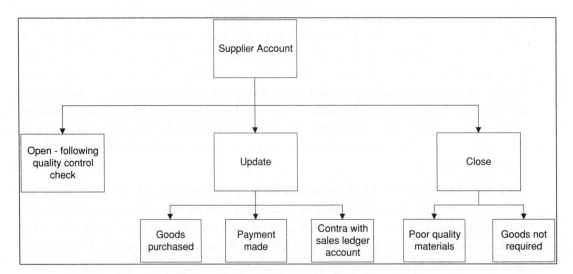

(c) Reasons for using an event model in designing information systems are noted below.

(i) A model shows the states that an entity can be in, eg create, amend or delete.

(ii) It provides information in a pictorial form, making it easier to see exactly how an entity changes over its life. Pictures generally provide a clearer representation of information than a simple explanation.

(iii) It provides a check for the physical design of the entity. All the states of the entity are identified and these can be included within the physical model design for that entity.

(iv) The model provides a check on the states of the entity, and helps to ensure that all entities are brought into being in some way and that the physical system allows this create event.

26   PREPARATION QUESTION: DATA FLOW DIAGRAM

(a) **Errors in the Data Flow Diagram**

The interview information states that the **order details are checked to ensure that the product and payment-type are valid.** This means that the two stores are checked with data flowing from the store to process 1. However, the data flow on the diagram shows data being written to the payment type store. This arrow needs reversing to show data going from the store to process 1.

The interview information also states that **the despatch-date is noted on the order file.** However, on the DFD, data is shown going from the order file to process 2 only. Another data flow is needed to show the despatch date being added to the order file.

At the end of the week, invoices are raised and sent to the *customer*. **However, the DFD shows invoice data being sent to an external entity called Invoice. The name of this entity needs replacing with** *customer*. Also, as the external entity customer is now duplicated, a line or similar duplication symbol needs added to both occurrences of the entity to identify this duplication.

(b) See next page.

Data Flow Diagram – Ordering Process

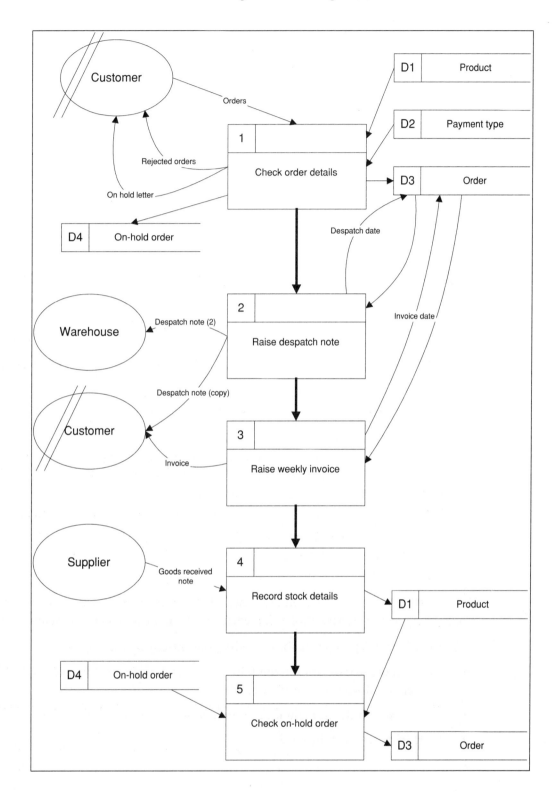

27   PREPARATION QUESTION: ENTITY RELATIONSHIP MODEL

> **Tutor's hint.** We have used the entity relationship model given below to exclude the many-to-many relationships that can be confusing when an entity-relationship model is built. These relationships will have to be broken down prior to programming. An alternative valid answer will show a many-to-many relationship between the Order and Product and the Invoice to the Cheque. Part (b) of the question does not require the ELH to be drawn. We have drawn one to help your understanding.

(a) **Entity relationship model – Customer order and payments system**

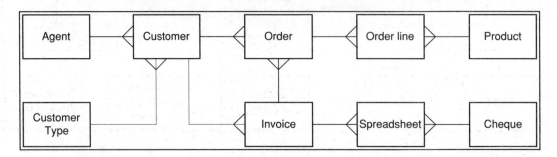

Assumptions made

Although there is no order line category in the narrative information, this has been introduced to break the many-to-many relationship that would otherwise occur between the Order and the Product entities.

Invoices can be part paid, and so one cheque can relate to many invoices. The Spreadsheet entity is used to break the many-to-many relationship between the invoice and the cheque. An invoice can be recorded in more than one part on the spreadsheet, in the case of part payments. However, the cheque can be recorded in more than one place on the spreadsheet reflecting payment of many invoices.

(b) An **alternative model** for documenting information about one entity in a system is the Entity Life History. The **ELH** shows the events that relate to an entity, particularly regarding the creation of the entity, the amendments that can affect it and the final removal of the entity from the system.

The small circles show that these events either result in the entity being **created or deleted**, while the asterisk shows that entity can be **modified**, perhaps many times.

The ELH is more appropriate for modelling the entity because:

- It is more **easily understood** by a non-technical person, especially if it is developed during an interview, and

- It **focuses on the document**, rather than the relationships to other documents.

The ELH is shown over the page.

Entity life history

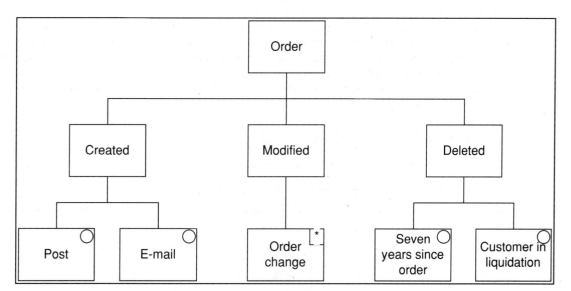

28   PREPARATION QUESTION: DATA FLOW DIAGRAM

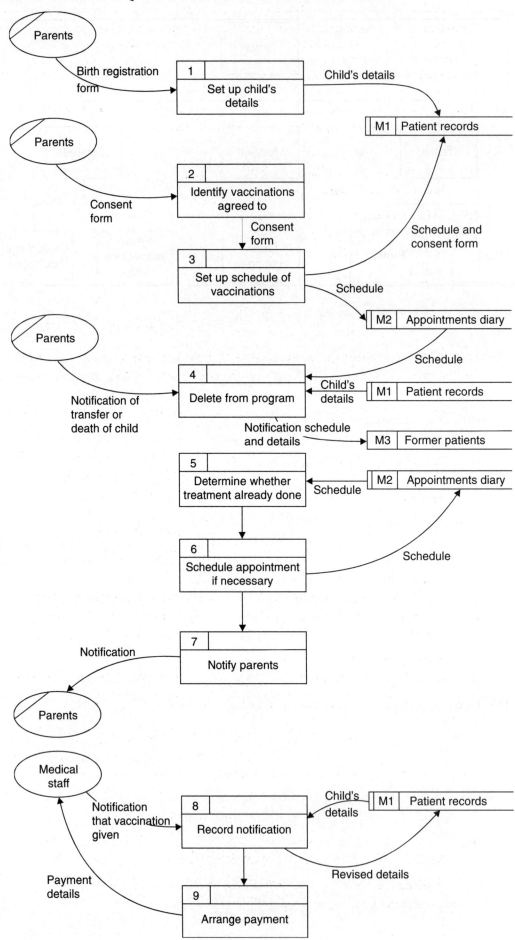

29   PREPARATION QUESTION: OUTPUT/SCREEN DESIGN

> **Tutor's hint.** This should have proved a relatively straightforward question for you. Our answer contains more than the required number of objectives and guidelines, to show a wider range of possible answers. You should *never* do this in the exam: in this case more than five suggestions would have wasted your time and would not have scored any extra marks.

(a)   The following **objectives** should be considered when designing **output**. The **key** objective is that output should only be produced where required and for the purpose(s) for which it is required.

   (i)   Output should be **clearly identified,** where necessary with sequential reference numbering and date of production.

   (ii)   The **content** of output should be appropriate, so that the user has **enough** information for the task or enquiry in hand, but is not presented with an information overload forcing him to perform unnecessary sorting and searching activity.

   (iii)   **Frequency** of production should be gauged with care. Some output is generated infrequently, for example a monthly payroll analysis or aged debtors analysis, while some is required daily or weekly (eg order books, cash reports etc).

   (iv)   Similarly, **speed** of production is important. Much 'urgent' output can be produced immediately on screen; some items such as large printouts may be run overnight.

   (v)   **Conditions** for the production of output may be specified. Some output is required regularly, some only on the occurrence of a specific incident/event.

   (vi)   **Volume** of output is important: it may be more appropriate to produce some outputs in the form of summaries or, often more useful, in the form of exception reports.

   (vii)   The output **medium** must be considered. It is not necessary to print everything out for users. One **hard copy** printout may be produced and microfilmed for archive purposes; other users may instead use **screens** to access relevant areas of the output. Screen output is transient in nature, so users who need to refer regularly to output may require hard copy. Of course, any user not connected to the system (suppliers, customers, external agencies etc) will also require hard copy.

   (viii)   **Distribution** of output also needs to be considered. Users who require output should receive it and it should not be sent to these who do not need it.

(b)   Good **input documents** should be designed with the following in mind.

   (i)   **Fields** for all data required should be included, but no unnecessary data should be added.

   (ii)   Documents should have a **clear title** and/or code number.

   (iii)   Documents should be designed to be **human-sensible** where input is manual or machine-sensible where bar-coding, MICR etc is to be used.

   (iv)   **Layout** should be **natural,** so that for example, customer name should appear before customer address. Related items should be grouped together.

   (v)   A **distinction** should be made between fields which **must** be filled in and those which **may** be filled in. Each type should be clearly marked with shading/border etc.

(iv) **Layout** should be **convenient** for the input assistant to follow, ie laid out in the same order as the fields appear on screen.

(vii) It must be clear that a document already has been input; ie appropriate **controls** must be designed to **ensure it is not input twice** or overlooked altogether, such as a box to show input is complete.

(viii) **Fields to be completed** must be **clearly titled**, with **narrative** if necessary, to show exactly what can be placed in each.

(ix) **Space** for each required **signature/authorisation** must be included on the form.

(c) The following factors should be taken into account in effective screen design. There are two broad areas to consider: ergonomics and presentation on screen.

Ergonomics

Health and Safety regulations stipulate that workstations must comply with certain requirements. The following are of particular relevance.

(i) VDUs must **not flicker,** must be free from glare and must swivel and tilt.

(ii) There must be appropriate **contrast** between the screen and the background; windows must have some sort of **blinds**.

(iii) **Radiation** must be reduced to negligible levels

(iv) The employer must offer **free eyesight testing** at regular intervals and provide any special glasses which may be needed for screen work.

Although these issues may seem **more relevant to the hardware** manufacturer than to the systems designer, it should be noted that some of the **problems** implicitly recognised in these provisions can be **countered by careful screen design**. Now that larger and better quality VDUs are available it has been possible, for example, for screen designers to replace the once-common **white-on-green** or white-on-black screen colouring with '**paper-like**' black-on-white **main screens**, and with blue and yellow on pale grey for **surrounding areas** and controls.

Screen design

The following issues are relevant.

(i) **Clarity** can be achieved by ensuring that **no extraneous information** is contained on any screen. Many screens are now designed with a **header bar** with some kind of **menu system** below it and **comments and narrative** at the **bottom** of the screen (the **status bar**), with a **large central working area**. Under Windows, the default working area is smaller than the available space, but groups of icons can be hidden or a 'full screen' option selected so that the working area's size is maximised.

(ii) **Consistency** of screen design within an application (and indeed between applications) makes it much easier for users to **navigate between** and use various **parts of a package** or **different packages**. Under Windows, for example, screens usually include a '**scroll bar** on the right to enable quick positioning within a document/file/dialogue box, and many **pull-down menus** start with '**File**' commands, next to which appear '**Edit**' commands, and so on. This consistency of approach also makes **learning/training** much easier.

(iii) **Mirroring of input documents** is an objective to be followed if users are to work with efficiency. If an input document is designed so that a customer's name and account number appear first, the **screen should be laid out in the same way**. (Of course, it may be that the input document needs revision!)

(iv)   The **overall look** of the screen is important too. This may include several features.

- **Different colours** for different screen areas

- **Reverse video** (where colours in a selected area are the reverse of the rest of it)

- **Flashing** items

- Larger characters for **titles**

- **Paging** or **scrolling**, depending on the volume of information

30   PREPARATION QUESTION: SOFTWARE DESIGN

> **Tutor's hint**. Our answer assumes that the computer system will perform as many of the calculations and completion of fields as possible – as this facilitates quick and accurate input of data.

The system may include the following items to assist in the quick, accurate and easy entry of order form details.

Check on data entered

The computer can **make a comparison** of data in many fields to information already maintained on the master files. These checks will help to ensure that only valid product codes, for example, are entered onto the form. Invalid codes will be rejected and on-screen prompts will request the correct code or even make suggestions as to what the code should be.

Completion of fields from entry of key information

Having some fields being completed by the computer can **reduce the amount of typing** on the form. For example, after a valid produce code has been entered, the computer can complete the product description by reference to the master file. Providing this description will also check on the accuracy of input. If the computer operator notes that the description is incorrect, then the product code can be amended prior to the form being completed.

Automatic calculation of some fields

One of the main types of errors on manual forms is arithmetical. Most errors can be avoided on this form by the **automatic completion and calculation of numeric fields**. In this example, having entered the product code and quantity ordered, the computer can calculate the total price, total value of goods, apply the appropriate postage and packaging expense and the total value of the invoice. The automatic completion of this information will provide timesavings and help to increase the accuracy of the form.

Completeness checks

Certain fields on the form **must be completed**, such as the customer name and address and at least one item to be ordered. If one of these fields is not completed, then appropriate messages can be displayed on-screen requesting this information. This will help to ensure that all forms have all the necessary information on them.

Form format

Ideally, the on-screen form should **follow the work method** required to complete it. So if the customer name and address are requested from customers first, then the first fields to be completed on the form should also be customer name and then address. Producing the form in this way make completion more accurate because it will be completed in a logical order.

If information is being transferred from a manual order form, then the form on-screen should be in the same format as the manual form. This will again make completion of the form easier because the operator will be able to see exactly where each part of the order has to be entered into the on-screen form.

31   PREPARATION QUESTION: END-USER DEVELOPMENT

(a)   (i)   **Fourth Generation Languages**

Fourth generation languages (4GLs) use English-like commands and are non-procedural languages. This means that **the software produces the program flows**. The programmer specifies the result required and the software codes the program to achieve it. This **speeds up program design and development** considerably and therefore reduces application backlogs.

4GLs are generally **easy** to learn; they have **on-line help** facilities, **graphical user interfaces** and are **fault tolerant**. These features mean that end-users can use them to develop their own programs; this again reduces applications backlogs and encourages the spread of **end-user computing**.

Applications and report generators are common types of 4GL. Report generators are now available with many standard applications packages and end-users are increasingly using these features to satisfy their varied information needs. Programmer time is therefore available, and better used, to develop more complex software where 4GLs may only have a limited use.

(ii)   **Information centres**

These are small expert units which provide **technical support and training** to end-users for their existing systems. Information centres may also encourage users to develop their own models or software.

Information centres should develop working relationships with all system users to encourage the imaginative development of new computer systems. They may offer a **'drop-in' advice centre** or a **telephone 'hot-line'**, or visit users at their desks. They are also likely to maintain a **bulletin board** service on the company's network or intranet.

Information centre staff provide the technical assistance to ensure that if **users develop their own software**, this is done efficiently and, if appropriate, utilised throughout an organisation. Without this level of support many users would risk producing poor quality models or macros each of which could only be used by the one user familiar with it; this is a potential disadvantage of end-user computing.

Further roles of the information centre are as follows.

(1)   To encourage users to **conform to any hardware, software or programming standards** that the organisation might use, for example to make sure that all the microcomputers purchased by the organisation are compatible, and so could be moved around from department to department if necessary or to make sure that if the organisation uses proprietary packages (for example, spreadsheets) in various departments, the same package (Lotus, Excel etc) is used in every department.

(2)   To provide users with **technical assistance**.

(3)   To ensure that applications developed are **replicated by others** in the organisation, where this would be of benefit to the organisation.

(4) To ensure that the **data** used in these disparate applications is properly **controlled** and is **consistent**.

(b) **Small computer systems and end users**

The introduction of small computer systems often **reduces the control on information** previously held by senior management. Whilst not necessarily a bad thing in itself, the **quality of information** and standards for **security** and **data flows** may fall. Applications and information may be duplicated in different functions of the organisation.

End-user program development can be inefficient, because staff may **lack adequate technical knowledge**, resulting in poor quality applications which only the developer can understand and use. Inefficient programs may also overload an organisation's hardware resource.

Addressing the risks

An **information centre**, as described above, is a useful means of controlling the quality and direction of end-user computing. **Networked** or distributed systems will help to ensure that information is generated and distributed efficiently, without duplication, and it will also allow senior management to maintain an adequate level of control. Organisations should also set **quality control standards** for all system users to adhere to. These standards should be supported by **internal audit** checks.

If end-user computing is to be encouraged then the provision of adequate **support and training** is essential. This may take the form of an information centre which is responsible for training users and encourages them to develop software for their needs whilst maintaining high quality standards. Information centres should be staffed by technical experts with good communications skills.

Encouragement of end-user computing will lead to increasing demands for applications development. The **demand must be fulfilled** otherwise users will see no benefits from their interest and enthusiasm. Fourth generation languages, report writers and other support tools should be used to speed up the development of programs.

32 OUTPUT DESIGN

(a) Standard items on a system generated report may include:

- Standard code to identify the report
- Distribution list for the report
- Date and time the report was printed
- Page numbering information
- Source of the data included in the report
- Standard to identify the end of the report
- Who printed the report

(b) The usability of the stock report may be enhanced in the ways outlined below.

The **main purpose** of the report is to **compare the stock value with the value at re-order level**. At present, these columns are separated from each other making a comparison very difficult. **The report could be improved by placing the columns next to each other** (preferably at the extreme left or right of the report to make the columns easy to locate).

The other main purpose of the report is to highlight items which are below their re-order level. In the report, products below re-order level are shown by a series of asterisks. While these products are shown, the whole report has to be scanned to locate all the product lines; and the report could run into many hundreds of pages given the product codes on this extract. **The report could be improved either by printing out the products below re-order level at the top of the report, or in a completely separate report which can then be used for re-ordering the stock lines.**

The presentation of the report as it stands is quite poor. Presentation could be improved by placing lines across the page to help read along each stock line. Similarly, alternate lines could be shaded in different colours to help users read along each line. The use of different colour writing to denote items below re-order level (perhaps in red writing) would ensure that these important items stand out in the report.

The totals provided at the foot of the report page appear to have little use; in fact the total of cost per unit appears to be completely irrelevant, as it cannot be used in any other calculation. Removing these totals will enhance the legibility of the report because users will not be distracted trying to work out what the totals mean.

(c) **A check digit is a number which is added to the end of a stock code to show whether or not that stock code is valid.** If the stock code is written down incorrectly, for example due to transposition or substitution errors, then the check digit will also be incorrect, showing the error in writing out that particular stock number.

The check digit works by a mathematical calculation being applied to the stock code; the remainder from that calculation becomes the check digit. When the stock code is written out again, or entered into the computer, the calculation can be re-performed, and the accuracy of the check digit verified. If the calculation shows that the check digit is incorrect, then the stock code is not valid and the error in writing out the code will have to be located. If there is no error in re-calculating the check digit, then the stock code is correct and the computer program will accept it.

As mentioned above, the check digit will help to **identify transposition errors**, where two numbers have been written down in the wrong order, and **substitution errors** where a number has been incorrectly replaced by a different number.

33   PREPARATION QUESTION: ITT

(a) Issues to be considered include the following.

(i)   **Compatibility**

The proposed new system may use **file formats**, field lengths and so on that are not consistent with the system in use at present. This may mean that **conversion software** will have to be written (either by the supplier, in-house or by another party) and rigorously debugged, probably involving item for item checking.

(ii) **Supplier reliability**

If the supplier is a **major world player** such as Microsoft or Oracle then there need be little doubt as to their reliability.

Suppliers of tailored solutions, however, are much **smaller** and their software is necessarily **less well tested** because it has a much smaller number of users. The company may be asking for a unique system, in which case it is the only guinea pig. Suppliers should be considered in terms of **financial stability** (their help with the system they provide may be needed for many years to come), **track record,** ability to provide fast **support** and **maintenance**, and so on.

(iii) **User friendliness**

This is often a factor that distinguishes one package from another. Two pieces of software may produce very **similar end-results** but one may be very much harder to use than another because it does not take into account the **needs of the user**. Most modern packages follow Microsoft **Windows** design principles, at least on the surface.

However, lack of care in this area is sometimes seen in poorly thought out **screen design** or lack of useful (context-sensitive) **Help facilities**. Often problems only become apparent when things go wrong, for instance when an error occurs and the **error message** only offers the user the option of abandoning all the work they have done so far (very widely used packages are far from innocent in this respect.)

(iv) **Performance**

This means that the system **does not crash** if it is given more than a certain volume of work to do, and does not take appreciably **longer** to process, say 750 transactions, than it does 500 transactions, or to compile a report covering a quarter rather than a month. Suppliers can be asked to provide figures for **speed of response** given different volumes but care needs to be taken that one supplier is not assuming, say, that Pentium PCs will be used while another's figures are based on 486s.

(v) **Overall fit**

The ITT is likely to be fairly demanding, and it may be that **none** of the tenders **exactly fits** what the company is looking for. Important issues in this case are how willing suppliers are to **tailor** their offering to **individual needs** (and at what cost), and what details in the ITT the company is willing to **go without** if a tender happens to fulfil other conditions particularly well.

(b) **Benchmarks**

One way of assessing the merits of alternative solutions would be to attempt to **run each version** of the software on the organisation's **current systems** and see which produced the most desirable result in terms of processing time(s), response, quality of output obtainable and so on.

The same data would be used for each test to make sure that the comparison was fair.

Key factors

Alternatively, or in addition, the company might identify a number of key factors such as **cost, security, support** available and so on and **weight** them in order of importance. Thus if **cost** were a factor a ideal score might be 100 and different tenders might score 60, 90 or 130 (or whatever), depending on how their cost compared to the ideal (130 would be cheaper than anticipated); if **security** were an issue an ideal might be 50 ('totally secure') in which case it is unlikely that a maximum ideal score would be achieved by any of the tenders.

The tender with the highest overall score would then be the first candidate for consideration, although there would no doubt still be certain **qualitative issues** to be taken into account.

34   PREPARATION QUESTION: SOFTWARE TESTING

(a)   **Systems testing**

Computer programmes are written and tested by programmers as the first major stage in writing those programmes. Systems testing then occurs when the initial programming is complete and the software is released by the programmers for additional testing by the systems analyst or a project leader.

Systems testing will seek assurance that the software **works correctly** in the following areas.

(i)   To ensure that the **specification for the system has been met**. Software will be designed to meet certain features in the initial specification for a project. If these features are not met, then the software will fail to meet user expectations and at the worst the whole system may be unusable.

(ii)   To check that the **user interface** is understandable and usable. Software must be easy to use; additional checks will be made to ensure that screen formats are consistent and the same keys are pressed to carry out common functions such as closing dialog boxes.

(iii)   To ensure that data is **processed correctly**. Checks need to be made to ensure that data is transferred between individual programmes (eg the sales program updates the stock balances in the stock system). Similarly, processing within one program should operate correctly (eg the correct sales ledger account is updated when an invoice is raised). Test data will be prepared and run within the program to meet these objectives. Further work will be necessary to ensure that appropriate error messages are generated (eg no sales ledger account is available for a customer), and that these are understandable by the user.

User acceptance testing

User acceptance testing will take place **after systems testing**. It is at this stage that users are involved with the software for the first time. User acceptance testing will seek the following assurances

(i)   The software **meets the systems specification** agreed by the users (this specification will normally be contained in flowcharts or entity-relationship models). Users will therefore want to check the design of the software, and in particular will check the individual screens to ensure that they are usable. Change requests may be generated where either the system has been incorrectly designed, or where users find that they need additional functionality building into the system that was not in the initial specification.

(ii)   The **workflow of each department is accurately reflected** in the software. Although the specification should reflect work flows, it is only when the system itself is available that a full check is possible. Again, change requests may be generated if the software does not meet the existing work practices.

(iii)   Appropriate **documentation** is being generated to provide training and reference material. Although this material is unlikely to be complete, users may be able to test the accuracy of draft material and provide valuable input into the important points that need to be included in both sets of material.

(b)   Both systems and user testing can use the actual system or software as a basis for testing. Other deliverables in a system project will never become a useable system and so this direct method of testing is not available. For these written documents (eg data flow diagrams and entity relationship models), alternative testing such as a **bench-test**

or **walkthrough** test will be necessary. This testing involves checking the accuracy of the document by literally talking the user through its contents. The aim is to ensure that the document is accurate and contains all the features or functions that the user requires. Other members of the systems team will also attend walk-through testing to confirm the accuracy and usability of the documentation.

In summary, demonstrating the documentation with the user and analyst in this way will ensure that the analyst has:

- **Understood the user requirements** and the business processes being used.

- Adhered to the **technical and quality standards** required of the documentation.

At the end of the testing, the documentation will be **amended** as appropriate and then signed off as being accurate by both the user and the analyst.

35   PREPARATION QUESTION: MAINTENANCE AND REVIEW

(a) (i)   **Definitions**

Corrective maintenance is carried out when there is a **systems failure** of some kind, for example in the processing or implementation procedure. Its objective is to ensure that **systems remain operational**.

Adaptive maintenance is out carried out to take account of **anticipated changes in the processing environment**. For example, new taxation legislation might require change to be made to payroll software.

(ii)   **Differences between the maintenance types**

(1)   **Computer activity**

Corrective maintenance is carried out when the computer system is '**down**' or **not working**. By implication, the maintenance is trying to correct a fault, so the **computer cannot be used**.

In contrast, **adaptive** maintenance is normally carried out when the computer system is working. Installing new versions of software or adding new users can **normally take place alongside other processing activities**.

(2)   **Reason for maintenance**

Corrective maintenance is concerned with identifying **faults** in the hardware or software that is being used. The aim of the procedure is therefore to **replace or repair** the defective hardware or software so that the system can be operational again.

However, **adaptive** maintenance is not concerned with finding or fixing faults. The changes that are required result from **normal changes to the operating environment** such as the addition of new users to the system or release of new software. The aim is to **make the required changes as soon as possible** while maintaining a normal service from the computer system.

(3)   **Software changes**

- **Replacing defective software** is corrective maintenance.

- **Upgrading existing software** with new releases is adaptive maintenance.

(b) **Measures of user-friendliness** and **frequency of use** of software can include the following:

(i) **Retention of knowledge**

Users can be asked to complete a short computer based **test** on the use and features of the software both **before and after training** as well as about one month **after they have started to use** the software.

The **results of all three tests can then be collated and reviewed**. If the software is easy to use then users should find they obtain a **higher score on each of the three tests**. A high score after a month of use indicates that users are comfortable using the software, and have even learnt new features. A lower score would indicate that the software is difficult to use and users are actually using less of the available features.

The data can be collected directly from the computer testing system. If the results indicate that users are not retaining knowledge of the software, the results can be analysed to show **which sections of the software need additional attention**. Short, focused training courses can then be arranged on those features to increase the user's knowledge.

(ii) **Number of calls to the HELP desk**

Users will tend to call the help desk when they cannot use or understand part of the new software. The **higher the number of calls** therefore, the less likely it that the software is user-friendly. Not being particularly user friendly in this case also indicates that the **help system in the software** is not particularly easy to use. Users would normally be encouraged to use the help system prior to telephoning the help desk for assistance.

Help desk staff can record the number of calls to the help desk. Many help desks **automatically record telephone calls** into a database. Every week or month, the calls can be **analysed by user, department and type of query**. A report can then be produced which will show particular **trends** of query from particular departments or on specific features of the software. The help desk can then issue **e-mails** to all users briefly **explaining common problems** and providing ideas for solving them.

(iii) **Monitoring the actual usage of software**

In many network situations, it is possible to monitor **what software is actually used** and **which reports are requested** by managers or other staff. If the software is easy to use, and users should be accessing the software as part of their job, then the software should be **accessed often**. Similarly, if managers require specific reports then these should be **requested on a regular basis**. However, if the software is not accessed or reports not requested then this may indicate that the software is difficult to use.

The actual data on accessing of software and requesting of reports can be obtained from **usage logs** on the computer system. However, care must be taken to ensure that **low access does not automatically equate to low user-friendliness**. The usage logs should be followed up with a **questionnaire** to users to identify why the software is not being used. If it is then found that users do not find the software easy to use then appropriate training can be arranged to assist the users.

36   PREPARATION QUESTION: USER OPPOSITION

Sources of resentment and opposition

New systems can generate hostility from the **staff** who are to **operate** them, from **middle management** who must **control** them, and from **senior management** who are ultimately **responsible to shareholders** for the use of a company's assets.

All businesses are social systems, and the computer system has to fit into that context. The degree of hostility encountered will partly depend on the **culture** of the organisation. If it has had **good experiences** with computerisation in the past, new systems are welcomed. However, if there have been one or two disasters, then the prospect of a new system will be greeted with scepticism, at least.

At senior management level, there is competition for resources, and questions might be raised as to whether it is worth spending money on computer systems as opposed to **other projects**. Some senior managers may be less friendly to information technology than others. This may be because they are **unaware of its potential** to offer competitive advantage. A way of coping with this is for an **IT strategy** to be developed and senior management approval to be gained by a process of education.

Commitment from senior management is an important factor in **persuading middle management** to be positive towards computerisation. Middle managers are often threatened by computerisation, as some of the control mechanisms which they exercise can be built into the computer system. Also, their subordinates will learn skills, which management might not possess.

Both management and staff have a number of fears related to computerisation.

(a) **Redundancy**. This fear may be justified, but in many cases it is not. New jobs are created, and staff are trained or redeployed.

(b) **Change in work practices**. It is sometimes felt that computers will eliminate boring and routine work. In many cases this is transparently false, but there are still gains of this nature to be made from computerisation. However, it might interfere with some of the working networks that have evolved.

(c) **Change in organisational structure**. Some computer systems (eg executive information systems) might have the effect of thinning out the layers of middle management. There will always be winners and losers where this is the case.

Some writers have argued that these problems are not inherent to **computerisation** as such, but in the **management culture** behind it. If computerisation is seen simply as a means of automating current procedures, it can **remove autonomy and fulfilment** from work. Alternatively, if it is used as an **opportunity to expand the skills of staff**, it can encourage a more dedicated work force. This might require an attitudinal change on behalf of management, who might benefit if they listen to the concerns and experience of those directly involved in computerisation.

Overcoming resentment and opposition

The task will be made if easier if the following conditions exist.

(a) There is a **clear commitment by senior management** to the computerisation project.

(b) Staff are **aware of the purpose and consequences** of the computer system. This can be communicated through staff magazines, lunch-hour video presentations, seminars, personal briefings. Any false rumours regarding redundancies should be scotched. The necessary training schemes should be publicised.

(c) During the systems analysis phase **end users should be consulted frequently** and their **views taken into account**. In some systems development methodologies, this is a required phase.

This latter requirement can be a real benefit as **users** are a source of invaluable information as to how a system works in practice. Users are **likely to support** a system more if they have been **involved** in creating it, as their own suggestions will have been incorporated in the plan. Also, users are best able to discern the **ideal man/machine interface**, although this sometimes might impede operational efficiency.

User co-operation is essential in the **implementation** phase, as users have to transfer the old data to the new system. Again, the involvement of users in planning implementation can make matters much easier, and reduce hostility.

37 TESTING: DECISION TABLE

(a)

Field accepts numbers only	Y	Y	Y	Y	Y	Y	Y	Y	N	N	N	N	N	N	N	N
Field accepts six digits only	Y	Y	Y	Y	N	N	N	N	Y	Y	Y	Y	N	N	N	N
Field accepts positive numbers only	Y	Y	N	N	Y	Y	N	N	Y	Y	N	N	Y	Y	N	N
Field must be completed during input	Y	N	Y	N	Y	N	Y	N	Y	N	Y	N	Y	N	Y	N
Test pass	X															
Amend field to accept six digits					X	X	X	X					X	X	X	X
Amend form exit conditions		X		X		X		X		X		X		X		X
Amend field to reject negative values			X	X			X	X			X	X			X	X
Amend field to accept numbers only									X	X	X	X	X	X	X	X

(b) (i) **The main purpose of user acceptance testing is to determine whether or not a system meets previously defined user requirements.** The aim is to determine whether or not the user should accept the system.

To help users decide whether to accept the system or not, user acceptance testing will be carried out. Users will be given a copy of the software, which has already been tested by the programmers, along with the systems specification and a test script. Additional testing will then be carried out.

(1) To try and find software errors which have not yet been detected.

(2) To check what the demands of the new system will be on the users of that system.

(3) To determine that operating procedures are as expected.

(4) To perform some stress testing on the system to ensure that it can cope with the volumes of data expected.

(5) To start to determine the training requirements of staff and organise the production of appropriate training material.

(b) (ii) The extent to which users can test the systems specification and action to be taken in event of any errors being found are outlined below.

Ability to process 5,000 orders each hour

In theory, users must try and input more than 5,000 orders to ensure that this requirement can be met. It is important that this feature of the software is tested, otherwise there is the possibility of errors occurring when the software is being used to its full potential.

In practical terms, this objective may not be possible due to lack of appropriate test data or sufficient on-line terminals to input this number of orders. With only 3,600 seconds in an hour, this level of input cannot be sustained from one workstation. Testing of this objective will have to be deferred until a full network version of the software is available.

Screen design will mimic the current manual order form

It is important that the screen design is familiar to the users to make the new system more acceptable and to enable quicker and more accurate input. This feature of the software can be tested, because the final screen design is part of the software.

If the layout of the screen is not correct, then it is likely that the individual fields can be moved relatively easily – the fields are simply "controls" that can be repositioned using 4GL screen design tools. If any fields are moved, then a re-test will be necessary to ensure that all required fields are still present on the screen.

Processing of one order will take no more than 5 seconds

Individual orders can be processed on the new software, and the time taken checked. It is important that processing is quick to minimise delays in inputting data.

However, processing time on the test system is unlikely to be representative of the final system. The software will only be used by one person, rather than a multi-user environment, while the hardware specification may also be different to the final configuration. These differences will mean that processing time is unlikely to be representative of the final system with more users and different hardware configurations (including the network).

If processing time is slow now, then it is unlikely to improve with the final system for the reasons noted above. The error will be noted by users, and methods of decreasing time such as using higher specification hardware will have to be investigated.

Order information will be automatically transferred to the production module

Within an integrated computer system, it is quite normal for output from one system to form the input to another system. This link will speed up overall processing while removing the need to re-input data.

However, in this situation, only the ordering module is being tested, so the link to the production system will not be available. Testing of this feature will have to wait for full system testing which occurs after each module has been tested and approved individually.

38   PREPARATION QUESTION: CONTROLS

REPORT

To: The Managing Director
From: The Management Accountant
Date: 30 April 20XX
Subject: Systems controls

Terms of reference and executive summary

To report on the controls used in our computing system (as set out in your memo of 6 April 20XX). Managers involved with the systems were interviewed and the controls were inspected. This report describes controls under three headings:

(a)   Physical access and security controls.
(b)   System software controls.
(c)   Application controls.

If we implement these controls we should be in a position to maintain our system's accuracy and security.

(a)   **Physical access and security controls**

The cost of data is very high when the cost of acquiring, capturing and storing it are taken into account. It is important for our commercial success to keep it secure, and physical access control is the first line of defence. Some points which have been considered for implementation are as follows.

The main risk on a system of the type installed **at head office** is the risk of a fault or breakdown in one area spreading across the system. This is particularly true of viruses. A virus introduced onto one machine could replicate itself throughout the network. All software and disks coming in to the organisation should be scanned using proprietary anti-virus software, and all machines should be virus-checked at regular intervals. Controls would also need to be established over the use of office software on home computers, including sweeping the latter regularly.

A second risk is that an unauthorised user using one network PC could gain access, not only to the files on that PC, but also to the other PCs in the system. This would require implementation of the controls described for Company A. A further risk, depending on the type of network configuration, is that an extra PC could be 'plugged in' to the network to gain access to it. The network management software should detect breaches of this type.

Other measures which should be taken at **both sites** to prevent physical access are as follows. A standalone computer, by its very nature, allows access to data files and program files held on the hard disk. Possible controls are as follows.

(i)   Installation of a password routine which is activated whenever the computer is booted up. This would need to be accompanied by rigorous adherence to password discipline.

(ii)   Physical access controls, for example door locks activated by swipe cards or PIN numbers, to prevent access into the room(s) where the computers are kept. Probably not feasible in an open plan office.

(iii) The use of keyboard locks.

(iv)   Virus controls, as described above.

(b) **System software controls**

All our users are on-line. We need to ensure that users' do not get access to data or systems which they are not authorised to run or use. Controls which should be implemented at both sites are set out below.

(i) Password control is activated on logging on to the system. The menus are tailored to users' needs, and start automatically when they log on (and therefore restrict them to systems which they are authorised to access).

(ii) There is a hierarchical system of control (based on the password system) which allows access to reading, changing and erasing files, all at different levels of authority. Individuals have different authority levels for each system.

(iii) Some data (particularly in the debtors and payroll/personnel systems) can be restricted on a per-field basis. This should be done through the database facilities, or the facilities in the payroll system, restricting access on a user authority level basis.

(c) **Application controls**

Our systems should be set up to ensure that data is captured and processed to retain as much accuracy as possible. To this end we should establish the following procedures. Most will be relevant to accounting and similar systems at head office more than to, say, proprietary WP and spreadsheet packages.

(i) Source documents should be authorised above certain limits, and for certain activities.

(ii) Batch controls should be used for all batched input.

(iii) Sequentially pre-numbered forms should be used where relevant (and then software checks implemented to ensure numbers are used, and are used only once).

(iv) Display of checking information on screen wherever possible when entering data.

(v) Programs must have validation checks built in to the data capture stage whenever possible.

(vi) If errors are found they should be logged for subsequent checking to ensure they have been corrected and re-submitted.

(vii) Routing controls should be established for all the reports we produce.

39   INPUT CHECKS

> **Tutor's hint**. This question requires you to do three things: describe the input check, explain the errors it is trying to detect and provide an example from the question information. You need to be careful that all these points are included in your answer. We have tried to include the first two points in the first paragraph of each section and included the question example in the second paragraph.
>
> *Other points*. Note in both parts (a) and (b) we have included more points than the question actually requires. Your answer will therefore be shorter.

(a) The checks over the input of examination data into the computer system will include the following.

(i) **Range checks**

A range check is used to ensure that the value being entered into a specific field **falls within a given range** or given **list of values**. The check is trying to ensure that only numbers within a given range or that appear on a particular list, are entered onto the computer.

For example, the **number of marks** obtained in the examination by one candidate must fall between **0 and 100**. Similarly, each candidate will be sitting the examination in a particular **examination centre**. That centre will have a unique **code number**. A check will also be made to ensure that the code can be found in the list of valid examination centre numbers. Some systems allow the code to be chosen from a list, rather than have to enter all the codes manually. **Choosing from a list** decreases the number of input errors.

(ii) **Format checks**

The data into each field must be in a specific format. The check is trying to ensure that all inputs contain a **set number of digits** or that they are in a particular **alphabetical or numeric format**.

Format checks are particularly useful where it is **not easy to specify all valid inputs in advance**. For example, format checks could be used to ensure that the examination number was entered in number format only; however checking to a **list of valid exam numbers** is a more reliable check given the low number of examinations. However, with 60,000 candidates taking the examination a check to the candidate database may not be practicable. Additional checks on the accuracy of the number can be used such as ensuring that **only 8 digits** were entered or that no letters were included in the number.

(iii) **Totals of items input**

Totals are used at the end of inputting data. The check is used to ensure that **all items have been input** (completeness of input) and within fields that can be added up (eg total of examination marks obtained), that the **individual marks** have been entered accurately.

For example, checks will include ensuring that a record has been entered for **each of the 60,000 candidates** entering the examination. A count can be kept of the **number of examination forms** entered onto the computer. Also, the marks for each question can be added up to check the total mark. The **marks obtained on each question must add up to the total mark awarded**.

(iv) **Consistency checks**

Consistency checks are used to ensure that otherwise **valid items** of data are actually **consistent with each other**. These checks tend to be used after range and format checks have been carried out as a further check on the accuracy of data being input.

For example, both a **candidate number and a desk number** could have been accurately entered onto the computer. However, a consistency check could be used to ensure that the candidate should be sitting at a particular desk. An error can still have occurred either because a candidate was sitting at an incorrect desk, or more importantly, a candidate number was entered which passed the format check but is still incorrect. So the candidate number 87654322 could be entered instead of 88765432, this number is still 8 numbers long and so passes the format check. However, **candidate 87654322 should not be sitting at desk A123**. The consistency check will identify this error and ask for a re-input of the candidate number.

(v)   **Check digits**

Check digits are used to ensure that long numbers are input accurately. For example, a number being input may have 7 digits. An arithmetical calculation is performed on the number, and the result of this calculation added to the end of the number. The 7-digit number is now 8 digits long. When the number is input, the computer recreates the check digit. **If any of the numbers have been input incorrectly, then the check digit will be wrong** and re-input of the number will be requested.

In the example, the candidate number could originally have been 7 digits, but the 8th digit was added as a check. Errors in entering the candidate number will therefore be identified before any consistency checks referred to above. The check digit in number 87654322 would be incorrect signalling an error before the consistency check against desk number.

(vi)   **Data verification**

Data verification can involve checking the accuracy of input by having another person check output reports.

This method of checking is not normally used due to the relatively high cost (employing two people) and because computer input checks are normally adequate to identify errors on input.

A version of data verification still exists in systems that accept input and then **redisplay** input for visual checking by the same operator.

(b)   The input of data could be made more speedy and accurate by using any of the following methods.

(i)   **Appropriate screen design**

The input screen on the computer could be designed to **look like the front of the candidate's answer book** where the data to be input can be found. Providing the screen in the same format makes it easier for the operator to **visually check** that the data being entered is correct. For example, entering a mark of 200 can be identified as being incorrect if the operator knows that the exam has a maximum of 100. Although the computer range check will also identify the error, seeing the place to enter data on-screen will enable the operator to think what the data should be rather than rely on the computer error messages.

(ii)   **Pre-input of data**

Entering data after the examination has been taken may be a **time pressured** activity, especially if the published results date is near. Rather than enter all the data at once, **some data could be entered prior to the marks becoming available**. For example, before the examination, the following items of data should be known: **Candidate number, centre number,** and **examination number**. Entering and checking this information prior to the examination will decrease the time pressure when the marks are entered so that fewer mistakes are made.

(iii) **Use of other input methods**

Using a different input method such as **Optical Mark Reading (OMR)** can also increase the speed of data input. If data on candidate number has already been entered, then an OMR sheet could be prepared showing candidate number as the key field, and then the marks for each question and the total mark attained for each candidate as separate OMR fields. **Scanning** an OMR document will be **much quicker** than manually inputting all the examination marks. Computer checks similar to those outlined above will still be used to check the accuracy of input.

40   PREPARATION QUESTION: PHYSICAL CONTROLS

Tutor's hint. Your answer should have provided a good selection of measures that could be taken in the two areas noted in the question - rather than dwelling on one or two points. The scenario appears unlikely to occur in many countries, but threats such as this are real in many parts of the world.

Preventing and recovering from physical attack

Physical defence of the site

If the risk from terrorist attack is considered to be significant, then **appropriate site security** such as perimeter fences, guard dogs and sentries will need to be considered. This will help to ensure that only authorised staff can actually approach the installation and breaching the security around the site identifies potential terrorists.

Site security – secret location.

A more extreme solution is to maintain the site at a **secret or at least heavily guarded** military installation where appropriate security is already available.

Ids required to enter building

All staff should show appropriate **identification** on entering the building, such as badges to security staff, swipe cards or even retina scans where security is essential. A 24-hour security guard will be required to ensure that these procedures are enforced.

Access to computer room and other sensitive areas restricted to selected staff

Within the building, **additional security** can be placed around the main computer room, with additional passwords or swipe cards being required to enter this area. All terminals provided for staff use should also have power on passwords and password protected screen savers to try and ensure that only authorised staff access computer files.

Daily backup taken and maintained at an off-site location

To recover from a terrorist attack, it is essential that appropriate **backup** is taken of all programs and data on the computer, and that this is stored in a secure, off site, location. Backup can be taken by transferring all information onto some storage medium (eg some form of tape or disk) and transferring this each evening to a secure location. Alternatively, data may be transferred by a **secure network link** to a backup computer system located again in a separate secure location.

Guaranteeing the supply and maintenance of essential services to the site

Power supply

An **Uninterrupted Power Supply** will be needed to ensure that any fluctuations in the power supply do not adversely affect the computer systems. A backup generator will also be needed to ensure that processing can continue even if terrorists interrupt the power supply to the computer system.

Disaster recovery procedures

Disaster recovery means that the computer system and the data and programs contained on it, **can be re-established** at any time. A full system backup will have been taken at the end of each day (see above). Backup is also required for transactions during the day, to ensure that data is not lost should an attack happen during working hours. This can be achieved by mirroring all transactions on a separate computer (preferably located in another secure location).

In the event of a disaster, the computer system can be re-built as follows:

- **Hardware**: a duplicate computer installation can be available at another location, or replacement hardware established in the existing location.

- **Software**: will be available from the previous end-of-day backup and the mirrored transactions up to time of any attack.

Testing and maintenance of backup provisions

Disaster recovery procedures should be **tested** on a regular basis to ensure that they are effective. This is particularly important where the risk of disaster is high. Similarly, a schedule of preventative maintenance should be used to ensure that all computers and other security equipment works effectively.

41   PHYSICAL THREATS

(a)   **Potential physical threats**

Threats to SCP's computer centre fall into two distinct areas - physical threats to the centre itself and threats to the software and data on the system.

Protection against natural and man-made disasters

(i)   **Power problems.** The electrical supply should be set up so as to be immune from any foreseeable interruptions or fluctuations. This could be done with standby or continuously running generators.

(ii)   **Flooding.** The facility should be constructed to be as secure as possible against the possibility of flooding, either from internal sources (eg fire control systems) or from external sources (eg leaking roofs, rain, rivers, and so on).

(iii) **Wind damage.** If the facility is in an area which might be susceptible to wind damage, or the building is not sufficiently solidly constructed, then precautions should be taken against the possibility of damage from freak wind conditions.

(iv)   **Storm and lightning damage.** Both direct lightning strikes and lightning strikes on the power grid should be taken into consideration, particularly if the installation is in an area where electrical storms occur. Other storm damage (wind and rain) also needs to be provided for.

(v)   **Fire.** Fire is an ever present threat. Smoking should be banned, and all electrical and heating apparatus should be checked to ensure that there is no likelihood of its being a source of fire. Smoke detectors, use of low-flammability materials and regular fire drills should all form part of control procedures.

(vi)   **Intruders.** Both outsiders and disillusioned staff should be guarded against. Protection could take the form of security guards, levels of physical entry prevention and careful adherence to entry checking.

(vii) **Dust.** For some parts of the system dust can be a major problem. Access controls for personnel will aid in preventing dust intrusion, and proper air conditioning, with a system of sealed/double doors to important parts of the installation, will manage much of the rest of the problem.

Protection against unauthorised physical access

(i)   Restrict the number of **entrances**. If the number of doors (taking into account safety requirements) is as low as possible the number of potential 'weak' access points which could cause a problem is restricted. Emergency exits should be fitted with **alarms**.

(ii)   **Graduated access** to different parts of the facility. Staff and other visitors should only be allowed access to those areas which they need to visit. If different areas have different levels of authorisation requirements, then control becomes more easily implemented.

(iii) **Key card controlled access** to the facility. Using magnetic or electronic key card facilities allows for sophisticated control on the time and place of access, as well as more mundane aspects such as preventing double entry of a card before an exit.

(iv)   **Time control** on access. Intelligent access control can limit access to staff to the hours when they legitimately would need it, and prevent access outside those hours except on override.

(v)   Wearing of **ID badges**. Wearing of ID cards with built-in photographs allows both staff and security personnel to maintain a check on people who have access and those who have used the access power. Visitors should also be given badges and asked to wear them.

(vi)   Voice, finger, palm or retina scan and **recognition systems** (if the investment warrants it). These systems can be expensive, but prevent card swapping and misuse.

(b) **Contingency plan**

The purpose of a contingency plan is to ensure that when a catastrophe happens, an organisation is **prepared** and is **able to continue working** in the face of a certain pre-determined level of interruption.

Catastrophes may have a wide range of causes. A contingency plan is usually invoked only in the event of a '**major' catastrophe**, typically fire, flooding, failure of the main processor or loss of a power supply. If a single system is 'lost', then an individual department must take appropriate action but this would not necessitate an organisation-wide contingency action.

The plan would be developed by establishing **how much interruption** could be tolerated in the system, what the **risks** of the various types of interruption are, what the **provisions** are that would have to be made for those interruptions and what **costs** would be associated with the failures and with the provision of the responses. Key to any contingency plan is **back-up** of data. However good the alternative hardware facilities, they will be of little use if SCP cannot load up with recent data.

Developing the plan

When a systems administrator sets out to ensure that the issues of security are fully covered, all these factors are taken into account. A team, led by the administrator, may be appointed to investigate the matter.

(i)   The team should assess **how vulnerable SCP is in principle** to any of these problems. It may help to do an estimate of the likely **costs** of any particular threat identified. It is obviously easier to identify the costs of replacing hardware than the costs caused, for example, by a virus infection.

(ii)   The team might review SCP's past history of security problems (eg any frauds discovered, and the **internal control** issues raised by them).

(iii) The team will then assess **how far current security measures are sufficient** to cope with the vulnerabilities discovered. This study might be quite a lengthy process, covering detailed technical issues (eg how easy might a hacker find it to enter the network? is there a proper lock system on new computer centre doors? fireproof cabinets? etc).

(iv)   Some analysis will be made of the extent to which the security procedures **theoretically** in force are in fact being followed **in practice** (eg users might share passwords which they are supposed to keep confidential).

(v)   Once some assessment of the risk, both qualitative and quantitative has been made, **additional security measures** may be suggested. These, too, will have to be costed, as far as possible, so that the costs of security do not outweigh the anticipated costs of the threats identified.

Standby options

Standby options would include some or all of the following.

(i)   **Replacement hardware** to be installed. This clearly involves some delay and does not address short-term operational problems.

(ii)   **Duplicate sites** to which communications links could be switched. These may be alternative sites already operated by the organisation, as in a distributed processing environment, or operated by a third party. **Third parties** may be either companies with which the organisation has some form of 'twinning' arrangement or dedicated companies providing standby services.

(iii) **Duplicate facilities** permanently installed. This is an expensive option, but one which should be considered for a mission-critical system.

42   PROCESSING CONTROLS

> **Tutor's hint.** Most of the general framework outlined in (a) can be widely applied. In (b) you needed to discuss a range of controls, but you should have emphasised the importance of specific controls over the database and access controls, since other controls would not operate very well in the system described or would be undermined by lack of segregation of duties.

(a)   Important general controls are as follows.

Organisational structure

Clear systems of authorisation of transactions and **delegation** of responsibilities should be important elements in any organisational structure.

A further significant element is **segregation of duties**. Segregation allows miscreants limited opportunities to cover their tracks and also acts to detect unintentional mistakes by allowing cross-checking of work done by a different person. Since there are a significant number of functions involved in data processing, it may be difficult to segregate all the duties. In any event, however, those responsible for maintaining and developing the system should not be responsible for the actual data processing.

Supervision controls

Management should be responsible for setting of **budgets** and **operational targets**, and reviewing performance against standards set. Management should oversee the overall development of the system. In particular they should be concerned with whether the information produced has resulted in **improved service** for grant recipients and **better information** for management.

As well as senior management exercising supervision, certain staff should be exercising full–time supervision over the system, particularly if there is a lack of segregation of duties. Key tasks of the system supervisor include ensuring **authorisation procedures** are **appropriate** and properly carried out, checking that the **necessary information** is available should problems occur, and **investigating problems.**

Operating manual

Guidance from management covering the system should include the following elements.

(i)   Clear statements of **targets,** such as length of turnaround period for all documentation

(ii)   **Organisational structure**

(iii)   **Job descriptions** containing responsibilities and duties of management and staff

(iv)   Controls, in particular documentation standards, security and integrity controls, and back-up procedures

(v)   A commitment to information security and details of legal data protection requirements

Staffing controls

Recruitment and **training** will be key controls. References should be requested for new recruits; this is particularly important because some of the information processed may be quite sensitive. Staff should receive sufficient training in both the technical knowledge required to carry out their work and also internal procedures.

Development controls

The system should be able to develop as the **needs** of **users change**. Development should however take place in accordance with defined guidelines covering **design standards**, requirements for **adequate documentation**, **testing procedures** and **training**. Each stage of development should be approved by both the management of the processing function and representatives of users of the information. **Internal audit** should also be involved in checking development standards have been met. However internal audit should not be involved with actually implementing developments since this would destroy its function as an independent check.

(b)   Real-time systems permit immediate updating of computer systems by a variety of users. An important feature is likely to be a lack of segregation of duties; the same person being responsible for originating and inputting data.

The most important controls are as follows.

Access controls

There should be **physical controls** over the computers, with access obtained only by an entry code, and the premises being kept shut outside operating hours.

A system of **passwords** should be in operation. This should be hierarchical with one level of password being required for access to information, another for the user to be able to process information. There may also be restrictions of certain users to certain files, for example restrictions on the amendment of standing or permanent data

The **effectiveness** of a **password** system will be improved by appropriate guidance and features built into the system. For example passwords should be changed regularly and no-one should use a password that could easily be guessed because of its simplicity or because of personal connection with the user. Terminals should automatically log off if no entry is made within a certain time or a wrong password is entered say three times in succession, and all attempted violations should be logged.

Input controls

Access controls should ensure **input** is only made by **authorised** staff. Various **accuracy** controls are likely to be required. Examples include check digit verification (a check on the validity of the coding of input), checks that input is within the permitted range, existence checks that recipients of grants have valid accounts within the system, and checks that all the necessary information is present.

Processing controls

Operating instructions should be clearly laid down, and updated whenever significant changes occur such as changes in the data dictionary. Controls should ensure that all input data is processed and the processing of each transaction is accurate.

The department should have **backup** and **emergency procedures** in place to ensure data processed is not lost through computer malfunction, and that processing can continue if a disaster occurs. Procedures include daily backup of processing and **storage** of what has been processed in a **remote location**. **Virus protection controls** should be embedded within the system. There should be **protection** of equipment against **fire** and other hazards, and arrangements to use **back-up facilities** if processing on the main site has to be suspended.

Output controls

Output controls may include an **audit trail,** the ability to trace output back to originating documentation. This may be difficult if only summary control totals are produced at the end of daily processing. A further problem with some output controls eg one-for-one checking with input is that they may be carried out in the real-time system by the person who input the information, and the lack of segregation of duties will mean that the control's reliability is undermined.

Hence other controls will be significant. **Exception reports**, highlighting rejected transactions should be printed out on a regular basis and reviewed by management. Management should also **review reports** of **changes** to **specified files,** particularly standing data files Internal audit can use computer assisted audit techniques to review output, in particular **SCARF**, which automatically writes transactions of certain types or certain amounts to a separate file for later review by the auditors.

The **distribution** of **output** should also be controlled carefully.

Controls over programs

These controls are particularly important because errors in programs may impact upon the processing of all transactions. **Password protection** is particularly important; no-one except computer support staff should be able to access live programs. An important review control would be periodic **comparison** of **live production programs** to **control copies** and supporting documentation. **Back-up copies** of programs should be stored away from the main site.

Controls over the database

The database system will also need controls to **maintain** the **integrity** of the database. Again restriction of access is vital; **access** to the **data dictionary** should again be **restricted** to computer support staff, because the dictionary contains what is integral to the running of the system, standard descriptions including definitions, characteristics and inter-relationship of data. There should be segregation of duties between the data processing and database administration functions.

43 PREPARATION QUESTION: DATA SECURITY

(a) **Threats to data**

Threats which a company holding sensitive data on a magnetic storage medium must guard against include the following.

(i) **Contravention of Data Protection legislation.** If the data falls within the scope of the legislation care must be taken that control to ensure compliance is exercised at all times.

(ii) **Losing the data through physical threats.** The data can be lost as a result of a number of factors, which include both external and internal influences: fire, theft, floods, physical damage to the storage media, or erasure of the storage media by magnetic or electrical means. 'Man-made' physical threats also exist, for example from hackers and disgruntled employees or ex-employees.

(iii) **Corruption of the data.** Many of the factors which might result in a total loss of data can also play a similar part in partially corrupting the data held on the medium. This corruption, if it goes undetected, is potentially more damaging than a total loss of the data would be, since there is a chance that the corrupted data is treated as correct. In addition, rogue software such as poorly written programs, viruses and misused utility programs can both corrupt and erase data.

(iv) **Releasing the data to unauthorised persons**. If the data is released to outsiders, then the value of the data can be negated as well as providing opportunities for the unauthorised person either to misuse the data, to sell it or just to pass it over to other parties. Data could be transmitted over communications links, or copied to floppy disks, Zip disks or CD-ROMs, which are easily concealed and very portable.

(b) **Logical access**

A logical access system is an entry system based on logical (program) controls rather than physical (keys, etc) controls. The logical access system will allocate passwords in a variety of forms at different levels of access to the system. A password may need to be given when first accessing the overall computer facility, when asking to use specific systems on the computer, and when accessing particular files, or specific fields within files. Whether passwords are allocated at a particular level would depend on the importance of the data at that level as well as the degree of sensitivity of the data.

When a user attempts to access a protected part of the system he or she would have to enter a password using the keyboard, or some form of input device and/or some form of physical scanning device to establish their credentials. Incorrect passwords would result in the attempted access being logged and perhaps shut down the terminal being used for the attempt.

When passwords are established they should be set by the person subsequently using them, and re-set at regular intervals.

(c) (i) **Encryption**

Encryption is the deliberate coding or altering of data, before transmission, so that any unauthorised party intercepting or eavesdropping on the transformation is unable to make sense of it. Encryption ranges from the simple substitution of one character for another to more secure methods, such as using a data encryption standard to change data to what is, effectively an unreadable state. Decryption of the data, which has to take place to allow it to be read, happens by reversing the substitution. Authorised recipients have the required decryption key (the process usually occurs without user intervention).

More secure methods of encryption make unauthorised reading of data difficult, and, therefore, discourage theft of the information. In addition encryption can make it more difficult to corrupt the data without the corruption being detected.

Encryption techniques are particularly valuable where data is transmitted electronically, for example via networks or over public telecommunications links.

(ii) **Hacking**

Hacking is the attempted or actual access to a computer system which the hacker is not entitled to access. Examples have included people looking at private mail on public network systems. Hackers can both steal data, with the attendant problems, and corrupt data without removing it. Both of these events are better prevented if possible.

Many hackers are children who see hacking as a game or a challenge. There are numerous examples of hackers accessing private systems, including those belonging to educational establishments, public utilities and defence ministries. Hackers access systems through the telephone network; they then try out passwords either by guesswork or by using simple programs. Once inside a system, a hacker's opportunity to cause damage is high.

(iii) **Computer viruses**

Computer viruses are small programs which, when executed, damage data and/or programs. Viruses have the ability to spread, replicating themselves like a biological virus. The damage or corruption can take the form of changes (such as an increase in the size of the corrupted program) to more complex ones (where the corrupted program might erase all the data on a disk when a specific event occurs). Both data loss and corruption are better prevented. Prevention on PCs involves using only software from recognised sources, running virus protection and detection software and not accepting e-mail attachments from unknown sources.

Two types of virus are logic bombs and time bombs.

(1) A **logic bomb** is a piece of code triggered by certain events. A program will behave normally until a certain event occurs, for example when disk utilisation reaches a certain percentage. A logic bomb, by responding to set

117

conditions, maximises damage. For example, it will be triggered when a disk is nearly full, or when a large number of users are using the system.

(2) A **time bomb** is similar to a logic bomb, except that it is triggered at a certain date. Companies have experienced virus attacks on April Fool's Day and on Friday 13th. These were released by time bombs.

An activated virus can show itself in a number of ways. The Jerusalem virus slows down the operation of the infected machine so much that it becomes virtually unusable, then deletes files. Cascade causes letters on the screen to 'fall' to the bottom of the screen and may reformat the hard disk. The Melissa virus corrupts Microsoft Office documents.

44   SECURITY

(a) **Encryption involves scrambling data before it is transmitted over a communications between two computers**, and then unscrambling that data again when it reaches the destination computer. If data is not encrypted during transmission, then if that data is intercepted by a third party during transmission over the Internet, it can be read.

Encryption is essential where personal information, such as credit card details, are being transferred over the Internet. Without encryption, the card details could be read and used by a third party. The fact that MN does not offer secure transfer of credit card information for sales will limit purchases from their Internet site. Customers will not make purchases when payment details are insecure.

A virus is a software program which causes damage to a computer system by making unauthorised amendments to program and data files and sometimes damaging the hardware of the computer system. Viruses are spread via e-mail attachments and in some cases by automatic download when an Internet site is accessed.

Anti-virus software is used to protect computer systems against the threat from viruses. This software detects and removes a virus from a computer system before it can do any damage. As the staff within MN plc have been provided with Internet access, then they could easily download a virus onto MN's computer system, by accident. Anti-virus software should be installed in a firewall to check all Internet access and so protect MN computer systems from virus damage.

(b) **Security procedures need to be implemented over any computer system to ensure that only authorised personnel can gain access to that system**. One of the main security features is the use of **password**; unless a valid password is entered onto a computer system, access will be denied. To be effective, passwords need to be changed regularly, as well as being difficult to guess. Passwords should also be required for accessing the computer system from any location.

Within MN plc, the passwords are changed regularly, although this is probably the only good feature of this system. The passwords are not particularly secure; the standard format of name and month number could be guessed, and when the format is known, any individual could access the computer by knowing the name of one employee. As Internet access is provided by MN, then it is possible that a hacker could break into MN's computer systems, especially as the password system is insecure.

The **password system needs revising** so that as well as being changed each month, passwords are set which are not related to the employee. For this purpose, employees could be allowed to set their own passwords, or new passwords are allocated using a sequence of random characters. The difficulty with taking the latter approach is that the password will be very difficult to remember, even for the person using that password.

(c) **The Computer Misuse Act was enacted in response to the growing threat of hacking into computer systems by unauthorised third parties**. In this situation, hacking means the unauthorised access into computer systems.

The Act created three specific crimes in relation to hacking.

Unauthorised access. This offence occurs where a hacker attempts to access a computer system they are not authorised to use. The success or otherwise of the access is irrelevant, the offence relates to the attempt to access the computer system.

Unauthorised access with the intention of committing another offence. In this situation the hacker does gain access to the computer system. If the hacker then starts to search through the data on that computer then there is an intention to commit a further offence. This offence carried stricter penalties than access alone.

Unauthorised modification of data or programs. The term modification includes the introduction of computer viruses into a computer system, as the virus is unlikely to be authorised software and it will modify data or program files. In court, guilt is based on the intention to impair the operation of a computer or programs, or to prevent or hinder access to data.

The Act is therefore relevant to limiting the spread of viruses because it makes introduction of a virus onto a computer system a criminal offence. However, the effectiveness of the Act is limited by difficulties in identifying the individual who carried out the access, as well as apprehending the individual where the access took place from a different country.

45   WRAY CASTLE

(a) The **steering committee** of an organisation normally includes the IT/IS manager, and senior managers from other parts of the organisation affected by the systems involved. The committee therefore acts as an **essential bridge** between IT professionals and the users they serve, assuming, of course, that the organisation concerned maintains a traditional staffing structure.

The role of the steering committee in deciding priorities for systems depends to a certain degree on the political structure of the committee itself, and whether the culture of Wray Castle leads to the **control of systems development being exercised by users** rather than by IT professionals. In some organisations users may determine systems development priorities, whereas in others, systems developments are largely under the control of the data processing department, especially if the organisation's processing function is heavily centralised. Here, a production system is likely to be run centrally, while a marketing system may be largely in the hands of end-users.

The steering committee, too, will have the responsibility for ensuring that other **organisational policies** are applied to IT systems. For example, a new system may be implemented with the cutting of labour costs as the desired outcome, which fits the organisation's overall strategy. Non-systems objectives set are generally imposed from outside, thus limiting the committee's freedom in choosing system development priorities. Systems development may be determined by other organisational issues.

The steering committee may either play a passive or an active role in systems development. In its **passive role**, the committee may **act as an arbiter** for a number of competing projects suggested by user departments, especially if resources are limited, as appears to be the case here. If it assumes an **active role**, the steering committee itself, assuming that this is in its terms of reference, **sets priorities** for computerisation.

Much of the detailed research is carried out by **feasibility study teams** for particular projects, and the steering committee may suggest parameters within which the feasibility study has to operate. The committee too will be responsible for co-ordinating the activities of the various study groups working on different projects, if more than one is undertaken.

Steering committees are appointed in large organisations to oversee the development of computer systems. A steering committee might, for example, **act as a filter,** referring some computerisation projects, whose costs exceeds an authorisation limit, to the Board or chief executive of an organisation for approval. Projects whose cost falls below a certain preset authorisation limit may be selected at the discretion of the steering committee alone. It may be that the marketing system falls into this latter category, but the production planning and control system, which is certainly a mission-critical system, will inevitably represent a major investment over the next couple of years at least.

The role of the steering committee in selecting computerisation priorities for Wray Castle is therefore likely to be a varied one. On the one hand it must bring to bear **general organisational objectives** on the organisation's systems and processing activities. On the other, it must support systems development against the possible scepticism of senior managers who are not familiar with technological developments and who need to be convinced of its importance. In addition it must arbitrate between the users competing for perhaps limited resources, acting as judge and jury in each case. This role becomes more pronounced with the growth of end-user computing, and the steering committee's role may include ensuring organisational standards are adhered to.

(b)

MEMORANDUM

To: Managing Director
From: Administrator
Date: 15 September 20X1
Subject: Systems prototyping

This memorandum sets out the weaknesses inherent in the traditional systems development cycle and explains how systems prototyping might help.

In the traditional systems development process the user is isolated from any close contact with the system during its development. Typically the user is intensively involved during the design stage during which the system functions and requirements are defined so that a system specification is produced. This specification then serves as a design document during the system design and implementation phase so that the system analysts and programmers know what to produce.

Two of the major weaknesses of this approach are described here.

(i)   The traditional approach involved consultation at an early stage in the development process with **user management rather than the actual people who would be using the system**. Although management was often responsible for authorising payment for a new system, they can not be expected to have a detailed knowledge of the processes the system will interact with. This ignorance is a very poor foundation for building a systems specification. In these instances, even if the systems professionals produced a system that met the user management demands, the system still may not be suitable. The actual users of the system need to be involved in the development process.

(ii)   **Users often have incorrect or unrealistic ideas** about what systems can do or how various functions might operate. In the traditional approach, users may be expecting the perfect system and do not see what actually has been built until the system is finished and delivered. In these instances users would feel let down and often regard the systems as failures. An additional problem arises because applications tend to evolve over time so that system specifications become less appropriate. If, as with many mainframe systems, the development effort takes a relatively long time the delivered system may no longer effectively perform the application it was intended to perform.

Systems prototyping can significantly reduce these problems by allowing the user to participate actively in the systems design and development process. Rather than producing a detailed specification the prototyping approach aims at producing a simplified version of the system, a prototype, which the user may then try out. Typically, the user might be able to try out data input screens or perform file enquiries.

The advantage of this approach is that the **user actually sees a system in operation and can judge its usefulness and operation.** This is extremely useful for users who are unfamiliar with information systems since they often revise their specifications as they become more familiar with the system's workings. The great advantage of this approach is the reduction in system modifications or enhancements - users can notice deficiencies before systems are delivered so that specifications may more fully address user needs.

(c)   A structured systems methodology could be applied to avoid the problems previously experienced by Wray Castle. An example of such a methodology is Structured Systems Analysis and Design Methodology, or SSADM. The key features of SSADM are set out below. Most of these could equally well be attributed to any structured systems methodology.

Project management

The structured framework of a methodology helps with planning. It defines the tasks to be performed and sets out when they should be done. Each step has an identifiable end product. **This allows control by reference to actual achievements rather than to estimates of progress.**

Techniques

Three techniques are used in SSADM: dataflow diagrams, logical data structures and entity life histories. These allow information to be cross-checked between diagrams and ensure that the delivered system is close to the final system, in other words that the necessity for later enhancements is minimised. For example, an event in an entity life history will match data flows which trigger processes on the dataflow diagrams. These techniques and others are available in different methodologies.

The specification

A logical design is produced that is independent of hardware and software. This logical design can then be given a physical design using whatever computer equipment and implementation language is required.

Users

Users are involved with development work from an early stage. Their involvement is a critical factor in the success of any development. SSADM encourages better communication between users and developers.

Documentation

Documentation is produced throughout the project. This gives a comprehensive and detailed picture of the system and helps understanding of the system. This makes the consequences of proposed changes clear. Recent excess programming and training costs are directly attributable to the lack of documentation for the SOP system.

Contractors

SSADM and other commercial methodologies are used widely enough to be known to many systems professionals. This is obviously an advantage, as it reduced dependence on individual suppliers or contractors.

Methodology

A methodology provides a set of development standards to which all parties can adhere.

Emphasis on graphical techniques

The emphasis on diagramming makes it easier for relevant parties to understand the system than if narrative descriptions were used. Some narrative can be used; however if this is excessive, the advantage of the diagramming techniques is lost.

(d) **Interviews**

Interviews are a useful means of assessing the information requirements of senior executives such as the marketing director. Each interview can be individual planned and tailored, and the reactions and requirements of the interviewee monitored, so that appropriate further investigation can take place immediately. Disadvantages are that they can be time consuming and expensive, particularly if several have to be performed. Also, it can be difficult to eliminate interviewer/interviewee bias, although this is perhaps less likely to be a problem where users are in favour of a system.

Questionnaires

These are probably not appropriate for this type of investigation, as the costs of designing them would be unlikely to be justified where a small department is involved. If sales staff are to be consulted as well, they might be worthwhile. Questionnaires can sample a wide range of opinion and collect useful statistics in a short space of time, particularly if those questioned cover a large geographical area. There are potentially many problems with a questionnaire. The response rate may be poor, analysis of a lengthy questionnaire can be costly and design of a good questionnaire is not easy, particularly if consistency of answer is needed to be checked by cross referencing answers.

Observation

This can be useful, but the nature of a senior executive's job is that it is not always clearly defined and often somewhat unpredictable, with the result that observation is unlikely to view a rounded (or adequate) picture of the executive's requirements.

Prototyping

This is as 'a technique commonly used in applications software development where, for example, input screens are developed and demonstrated to the users in advance of detailed development work on processing. The intention is that the feedback thus obtained from the users can be incorporated into the systems design.'

Screens can be mocked up, with some example data included, so that the marketing department can experiment with data retrieval and comment on screen layout, hierarchy of screens/menus, and general user-friendliness. The underlying processing is added later. The disadvantage is that staff may wish to keep on 'tinkering' and be unwilling to give final approval to a design.

Critical success factors

Critical success factors can be used to help to determine the information requirements of senior management. The critical success factors method was developed by John Rockart in the late 1970s in order to define executive information needs. Once CSFs, which are matters fundamental to business success, have been identified, they can be used to generate performance indicators. It is these performance indicators which possess inherent quantitative (or sometimes qualitative) elements which might be used to define the type of information required, for example repeat orders, market penetration, success of campaigns and market share (an example of information which has an external element). The disadvantage is that some of these types of measure might be too vague to be incorporated into a system.

Bank of existing requests

A good systems analyst will, during the course of a development project, keep notes and records of other ideas suggested or requests made to him or her during the course of his or her work. At the outset of any new project, this file should be examined to see if any relevant information is already held, for example from the previous sales order processing project. Other sources of requests might include user group meetings, minutes of steering committee meetings and so on. Particularly as marketing people may be difficult to 'pin down', any background 'fill-in' information of this type could be extremely useful.

46   ISEC

(a) (i)   **Benefits** that may come about following the **integration** of the three departments systems via a network include the following.

(1) Data will only have to be **input once**, saving time and money. At present, for instance, details such as name, address and candidate number have to be recorded by Administration, who track the progress of an entry, by the Education staff, who have to issue certificates and keep records of successes, and by Finance, who collect payments from candidates.

(2) Because data is held only in one location it is easier to ensure that it is **up to date and consistent**. For instance, poor communication may mean that Administration update their records with a change in an candidate's address, but this information does not reach Finance, who continue to pursue payment from the old address.

(3) Data can be **used more flexibly**. New programs can easily be introduced to make use of existing data in different ways. For instance, linking up Administration information with the Education department's information should lead to a **more sophisticated analysis** of exam performance than has been possible in the past, perhaps forming the basis for revisions in the syllabus or standards.

(4) **Control of data will improve,** because it will be necessary to set and adhere to common **standards** for the input of data and its definition (for example one section might refer to an candidate as a 'student', another as 'trainee' in one place and 'candidate' in another, and so on). Standards will also be set for storage structures, security and integrity of data and backup and recovery strategies.

(ii) **Costs**

Categories of cost will include [**four of**] the following.

(1) **Equipment costs**

It may be possible to use the present equipment owned by ISEC, but it seems likely that **more powerful PCs** will be needed to cope with the system's networking requirements and the software that it will run. A **server** will be needed, and each member of the administration department will need a PC (they appear to share one at present).

New or extra **peripherals** such as printers will also be required.

(2) **Installation costs**

In this case installation costs will include the cost of putting in **cabling** to link up the network, and possibly **telecommunications links** if the network is to be linked up to other bodies such as the government or training colleges. There may also need to be some re-organisation of **workspaces**, and this may incur costs (new desks, building or knocking down partitions, etc).

(3) **Development costs**

These include costs of measuring and analysing the **existing** system, costs of looking at the **new** system, and **changeover** costs.

A major sub-category is the cost of the applications and networking **software** that will be used, whether it is purchased **off-the-shelf** (multi-user **licences** will also be needed), or programs have to be **written specifically** for this application.

(4) **Personnel costs**

These will certainly include costs of **training,** and inevitable **time wasted** while learning the new system. There may also be **redundancy or recruitment** costs, and **changes in salaries** to pay for, following reallocation of responsibilities.

(5) **Operating costs**

These are ongoing costs such as **consumables** like disks and paper, **maintenance, insurance,** and **back-up and standby** arrangements.

(b) (i) **Payback and DCF**

(1) The payback method calculates the length of time a project will take to recoup the initial investment; in other words **how long a project will take to pay for itself.** The method is based on cash flows and, all else being equal, the project that takes the shortest time to pay for itself is the one that is preferred.

(2) Discounted cash flow (DCF) techniques may be subdivided into two approaches.

Net present value (NPV) considers **all relevant cash flows** associated with a project over the whole of its life and adjusts those occurring in future years to 'present value' by **discounting** at a rate called the cost of capital. The preferred choice is the project with the highest NPV. Projects with a negative NPV (a higher PV of outflows than of inflows) should not be undertaken.

Internal rate of return (IRR) involves comparing the **rate of return expected** from the project calculated on a discounted cash flow basis with the rate used as the **cost of capital**. Projects with an IRR higher than the cost of capital are worth undertaking.

Advantages [two only are requested in each case]

(1) Payback is intuitively **easy to understand** (it is often used by individuals in reaching personal financial decisions) and **easy to calculate**.

It gives greater weight to cash flows generated in **earlier years** which are **easier to predict**, represent a **faster return**, and help to **improve liquidity** so that money is available for more projects sooner.

(2) DCF considers **all of the cash flows** over a project's life, not just the early ones (a project may start slowly but be highly profitable in the long term).

DCF takes account of the '**time value of money**', in other words the fact that due to inflation and opportunity costs, £1 today is more valuable than £1 in a year's time.

Disadvantages [one only is requested in each case]

(1) **Payback** ignores cash flows (inflows and outflows) that occur **after** the project has paid for itself, which may be considerable.

(2) **DCF** requires a **cost of capital** to be accurately determined. This is very difficult in practice.

(ii) **Difficulties**

Besides the drawbacks already mentioned, problems may include the following.

(1) **Collecting cost information**. Certain facts, such as the consultant's fee or the cost of a standard package, may be known reasonably well in advance. However, the true extent of, say, **training** needs or the effect of any **teething problems** cannot be easily anticipated.

(2) **Collecting information about benefits**. Many benefits, such as **less stress** on staff due to overwork with inefficient systems, and **earlier publication** of results may be very difficult to quantify. Others, such as the value of extra information availability, will be very unclear until the system is up and running: some new benefits **may not be thought of** until some time after the system comes into operation.

(c) (i) **Pre-recorded information**

Possibilities include the following.

- Candidate number
- Paper number and title
- Examination date
- Designated marker code
- Exam centre

125

Difficulties

The main difficulty that may arise is that a candidate may need to continue his or her answers in **extra booklets**: should there only be one booklet for each candidate or should several be produced just in case? Clearly the latter approach could be very wasteful.

The problem is probably fairly easy to solve: it should be possible to produce **one booklet with pre-recorded information** and with sufficient space to accommodate the answers of all but the most industrious candidates or those with the largest handwriting. If extra space is needed **continuation sheets**, with **no** pre-recorded details could be used, so long as they can be securely attached to the booklet and the booklet is marked to show how many continuation sheets exist.

(ii)   **Data collection methods**

Only **one** of the following methods should have been described.

(1) **Optical Mark Recognition**

Optical mark reading is generally used for **numeric characters**. Values are denoted by a pencilled, ball-point pen or typed line in an appropriate box, whose position represents a value, on the pre-printed source document or card. The card is then read by a device which senses the **mark** in each box using an electric current and translates it into machine code.

The most widely known application of OMR in the UK is the entry form for the National Lottery. OMR is also widely used for multiple choice exam questions: candidates mark a box representing, say, A, B, C or D as their choice of answer to a question.

(2) **Optical Character Recognition**

Optical character recognition is a method of input involving a machine that is able to read characters by optical detection of the **shape of the characters**. Optical scanners can read printed, typed and sometimes handwritten documents at very fast speeds. They recognise the characters, convert them into machine code and record them.

OCR is now quite widely used (for example in publishing and legal work) for **scanning typed documents** and converting them into computer sensible form, but although the technology is improving, certain aspects of the **data** such as font or layout **may be lost** in the process.

(3) **Bar coding**

A bar code scanner is a device which reads bar codes, which are **groups of marks** that, by their spacing and thickness, indicate specific codes or values. The actual **number** represented by the code is printed below the bar code, in case the bars themselves are accidentally damaged (for example partly obliterated or torn off) or in case the scanner refuses to function properly.

Bar codes are now very common on almost all **consumer goods**, and scanners are widely used in **retailing**. They are also used in stock control systems and fixed assets management. In such applications bar code data entry enables highly accurate data and analyses to be produced very quickly.

(iii)   **Potential application in the examination system**

(Only **one** of the following methods should have been described.)

(1) **Optical Mark Recognition**

In this case, optical marks representing the data items listed in (i) could be pre-printed on the booklets (though this is not much different from using bar codes). In addition blank boxes could be provided, allowing markers to summarise what questions they had marked and what score they gave to the candidate for each one. If markers are not designated in advance, numbered blank boxes could be provided for them to mark in their own code.

The problem with this method is that it is easy to put the marks in the wrong place. A possible safeguard is for the marker not only to insert the optical marks but also to write in the candidate's scores in conventional number, facilitating manual cross-checking and quality control. Control totals could also be completed in both optical mark form and numbers: if the optical marks under individual headings did not add up to the same amount as the optically marked total, the optical mark reading software could detect that there had been an error.

(2) **Optical Character Recognition**

In this case, although handwriting can be scanned, systems cannot cope with all the possible variations between individuals' scripts and so some letters or numbers are always likely to be unrecognised.

OCR may be suitable for items such as those listed in part (ii), but it is far too unreliable to be used to obtain a true record of markers' handwritten scores or comments.

(3) **Bar coding**

Bar codes would be ideal for recording some, but not all, of the data that needs to be collected. Each of the items mentioned in (i) could be coded on the pre-printed booklets in this way. Markers could be issued with sticky labels showing a bar code, which they would stick onto each booklet that they marked.

However, it would not be possible for the scores given by markers to questions to be recorded in this way. A bar code system would need to be supplemented by Optical Mark Reading to achieve this.

(d) (i) **Operational feasibility**

A study of the operational feasibility of the proposed new system will be concerned to discover whether it would conflict with the way the organisation wishes to do its business.

Examples include [**three of**] the following.

(1) The new system might entail a change in management responsibilities, status or chains of command.

(2) The system might lead to such a high level of redundancies that it was considered too damaging to organisational morale.

(3) It might involve extensive retraining of staff who were not likely to be able to cope well with computers.

(4) Operational feasibility cannot be considered apart from economic feasibility: each of the previous points involves costs such as changes in salaries, redundancy costs, costs of retraining and/or new recruitment.

(ii)   **ISEC**

Aspects of ISEC's operations that may be affected include the following.

(1)   At present it seems likely that the spreadsheet operated by Administration is regarded as the central point for information, and other departments no doubt rely upon Administration for help with their own work. If information is shared across a network, this will undermine the organisational power of Administration.

(2)   Redundancies are unlikely to be an issue, since ISEC appears to be considerably overworked already.

(3)   Retraining may be needed. There is little evidence in the case that the staff are highly familiar with computers, and they certainly have no experience of managing information shared in databases. Learning to operate the controls necessary with networks as opposed to stand alone computers is a key issue.

(4)   It may be necessary to recruit a new person with appropriate experience of information management. Besides the political problems that this may cause, a new member of staff in a relatively senior position will be expensive.

47   AMALCAR

(a)   (i)   **Parallel running**

Parallel running means that the old and new systems are run together for a period of time. This means that the output from both systems can be compared or cross-checked to try and identify problems and errors in the new system. When comparisons between the two systems are satisfactory, the old system is abandoned and processing continues on the new system only.

Parallel running can be an **expensive exercise** because of the need to maintain two systems throughout the parallel run. The organisation may need to hire temporary staff and make overtime payments to ensure that all processing of data is completed. The effectiveness of the checking may also be limited where the two systems produce output in different formats.

Some of the **advantages of parallel** running are as follows.

(1)   Running the old system in parallel with the new system means that **reliance can again be placed on the old system should the new system develop significant problems on implementation**. The old system provides a safety net; processing within the organisation can continue while problems with the new system are rectified.

(2)   The **accuracy of the new system can be established relatively quickly**. Assuming that the outputs from both systems are compatible, then comparison of outputs provides assurance that the new system is processing data correctly. Without this assurance additional testing of the new system using test data would be necessary to prove the integrity of that system.

(3)   **Users of the system will be able to compare how the two systems operate by direct comparison**. This avoids the sometimes-artificial environment of a separate training course where the new system is taught using dummy or trial data, which is not always relevant to the organisation itself. Seeing how 'live' data is processed on the new system will help users relate to it more quickly which in turn will decrease their learning time for the new system.

Direct changeover

In a direct changeover, an old system is completely replaced by a new system in one move. The old system will be shut down one evening and the new system will start processing on the next day. This method of changeover allows no time at all for parallel running and so will be relatively risky should problems or errors occur with the new system. In a worse case scenario, the new system may fail leaving the organisation with no computer processing system.

Direct changeover is used where two systems are significantly different or where parallel running is not possible due to resource constraints like lack of staff or spare computer-processing time. To minimise the dangers of direct changeover, the change will normally take place during periods of low computer activity or usage, for instance during a holiday or near Christmas.

Some of the **advantages** of direct changeover are:

(1)   It is a relatively **cheap** method of systems changeover. Direct changeover does not incur the additional costs of parallel running such as additional staff, overtime or increased computer processing requirements.

(2)   **Training** for the new system can be **prior to implementation** rather than training being given 'on the job', as in many parallel runs. This will allow staff to become familiar with the new system in a 'safe' environment using test data rather than making mistakes with live data as in a parallel run. Also, the absence of the old system after implementation means that staff are less reliant on old ways and cannot be tempted to revert to using the old system because it happens to be more familiar.

(3)   It is possible that the new system will be **more reliable** because more time will have been taken **testing** it than in a parallel run situation where testing can take place during the parallel run itself. However, there is no guarantee that all errors will be found in any changeover method, so care will still be needed during the first months of operation to ensure that the system is working correctly.

(ii)   **Recommendation**

The staff at Amalcar face one major **constraint** in the choice of systems changeover. The contract with the bureau expires in two months time, so any method of changeover must therefore be complete by this time if additional (and higher) processing costs at the bureau are to be avoided.

Although a new system has been identified for use, it is unlikely that it can be implemented and tested effectively within two months using a parallel run. There will simply not be enough time to organise systems changeover, hiring of additional staff and upgrading computers and then do a parallel run.

Amalcar's main option is therefore a direct changeover. The new system can still be installed and tested using some test data in the two months. A one-off conversion of files, probably at a weekend, will then be required to complete the change.

(b)   **Training**

Advantages and disadvantages

(i)   **Sending employees on a standard three day training course**

The billing office manager has already attended this training course so she will be able to provide first hand comments on its usefulness to the organisation.

Advantages

(1) The software company runs the course. Their trainers will therefore be very knowledgeable concerning the new software and will be able to answer any query about it.

(2) The course is held away from Amalcar's premises. Staff will therefore not be interrupted with work-related queries while they are being trained.

(3) Employees can be trained individually or in small groups. Some employees are therefore always available to run the existing system while others are being trained.

(4) If the software company is ISO9000 registered then training should be high standard and consistent quality for all members of staff.

(5) Amalcar's employees will be able to meet other users of the software and learn from their experience.

Disadvantages of a standard training course

(1) The course may not take into account the specific needs of Amalcar's employees. The course may have to focus on general issues rather than the specific parts of the system that Amalcar's employees need to know about.

(2) The quality of the tuition will depend partly on the number of participants attending the course. Amalcar will have no control over the size of the class. Participants in larger classes will have less direct contact time with the tutor and so may learn less.

(3) The option is relatively expensive compared to running a course in-house. Sending staff on standard training courses will cost £3,750 compared with £2,000 for an in-house course.

(4) No information is available to show whether the standard course can be amended to cater for the individual skill requirements of participants. Some of the managers at Amalcar may only need to know about interrogating the data; sessions dealing with the input of data will therefore not be relevant for them.

(5) Care will be needed to ensure that all employees are booked on a course prior to the new system going live.

(ii) **Running the course in Amalcar's offices**

The standard course can be run in Amalcar's offices. Many of the advantages of attending the course at the software company itself still apply. However, additional advantages and disadvantages include the following.

Advantages

(1) Because the participants will all be from Amalcar, the course can be tailored to the specific requirements of the employees from Amalcar. Trainers can therefore focus on the specific needs of Amalcar employees and specific use they will be making of the software.

(2) A separate course may be available for managers who will be using only part of the functionality of the software system. Alternatively, the course can be structured so that managers may only have to attend for the last few hours of the day.

(3) The cost of an in-house course is less than sending all employees on a course at the software company itself.

(4) All users will be able to attend the course at the same time. They will therefore be able to pool their knowledge of the system and help each other both during and after the course.

Disadvantages of an in-house course

(1) If all employees attend the course on the same day, then it will be difficult, or impossible, to maintain processing on the old system. The alternative of sending one or two employees on an external course may not be an acceptable solution from the point-of-view of the motivation of employees involved.

(2) Holding the course in the office means that there will be a temptation to check for messages or undertake some processing during coffee and lunch breaks. It will be more difficult to maintain good timekeeping than running the course away from the office.

(3) More junior staff may not feel comfortable being in the same 'classroom' as their managers. Learning may not be effective if junior staff feel inhibited about asking questions because they don't want to look as if they don't understand what is being taught.

(iii) **Billing officer teaches other staff**

The billing officer has already attended the course, so she should have the knowledge to teach the other staff.

Advantages of the billing office teaching other staff

(1) The officer will have detailed knowledge of the system both from the training course she attended, and also from being involved in the system selection and planning for implementation. She will therefore be able to explain precisely how the software will be used in practice within Amalcar.

(2) Tuition will be provided on an individual basis within the department. The department can be kept running because the manager and staff will always be available to resolve queries on the old system.

(3) In pure cost terms this is the cheapest solution because there is no direct costs involved.

Disadvantages of the billing officer teaching other staff

(1) The billing officer has a limited amount of time while the training of 6 employees for three days each means that the office must find 18 days for training. Given the importance of implementing the new system it may be more important for her to concentrate on the implementation itself. A possible solution would be train another senior member of staff who would in turn training the remaining employees.

(2) Employees may not feel comfortable learning from their manager. As in the running of a course in-house, employees may feel inhibited about asking questions, which will limit the effectiveness of the training being provided.

(3) The billing office may not be a recognised trainer. Although she may be willing to provide the training she may not have the required personal skills to provide this effectively. This issue will severely limit the learning value of this option.

(4) The billing officer may not be confident about using the new system. This will mean that she will not be able to train the other staff, and may feel defensive when asked questions that she does not know the answer to.

131

(iv) **Use of a Computer Based Training package**

Advantages of using a CBT package

(1) Employees will be able to learn when they have the time, rather than on three specific days. Training can be tailored around existing workloads.

(2) The CBT system should provide some form of assessment software to check the progress of learning. Employees will benefit from this system because they can check their knowledge retention in private rather than being embarrassed about getting questions wrong in a classroom.

(3) The system appears to be very cost-effective, with a 6-user licence at £240 costing less than sending one employee on a training course at £750.

(4) New employees can work through the CBT as soon as they join the company rather than having to wait for the next available training course.

Disadvantages of using a CBT package

(1) The CBT may be badly written and lack the interaction of a face-to-face training course. Users may therefore not gain the advantage of using either the live software itself or being able to ask questions on demand of the trainer on the course.

(2) The package must be compatible with the existing computers, and a computer must be available for training when needed.

(3) Using the package can be quite boring and employees may find it difficult to concentrate on a computer screen for the require length of time. This is particularly an issue because employees will be using a computer system as part of their job anyway.

(4) There will be no opportunity to learn from the trainer, other employees or staff at other organisations when the CBT is being used.

Recommendation

I would recommend running a course for all staff in-house, but perhaps on a Saturday to avoid having to close the department on a weekday.

This has the benefit of training all staff at once while allowing the course to be tailored to the precise requirements of Amalcar. Staff will also be able to share their concerns about the software and implementation away from the pressures of work. Implementation can then proceed effectively because all staff will be trained and have knowledge of the precise implementation issues affecting Amalcar. If Saturday working is an issue, then staff can be given an extra day off in rotation during the following week.

(c)

(i) **Support contracts**

A support or maintenance contract is a legal agreement between the software supplier and the purchaser of that software. In general terms, the contract will explain the legal obligations of the supplier in providing and maintaining the software as well as stating what rights the purchaser has regarding use and upgrading of the software.

The following are some of the facilities and services that will normally be included in a maintenance contract:

(1) **Help**

A system of support for users who are having difficulty using the software is provided in almost all maintenance contracts. Users will be able to obtain answers to queries either by telephone hot line or e-mail. The hours of operation of the hotline and guaranteed response times to solve queries will be given in the contract.

(2) **Information**

The supplier will normally provide general information about how to use the software. This information may take the form of a newsletter or fact-sheet and will normally include examples of how the software is being used in different companies.

(3) **Fixing errors**

It is unlikely that software will be issued without some 'bugs' or undetected errors. Most suppliers therefore issue 'bug fixes' to provide minor amendments to their software. These fixes are often available via the Internet, free of charge. Customers with a support contract should be automatically notified of any such amendments.

(4) **Updates**

Software updates are also provided to amend the software if the external environment changes. For example, upgrades to the payroll package would be produced to take account of revised taxation rates and personal allowances.

(5) **Upgrades**

When a software package is significantly amended, then a new release will be available in the form of an upgrade. A maintenance contract will allow users to purchase the upgrade at a heavily discounted price.

(ii) **Why it is essential to subscribe to the contract**

The payroll software the Amalcar will be using will be subject to fairly frequent revisions as tax law within the country changes, or tax rates are amended. If Amalcar wanted to amend the software itself, it would mean an increase in staff costs of additional computer staff. Also, there would be no guarantee that the all amendments would be accurately carried out due to the specialised nature of the software.

By taking out a support contract, Amalcar place the responsibility for providing updated software on the supplier. The supplier will have the specialist staff needed to make the programme amendments. Furthermore, should any amendment prove to be incorrect, Amalcar can rely on the supplier to make the required adjustments. Avoidance of additional programming cost and the knowledge that the supplier must provide the amended software as required are easily worth the cost of the support contract.

(iii) **User groups**

A user group is a forum for users of some particular hardware or software. These users, who are the people actually using the software rather than professional developers, maintain some form of regular contact, perhaps via the Internet. They share ideas and experience about the software and may also act as an arbiter if there are any disputes with the supplier.

The benefits of Amalcar becoming a member of a user group are directed mainly to the staff of Amalcar rather than the organisation itself. The benefits include the following.

(1) Obtaining **information about problems** that staff may encounter when using the software. Because the software already has a large user base, it is likely that another member of the group has already come across the problem. A message on the group's Internet site will hopefully produce a quick solution.

(2) Attendance at **user group meetings**. Employees from Amalcar can attend meetings of the user group where uses of the software are discussed and methods of overcoming problems with the software are shared. This sharing of knowledge may help Amalcar use the software more effectively.

(3) **Recommending changes** to the software. Many suppliers will obtain the opinion of the user group concerning changes that could be made to the software. The staff at Amalcar will therefore be in a good position to influence the development of the payroll package.

(4) Obtaining **early copies of the upgraded software**. User group members are normally issued with 'beta' copies of new software to subject to trial and testing before the new version becomes generally available. Although there is an element of risk in checking new software, working on a beta copy means that Amalcar gets new features in the software early. Beta testers may also receive the upgrade free of charge.

(d) (i)   **Further information**

The additional information required to draw a network will include:

(1) **The length of time taken by each activity**

The first stage in drawing a network diagram is to find the length of time, which is required to complete each activity. The length of time is required to identify whether any **activities overlap** and to find the **critical path** of the network. In this situation, timings may also be affected the method of training chosen, for example. If there is any **uncertainty** regarding the length of time an activity will take then this must also be recorded before the network diagram can be produced.

(2) **Finding out which activities are dependent on other activities**

The point of a network is to show the order in which activities are undertaken, and whether a particular activity is dependent on any previous activities. For example, the installation of the software in Amalcar should only be attempted after the project plan has been produced and the staff trained in the new system (to give but two prior activities).

(ii)   **Terms and explanation**

The **critical path** is the duration of the longest path through a network. When a network diagram is completed, the amount of time taken on each of the paths from the start to the finish node in the network can be calculated. The path with the longest time is the critical path; it is critical because if any additional time is taken on this path, then the total time to complete the whole project will also increase.

Other paths in the network will have some slack in them; taking additional time on these paths will not affect the overall project time.

It is essential that the billing manager knows what activities lie on the critical path for a number of reasons including the following.

(1) So that she knows which **activities are critical** to the overall project. She can monitor those activities to ensure that they are not delayed; any delay would increase the overall project time.

(2) To **ensure that critical activities are being carried out** by trusted and more experienced staff, because they are less likely to make mistakes and therefore delay the overall project.

(3) **To try and find ways of decreasing the time taken on the critical path**, if the overall project time is excessive. She may find that the estimated time for completing one activity has some budgetary slack built into it, which can therefore be removed. Alternatively, it may be possible to split a critical activity into two smaller activities, which together take less time.

48   ELEX

(a)

> **Tutor's hint**. This question required you to review the case study material in the question and use this information to provide relevant examples. You should have stated the problem, explained how the problem is relevant to the case study, and given a solution.

(i)   Functional shortcomings

Functional shortcomings relate to whether or not the software supports the **procedures and operations** of the organisation. It is unlikely that the chosen software meets these objectives for the following reasons:

(1) **Lack of specific objectives for the software**

A post-implementation review will establish whether or not the **objectives and targeted performance criteria** of the organisation have been met. This helps to ensure that any software purchased will actually meet the requirements of the organisation.

However, in this situation, the **actual requirements** of the organisation were **not specified**. The IS manager did suggest that the organisation requirements were stated when she asked for a formal requirements specification. This advice was rejected and the package was chosen on the basis of the **intuition** of the Warehouse Manager and the Operations Director. This approach was unsuccessful because one of the first complaints from users was that the package 'does not work in the same way that we do' and the package only met 80% of the organisation's requirements. The package was therefore **inappropriate** for the organisation.

To avoid this situation occurring, any future project should start with a **formal statement of the organisation's requirements**. This document can be used as a reference when investigating different packages. Only packages that meet the statement of requirements should then be considered for use within the organisation.

(2) **Lack of checking of functionality of the software**

The selection of new software will normally be carried out against a series of **pre-defined criteria** that will include **cost** and the **functionality** of the package as well as an analysis of the **background of the supplier**. In this situation, the package was selected on the basis of a half-day demonstration

135 **BPP**
PUBLISHING

and a telephone call to one existing customer. While the demonstration was useful, and the customer could provide some information, it is not surprising that the package did not meet the organisation's requirements because:

- A review of the **background** of the supplier was **not undertaken**.

- A half-day demonstration is **unlikely to provide a full evaluation** of the package.

- The software was **not compared to performance criteria** (as noted above).

As the case study information shows, the evaluation resulted in the wrong package being chosen because it did not meet the functionality requirements of the organisation, and there is concern over the reliability of the supplier.

To avoid this situation occurring in the future, a **formal tender** should be drawn up listing **all the organisation's requirements** regarding not just the software but also supplier evaluation and the other areas mentioned above. When tenders have been received back from potential suppliers they can be compared to business requirements and only suppliers meeting those requirements and providing acceptable references should be chosen.

(ii)   **Performance**

Performance analysis looks at whether an organisation's **current systems** can be supported by any proposed software. The software may not meet the performance requirements of the organisation for the following reasons.

(1)   **Lack of user input**

It is normal to include **users** in the evaluation of software to check that the new software meets their requirements.

User input did not appear to have been taken in this implementation because the need for quick entry of customer orders had not been identified by the steering committee.

To avoid this problem in the future, a **full analysis of user requirements** should be undertaken to ensure that the proposed software would help users to do their jobs.

(2)   **Checking software meets requirements of the whole organisation**

Before purchasing any new software, it is important to ensure that the software will meet **all the requirements of the organisation**. Not only must the software meet user requirements (as noted above) but it must also meet overall organisation requirements in terms of **provision of correct reports**, ability to **run alongside existing systems** etc.

However, in this situation the steering committee did not make any attempt to assess system performance prior to implementation. This implies that **the requirements of the organisation as a whole were not known**. There could therefore be no confidence that the new system would provide the correct reports etc.

To avoid this problem in the future, a **full analysis of the organisation** should be undertaken including detailed **job requirements** and **requirements for provision of information** at all management levels. The software can then be reviewed to ensure that its functionality meets these detailed requirements. If the software cannot meet the requirements, then it may either be tailored so that it does, or rejected as being unsuitable.

(3) **Reviewing reports from other users**

One method of checking the acceptability of software is to review reports from **other users** and in many cases even **visit their sites** to obtain first hand information on the use of the software. Although this will not provide evidence that the software will tie in with the organisation's own working methods, it will provide some input on **how easy it is to use** the system as well an indication of the **support provided** by the supplier.

In this situation, only one user was contacted, and even this user had been supplied with a different version of the software. This was probably not, therefore, a particularly good reference.

To avoid this problem in the future, the sites of other users should be visited and a check made to ensure that the **same version** of the software is actually being used at these sites.

(iii) **System down-time**

System down time relates to the amount of time that the computer system cannot be used. This will be a significant problem for any organisation because it normally means that **processing cannot be undertaken** during down time, and consequently orders may be lost if stock and customer details cannot be accessed. Reasons for excessive down time for this particular software are as follows.

(1) **A lack of training of staff**

In most systems implementations, staff are trained to use the system **prior** to the new system going live. Training ensures not only that staff **understand how to use the system**, but also that they **know the major system weaknesses and errors** and how to deal with these.

In this situation, **staff were not trained** on the new system. A lack of training will affect the efficiency of use of the system, but more importantly, **errors may be made in using the system**, which may actually cause the system to crash.

(2) **Possible hardware constraints on software usage**

It is important to ensure that computer **hardware will support the software** that is to run on it. Hardware purchase will normally carried be out after reference to the software supplier or at least by reference to the software requirements. If the hardware, particularly the RAM and hard disk size, does not meet the software requirements, then the software may become unstable and 'crash'.

In this situation, it appears that the software supplier was not consulted. This means that there is no guarantee that the new software will actually run on the hardware. Some of the system downtime could therefore relate to **inadequate hardware** being used.

To avoid this problem in the future, the **organisation should contact the supplier** to check the hardware requirements prior to purchase.

(3) **The new software was not fully tested**

If software has not been fully tested or crashes regularly, then this will lead to system down time while the software is checked and reinstalled if required.

The case study indicates that the software was experiencing **reliability problems** at the only other user site. Some of the system down time could relate to the software crashing resulting in the computer system being unusable.

To avoid this problem in the future, software should only be purchased either when a **more established user base** has been built up or a **comparable reference site** has been visited to see that the software is reliable.

(b)

> **Tutor's hint**. We have given more than the minimum number of comments so you can see the range of valid answers that could be used.

Resolving the current problems

The current problems with the software could be resolved in three different ways, as explained below.

(i)   **Purchase the source code**

Purchasing the source code would mean that Elex would be able to **amend the program code directly**. Most software is sold in the object code, which makes amendments **difficult or impossible** in most cases.

(1)   **Advantages**

The organisation should obtain the software system that is required. In-house programmers will be able to amend the code to **make the software specific to Elex's systems**. This may be a better option than relying on the software house to make amendments because Elex's own staff will be able to provide a **more accurate tailoring** of the software.

Software support can be moved in-house. The software developers in Elex will learn how the package from HR SOFT works. **Technical queries** on the software can therefore be **resolved in–house** rather than relying on support from HR SOFT.

Amending the existing package should be **quicker than writing software from scratch**. The existing software already provides 80% of the functionality required by Elex.

(2)   **Disadvantages**

It is **unlikely that HR SOFT would continue to support** the software after Elex purchases the source code. Elex would want to make changes to the code that HR SOFT would have no knowledge about. HR SOFT could not support the software in these circumstances.

Any **new developments** in the software produced by **HR SOFT** would have to be **implemented separately** into Elex's version of the software. Because Elex had amended the source code of the software, **software updates from the supplier could not be automatically rolled out** in Elex. This means that Elex must retain the in-house development team. Furthermore there will be a **delay in implementing upgrades** in the software as the programmers in Elex work through the changes and then implement these into the Elex software.

The staff at Elex **may not have the necessary knowledge and skill** to amend the software. The software has been written in a **new programming language,** so programmers in Elex would have to learn this language before working on the software. Given their lack of experience it may be quite difficult to make acceptable amendments in a realistic timescale. The alternative of employing programmers with experience of the software may be an expensive option; if the language is new then few programmers will be familiar with it and they are likely to command relatively **higher salaries.**

(ii)   **Replace with in-house software**

The **whole system could be re-written and replaced** using the in-house development team. Advantages and disadvantages of this solution include the following.

(1)   **Advantages**

COBOL was the programming language used for the old software. The programmers at Elex will therefore **already be familiar with this** language and there will be no need for the organisation to employ new staff or retrain existing staff.

Writing software in-house means that **control** of the development is **retained within the organisation**. This will help to ensure that the exact program that Elex requires is actually produced. **Users** will also be on-hand to make comments on the system as it is written so hopefully the software will meet their requirements.

The COBOL language has a **large and established user base** with many programmers trained in COBOL. Hiring additional staff, to cope with short-term problems like development timetable slippage, should be easy.

(2)   **Disadvantages**

The system is programmed to run on **dumb terminals**. Although it is not clear from the question, it appears that the **investment in PC's will be wasted**. This alternative may therefore result in higher capital expenditure. Also, users are unlikely to want to return to dumb terminals having experienced some of the flexibility of **Windows** with the more recent version of the software. **Employee morale** may also be an issue if this solution is chosen.

Care will have to be taken if code is borrowed form the old system when writing the new program that appropriate checking is carried out to ensure that the software will be year 2000 compliant.

The program will have to be written from scratch. This means that the overall development of the program **may take a long time**. Given that proprietary systems are available now (one was rejected on cost grounds by Elex), then the organisation may find itself at a **competitive disadvantage** if the new system cannot be implemented quickly enough.

A further problem with writing the program from scratch is that the whole systems development process must be undertaken. A large amount of time will be taken **working through the whole development cycle** from systems specification to delivery of the final product. Again, Elex may be at a **competitive disadvantage** if it has to **wait a long time** for the new software.

Writing a new program implies that there will be another round of **systems changeover**. Extreme care will be needed to ensure that all **data is completely and accurately transferred** again to the new system. Staff **training** will also have to be planned carefully so that employees do not become demotivated by yet another systems change without adequate user training.

(iii) **Software house makes the required program changes**

Finally, the **software house** could be asked to make the changes to the software so that Elex still receives a system, which is suited to its precise requirements. Some of the advantages and disadvantages of this option are as follows.

(1) **Advantages**

The software house **wrote the original program**. Programmers at the software house will **already be familiar** with the source code of the program and should be able to make the changes **quickly and accurately**.

The **software house is made responsible** for the accuracy and running of the program. If the software requires any amendments because of design errors, then the software house will have to make these changes. The **cost of rectifying errors lies with the software house** and not Elex.

Elex **does not need to maintain resources in-house** to write or maintain the software. The organisation may therefore experience some **cost savings** from not having to employ programmers and purchasing suitable computer equipment and provide office space for them.

The **supplier** will make **software updates** for an agreed fee. Although the fee will be more than it would be for purchasing simple upgrades to a proprietary package, Elex will still be able to draw on new features of the software that have been added at the request of other users. These **external ideas and new features** may not have been available had the software been written in-house.

(2) **Disadvantages**

There is a **physical separation** between the users of the software and the development team at the third party. It may therefore be more **difficult for Elex to control** the changes being made to the software and to obtain appropriate **user input** to test and check the changes made. Some arrangement will be needed to ensure that appropriate user input to the software can still be given.

Elex will be **dependent** on the software house to continue supplying the software. If the software house is **late** supplying an upgrade, or even **goes out of business,** there is little Elex can do to resolve the situation. Current experience with the software house shows that developments have been late and the software tends to be unstable. Elex takes a risk that it may not be able to continue trading if the software is not available when required.

It may be **difficult to manage the costs of upgrades** to the software. Elex will effectively 'lock' itself into purchasing software from this supplier. HR SOFT will realise this and could try and increase the cost of software support to exploit its monopoly situation. Care will be needed in negotiating the **support contract** to ensure that cost increases are reasonable and accurately reflect the work done.

(c)

In the **short term**, Elex has to continue operating using some sort of computerised system. The options available to the Managing Director regarding the order processing system in the short term will include the following.

(i) **Use the new software, but upgrade the hardware**

When the new software was purchased, the suppliers were not involved in the hardware purchase. Some of the errors that are currently being experienced could arise from an **inadequate hardware specification**.

A **review** can be undertaken of the **errors** being experienced to identify **why these are occurring**. If necessary the hardware configuration can be upgraded to try and stop some of the errors occurring. It would be relatively easy to upgrade the RAM or hard disk sizes.

(ii) **Use the new software, but train staff**

When the new software was implemented, **staff were not trained** on how to use the system. This will have resulted in **poor working practices** and could have caused some of the system failures because staff were using the software incorrectly.

The Managing Director could now take the opportunity of training staff in the use of the new software. If necessary, the **HR SOFT manuals can be amended** to take account of **specific work practices** within Elex. Within a few weeks, training material and courses could be run, directed at how the staff at Elex use the system, and **short functional guides** produced for reference. These actions will help **motivate** staff, **cut down system errors** and hopefully provide a **more efficient use** of the new system.

(iii) **Use the new software, but amend work practices in Elex**

A complaint from staff regarding the new software was that it did not operate in the way that they were used to working. It is possible that some of the errors in the new software resulted from employees **trying to make the software work in ways it was not designed to.**

An action to resolve this problem is to **amend the way in which staff actually work**. This may not be very popular with the employees, but may provide a workable solution to decrease software errors. If the employee's jobs are restructured to follow the procedures in the software, employees should find the software easier to use. After some initial complaints, the MD should find that this an acceptable alternative.

(iv) **Revert to using the old software**

The old software will still be available in the organisation, so it is possible to re-load this onto the computers and start working again with it. **Current data** will have to be reloaded into the system because the old software has not been used for six months.

This option will be **more acceptable to employees** because they are already familiar with the old software. The software has also been in use for 10 years so it is likely to be **error free**. A wait of a further six months before a new system is

141

introduced is a relatively short amount of time compared to the last 10 years of usage. This alternative therefore provides a useful **breathing space** where employees can use a familiar system before a more important change is undertaken.

(v)   **Error recording in new software**

If the new system is used, with any or all of the modifications in (i) to (iii) above, then there will still be a need to **record software errors**. It is still not clear what is causing these errors.

If the errors are found to result from **faulty software**, then the information can be passed immediately to the software house. It is possible that a more robust version of the software can be made available in the near future which will make working conditions easier for the employees at Elex.

(d)

> **Tutor's hint**. The question referred to the responsibilities of the project manager. Your answer should have repeatedly referred to these responsibilities rather than simply explaining the stages in project management.

A **project manager** is the individual who is in overall control of a project; he or she literally manages the project. Many project managers, like the Operations Director, will have **IT skills**. It will be important to ensure that the manager has the **project management** and **people skills** to run the project.

Some of the responsibilities of the project manager are as follows.

(i)   **Producing the project quality plan**

The project quality plan contains the detailed **terms of reference** for the project. It explains in detail important points concerning the project such as:

(1)   What the **aim** of the project is.

(2)   How the project will **proceed** and what **standards** are to be followed during the project.

(3)   What the **deliverables** of the project are.

(4)   How the project will be **reviewed** to ensure that the initial objectives have been met.

The project manager will **need to be involved** in the production of the project quality plan because he will need to be happy that the project can deliver the required product in the timeframe given. If he is **not convinced** that the project is feasible then it is likely to **fail** because he will not be able to pass on any enthusiasm or commitment to his fellow workers.

(ii)   **Project scheduling and monitoring**

Project monitoring involves detailed **budget preparation** as well as setting of **individual measurable targets** for the project. Important responsibilities at this stage include:

(1)   Setting of **time and cost budgets.**

(2)   Identifying the **activities** of the project, including the **critical path.**

(3)   Setting up the framework of **procedures** and organisational **structures** to manage the project.

(4)   **Allocating resources** to each section of the project.

(5) Arranging **training**.

(6) Confirming **reporting and monitoring** procedures.

The project manager will need to be involved with all the planning because he has overall responsibility for the project. He therefore needs to be happy that appropriate structures are being established to run the project and report on the progress of the project. A **computerised planning tool** will normally be used to help prepare the various plans.

(iii) **Communication**

The manager will be responsible for **briefing the staff involved** in the project and for **communicating the progress of the project** to the steering committee or Board.

(iv) **Co-ordination**

The manager will also be responsible for the initial **co-ordination between the project team and the users** and any **third parties** involved in the project. By providing some initial control in this area, the manager can ensure that appropriate communication systems are implemented with users. Also, he can ensure that there is no duplication of communication, such as a third party being approached by two different sub-teams.

(v) **Monitoring and control**

The main responsibility of the manager when the project is running is to **monitor and control the progress of the project**. Appropriate reporting structures to provide information on the progress of the project should already be in-place. Information will now be collected in the form of reports from those structures and reviewed by the manager.

The manager will need to take various actions as the project progresses, depending on the actual content of the reports received. The running of the project will be affected by **problems** such as staff illness, late deliveries from suppliers, tasks taking longer than budgeted and requests for more resources because the initial plan was incorrect. The manager will monitor the reports and then **make decisions regarding the action to be taken** on the problems. The manager's overall responsibility is to keep the project running, so project tools such as Gantt charts and network diagrams will be continually updated to identify areas where time may be a problem.

Having taken decisions on the running of the project, these **decisions need to be communicated** to the staff on the project and also to the steering committee or Board. The manager will also be responsible for producing regular progress reports for the committee, which will incorporate any key decisions made affecting the overall time, and costs budgets for the project.

(vi) **Post project review**

Towards the end of the project, the manager will be responsible for producing the post project review. This review will investigate two key areas:

(1) Whether the project **produced the required deliverables** including a review of **budgets** and investigation of significant **variances.**

(2) Whether the project was **organised correctly** and **managed** to an acceptable standard.

The aim of the review is to provide key **learning and action points** so that errors are not repeated on future projects.

(vii) **People management**

Throughout the whole project, the manager will also be responsible for managing the staff involved with the project. This will involve keeping staff **motivated**, dealing with **conflicts** in the team, maintaining **staff development** and **appraisal** systems, awarding **bonuses** and if necessary **hiring and firing** staff. The project manager will therefore need to be a good manager of people. The overall success of the project may well depend how well the people on the project are managed.

49 CAET TEXTILES

(a)

> **Tutor's hint**. You should have related the points raised in your answer to the specific issues from the case study.

The advantages to CAET of outsourcing its information services function will include:

Focus on the core activities of the business

One of the managers has already commented that 'We are not a software house' reminding the Board that the main function of the CAET is **producing clothes, not IT systems**. Retaining the information services function in-house means that the Board's time will be split between managing the core business as well as making decisions about the IT systems. Outsourcing the information services function will enable the Board to focus on the areas of activity that the members understand and can make informed decisions about. Given the specialist nature of IT, decisions made in this area by the Board may be incorrect or inappropriate, due to a lack of knowledge.

Outsourcing may also help individual departmental managers **focus** on maintaining and developing their non-IT staff. The present situation seems to involve managers spending considerable time discussing problems with the information systems department rather than supervising the manufacturing operations of CAET.

Better control of costs

The current system of financing the IS department is via a standard level on each of the user departments. While this has the advantage that it is **easy to administer,** it does lack apparent need to justify expenditure on the part of the IS department. The managers in the individual business departments are therefore concerned that the IS department is not providing value for money. Similarly, a significant number of demands for system changes and enhancements may be made on the IS department by managers because there is **no additional costs** in making more requests.

Outsourcing the IS department would place the work being performed by that department on a definite contractual footing. This will benefit the IS department because all project requests would **have to be cost justified** prior to being submitted to the department. Requests will only be made in accordance with the budgets available in each department. However, each project will now have a definite cost, so the managers in each user department can see that the IS department is providing a useful service to each department and CAET. The IS department can therefore be seen to be working efficiently by providing projects within pre-defined budgets.

More rewarding career structure for IT personnel

Although CAET employs 30 IT personnel, this does not necessarily make a large IT department. Opportunities for career advancement and job satisfaction may therefore be limited. A relatively **high turnover** of IT personnel could be expected.

By outsourcing the IS department, the personnel would become members of a large company offering enhanced job variety and career prospects. This should increase staff motivation. Some improvement in the standard and efficiently of the department could also be expected. Because the IS personnel work for a different company, the standard of work will be **defined contractually** with the outsourcing company. Complaints concerning standard of work may be easier to resolve in this situation rather than being involved in inter-departmental disputes.

User sign-off on projects

Under the current system, user departments appear to be unwilling to commit to signing off on specific projects. This leads to aggravation between the user department and the IS department.

Outsourcing the IS department will place a clear emphasis on agreeing an **accurate systems specification** prior to programming work commencing. The outsourced IS department is extremely unlikely to commence work on a project where users cannot specify what they want because they could be held accountable for not meeting specifications when the project is finished. Realising that work will not commence until the specification is agreed will help the user departments to state exactly what they want from any IT system. Providing **sign-off** confirms what the requirements are and ensures that users are involved in the ownership and development of the system; keys points that did not happen under the existing system.

(b)

> **Tutor's hint.** This question asked for an explanation of CASE tools and fourth generation languages, without actually referring back to the case study itself. We have included direct references to the case study information to ensure the relevance of the answer is maintained.

(i)   Structured techniques are normally used in a systems project. While they do not guarantee that the shortcomings of the design processes at CAET will be overcome, they do help to provide **more structured processes** and models which will help to ensure that user requirements are correctly translated into a workable system.

The actual technique used will vary according to the stage of the project. Some of the main techniques used include:

- **Data flow diagrams** – to show how processes are currently carried out in an organisation

- **Logical data models** and **Entity life history** - to show how data in a new system will be processed and to show complementary views of a system to make it easier to understand

- **Physical data models** to show that actual transfer of data within a new system

A Computer Assisted Software Engineering (**CASE**) tool can assist the production of many of the models. The CASE tool allows a logical data model, most of which are graphical, to be drawn quickly and easily using support programs like an integrated data dictionary to establish relationships in the model. Other support programs within the CASE tool may also allow logical designs to be converted into a physical design, saving further time and expense.

(ii) **Prototyping** may help the systems development at CAET because it provides a useful vehicle for obtaining user input as well as demonstrating the system prior to final development. Using prototyping will also help ensure that user requirements are met, and check that users have "bought into" the systems development and so are more willing to accept the new system.

A prototype is essentially a model or mock-up of the input and possibly output screens that users will be using. The screens are written in a development tool, normally called 4th Generation Software (**4GL**), as opposed to older third generation languages like COBOL, which do not easily support prototyping. The 4GL is used because screens can be designed and amended quickly in accordance with user requirements. The design process is a series of iterations revolving around producing a design, obtaining user input, modifying the design and obtaining further input and modification until the screens are acceptable to users and programmers.

The final design may either be used as basis for the final software directly, with the code being transferred to the release version of the software, or it may simply be used as a template to model the final software on. Either way, having obtaining user input, the software should meet user requirements and so help stop rejection or lack of ownership of the system by the users.

(c)

> **Tutor's hint**. Ensure your answer applied your knowledge of structured techniques and prototyping to the specific problems raised in the case study.

(i) **Problems of operational understanding**

Software must be **appropriate for the needs of users,** and users must also be able to understand that software in the design stage so that they can accept it. The operational design referred to in the question was a flowchart which users 'could not be bothered to read'. The flowchart therefore failed to meet user requirements because it was **potentially difficult to understand** and they could not relate this to the way that they worked.

Using structured techniques and prototyping would help overcome these problems by:

Providing a system that matched **more closely with the actual work patterns** of the managers. User involvement would be obtained and prototypes produced so users could clearly see the sequence of operations in the software and check that this matched their own procedures.

Providing a system that they **could relate to**. Prototyping enables programmers to show what the actual input and output screens will look like, rather than relying on a flowchart which is a simplification of the system. Users will be able to see the different screens and error messages etc. and make constructive comments for amendments to ensure that their requirements are met.

(ii) **Fulfilling user requirements**

It appeared to be difficult to fulfil user requirements at CAET because these were **not defined** at the beginning of the project. So, while users recommended some changes to the software, these amendments only showed other features and functionality that could be useful. This placed the users and programmers at odds with each other because it appeared that user requirements could never be satisfied while users thought that programmers were being inflexible.

Using structured techniques will assist the situation because one of the key elements of this process is to obtain **a statement of user requirements** early in any project. While this may be amended later, having a definite statement of requirements will assist programmers because they can build a system to meet those requirements. Similarly, users can check that those precise requirements are met, rather than making apparent ad hoc amendments as the project progresses. Any amendments can be considered, along with the time and cost implications associated with them.

The use of prototyping will also help users assess their requirements, because they will be able to **see the possibilities** of system design before detailed programming takes place. This initial exploration of requirements will assist both users and programmers because a **detailed specification can be agreed**; programming can then continue without any major changes being made to this specification.

(iii) **Lack of user ownership**

Lack of ownership by users makes the work of analysts and programmers difficult because they will not be sure that the system being designed **meets user requirements**. Also, without having formal signoff of the different stages of a project, progress may appear to be slow.

Structured techniques will assist in the issue of obtaining signoffs because users will be asked to confirm that various stages of the project have been **completed**. The analyst may present models of the system at various stages simply to confirm that the system is being produced correctly. While this may not remove completely the fear that requirements cannot be changed, the process will show that progress is being made as well as identifying the costs of making amendments as the project progresses. Prototyping can be used to display models of the system at the signoff points, so users can see progress, rather than rely on the word of the analyst.

Obtaining **formal sign-off** will also confirm joint ownership of the project. In fact, delaying the next stage of the project until signoff has been achieved will help to show the importance to users of being involved in the project at all stages.

(d)

The current situation is that the IS department is funded by a **standing charge** on the user departments. This implies that there is no need to construct a business case for the use of IS department services, rather the user departments simply make requests for any IS system that may seem appropriate to them. It is therefore almost impossible for the IS department to prioritise work.

One solution is to require user departments to present a business case for each project requested. This will help to ensure that there is some **benefit** to that department and that the **costs** of development are acceptable in relation to the benefit. Providing a business case will also help the IS department allocate resources to those projects providing the largest benefits to CAET, as a whole. The main issue to be resolved with this proposal will be the quantification of the benefits of any project, because many benefits are likely to be intangible.

Providing specific projects for the IS department to produce may also assist in the issue of justifying the funding of the department. The IS department will have to provide specific quotes for each project, showing some **accountability** to the user departments. Allowing third parties to bid for the contracts could also test the efficiency of the department. The main problems with allowing external bids are maintaining **control** of the overall direction of the company's IS strategy and ensuring that the IS department can maintain sufficient staff to provide the basic IT service that CAET will require. The option of full outsourcing of the department could also be considered.

50   BARNES PLC

(a)   (i)

> **Tutor's hint**. Your answer should have focused on the situation explained in the scenario. Examples of software should be specific to the scenario, you would not have scored well if you simply provided general information on spreadsheets or operating systems.

- **Software package**

  A software package is a computer programme which has been written to perform a specific task such as order processing or payroll. It is normally written by a specialist software developer (or software house) to meet the general needs of individuals or organisations rather than any specific requirements. For example, in a stock system the software package could offer re-ordering of goods below a specific quantity because this is a commonly used features of this package, but possibly not compute the Economic Order Quantity if few organisations need this feature. The software package is therefore not tailored in any way; it is up to each organisation to purchase the package that most closely fits its own requirements.

- **Bespoke solution**

  A bespoke solution means that software is written to meet a specific business need within an organisation. The software is therefore written to a precise functional specification, which will have been produced by the organisation ordering the software. The software can be written either by a software house or by an in-house programming department. The main difference between the bespoke solution and a software package is that the former will be written to meet the specific requirements of the organisation. The software developer must ensure that the specification has been met before the software is delivered to the purchasing organisation.

(ii)   (1)   **Cost savings**

There are normally significant cost savings to be gained from purchasing software packages as compared to bespoke solutions. The main savings will result from some or all of these areas.

- Shared development costs. The cost of writing the software is spread over all the purchasers rather than one organisation having to pay for producing the specification as well as the writing and testing of the software.

- Cheaper maintenance and upgrades. The cost of annual upgrades for the software will be shared in the same way as the initial development costs. All users will pay an annual software maintenance fee for which they will be entitled to enhanced versions of the software.

- Potentially higher quality product. A larger development budget, and selling to third parties who expect high quality software may mean that software has fewer errors than software written in-house. Further cost savings will arise from decreased computer systems downtime and less disruption to the overall running of the organisation.

(2) **Time savings**

The main time saving in purchasing a software package is that the package is already written and ready for implementation. In an extreme situation, the software could be purchased today and implementation begins tomorrow. A bespoke solution will need the specification agreeing and the software written and tested before implementation can begin, which can take a considerable amount of time. Further time delays may also arise during the development process if the specification has to change due to revised user requirements or changes in legislation.

(3) **Guaranteed quality**

Software packages will normally have a higher quality for two main reasons.

- The software writing company will perform detailed testing on the software because, where is it is being sold to third parties, users will expect the software to work. If the software has many errors then this will provide adverse publicity for the software writer resulting in liquidation if the software cannot be sold. It will be more difficult to guarantee the quality of bespoke software, especially where testing facilities are limited because software has never been used before.

- The software will be used by a large number of users. This means that even relatively minor errors in the software should be discovered compared to bespoke software where the user base will be relatively small. Purchasing an established software package may not guarantee that is it 100% free from error, but the significant use will mean it will have fewer errors than bespoke software with little or no user testing. Note that staff at Barnes have already complained that the bespoke software has errors in it.

(b)

> **Tutor's hint**. One approach that may have proved useful, would have been to check the IT directors comments, looking particularly for the benefits of using the third party supplier. Turn these around and you have the disadvantages of using that supplier. For example, the benefit of the supplier meeting 80% of the business needs is up to 20% will not be met.

(i) The risks of using standard software packages will include the following.

- **Forcing the business to change to the software package**

The standard package is unlikely to provide all the functionality required by the business. In fact the IT director is looking for packages that fit 80% of more of the business requirements; this implies that up to 20% of the requirements will not be met. It is possible that the business will not be able to change to meet the requirements of this package, or that any change will be both costly and time consuming. There is a further danger that the focus of the business may be directed to adapting to the software, which may lose any emphasis on providing service to customers. Some loss of customer goodwill and orders may occur.

- **Reliance on an external supplier**

  The current situation is to develop software in-house and so have available an experienced team to write and amend that software as required. Barnes plc can hopefully maintain that team and provide the necessary support for the company software.

  Purchasing a third party product means placing reliance on a third party supplier, and in particular on that supplier continuing to produce and support the software product. There is also the issue of the long-term financial and technical viability of that software house to consider. Barnes plc will also have to purchase the software 'as is' and will not have the option of amending the software to meet its own requirements.

- **Lack of competitive advantage**

  Producing unique software in-house may provide Barnes plc with some competitive advantage compared to similar companies, especially where the in-house software provides unique or enhanced facilities against standard 'off the shelf' software. Using a standard package means that any competitive advantage will be lost as only the features in the standard package, as used by similar suppliers, would be available.

(ii)   **Forcing the business to change to the software package**

If the third party software is to be purchased, then the focus of the implementation must be on providing continued good customer service. This may mean additional changes within Barnes, however, good customer relations must be maintained. The selection of software will focus on the customer interface, as well as ensuring that internal requirements are met. The change may be sold to staff by providing appropriate training explaining the new package and any changes to business processes that are required. Explaining the benefits of moving to an external supplier rather than maintaining the in-house software development team will also help staff accept the change.

- **Reliance on an external supplier**

  Obtaining credit references and copies of past accounts from companies' house can provide reassurance about the financial reliability of the supplier. The length of time in business may also be an indicator of the future financial stability of the company.

  The issue of ensuring that the software is updated and continues to meet the 80% requirement rule for Barnes is more difficult to address. If the supplier has a user group, then Barnes can attend meetings and provide input into future functionality via this group.

  As a last resort, the source code of the software can be lodged with a third party; if the supplier does go out of business then Barnes can obtain this code and continue to update the software.

- **Lack of competitive advantage**

  Barnes may have obtained some competitive edge from using their own software; using a standard package will result in this edge being lost unless the software can be amended, just for Barnes. Assuming that amendment is possible, then this will have the same problems as before; namely time and cost of making and then checking the amendments. Barnes may have to accept that any competitive advantage from using the software will be lost and concentrate on providing better service in other ways to their customers.

(c) (i) **Feasibility study**

A feasibility study seeks to ensure that any new system is technically, economically, socially and operationally feasible. The study compares costs and benefits and provides a recommendation as to whether to continue with the project. Costs are normally relatively easy to ascertain, benefits are more difficult to quantify.

Systems specification

The systems specification provides a detailed analysis and definition of the functional requirements of the system. Various modelling techniques are used to show these requirements such as Data Flow Diagrams and Entity Relationship Models. The user will formally sign off these models, along with prototypes of the system, before any new software is written.

Programming and unit testing

Programs are written and tested using the systems specification to provide the detail for each program. Programs are tested individually at this stage.

Systems testing

The systems analyst will test all the programs making up the software suite to ensure that they work together correctly, and that they meet the systems specification. Any amendments to programs will be made before they are passed onto the users for additional testing.

User-acceptance testing

The software is tested by users to ensure it meets their requirements as laid out in the systems specification. Users will also check that they can use the software, and that it meets their business's process and unusual transactions such as year-end adjustments. Testing is carried out by staff from the department commissioning the software.

Implementation

Implementation normally consists of a variety of tasks such as producing user manuals, completing system documentation, training users and converting data files onto the new system.

(ii) **Feasibility study**

A feasibility study will still be required. Technical and operational feasibility will be easy to assess because the software already exists. Software development costs are likely to be less so that the project has a greater chance of continuing.

Systems specification

A formal specification will also be required. The functionality required from the software must be understood before possible solutions from vendors are reviewed. Demonstrations of live systems may well take the place of prototyping, as completed software will be available for review.

Programming and unit testing

This stage will not be required when third party software is purchased. The vendor will already have written and tested the software programs.

Systems testing

The software vendor will already have performed this testing, so it will not be required.

User-acceptance testing

User acceptance testing will still be required, because users in each department still need to ensure that the software meets their individual requirements. Vendors will normally make their software available for a trial period to allow this testing to take place.

Implementation

All the activities in the implementation stage will still be required; users will need training because the software is changing; manuals will be needed and data will be input to the new system. The implementation stage may be quicker and cheaper using third party software because documentation and training courses should be available from the vendor. However, software conversion may still be difficult, although the vendor should be able to provide specialist advice and assistance to minimise the problems encountered

(d) **Arguments for the IT director's view**

Many organisations change their business processes to meet the functionality of software because this provides a relatively quick and cost-effective method of using that software. Writing the software in-house, or commissioning the software house to amend the software is relatively expensive, and will incur time delays before the software can be used. While the revised software may meet exactly the business requirements, the benefits of using the software 'out of the box' will have been lost.

There is also no guarantee that making changes to the software will meet either the organisation's or employee's requirements in the future. It is therefore better to accept some minor changes to processes rather than spend time and money to achieve what may be a transient benefit.

Arguments against the IT director's view

One of the main benefits of providing bespoke software is that customer requirements can be programmed into that software. CAET can therefore gain competitive advantage by using software which accurately supports their business processes and provides customers with exactly the information or services that are required. Not being able to use this software may have a negative influence on staff and on customer relations. Having to explain that software features are no longer available may result in loss of competitive advantage and therefore poorer customer service.

Not being able to produce software to meet CAET's own requirements also means that the organisation may have to change its processes each time a new version of the software is released. CAET may also have little input into the functionality of these releases, which again will limit the possibility of the software meeting its own internal business processes.

51   X COMPANY

(a)   **Data Flow Diagram to show preparation of insurance quotes**

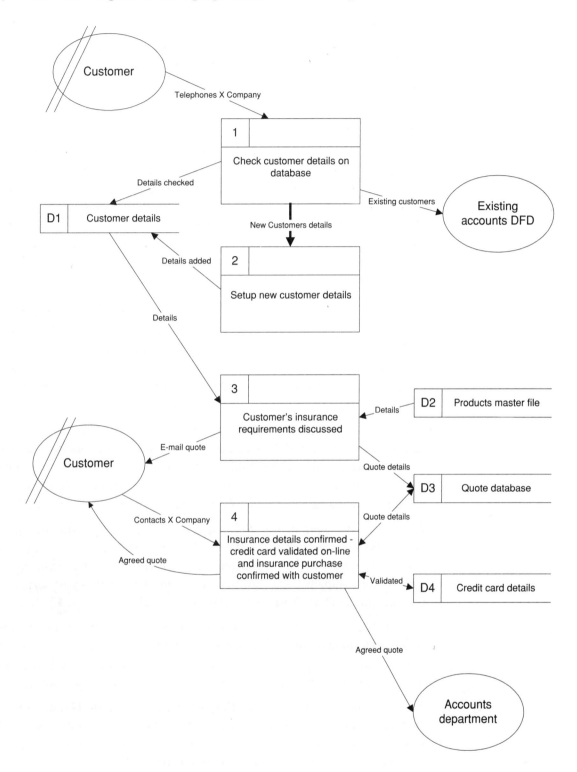

(b)   (i)   There are **two main aims of the Data Protection Act 1998**.

Firstly, to **protect individual privacy**. Data protection law in the UK prior to the 1998 Act applied to data held on computer systems only. The 1998 Act applies to all personal data in any form.

Secondly, to **harmonise data protection legislation across the European Economic Area** (basically the European Union). The aim is to promote the single European market by allowing for a free flow of personal data between the member states of the EU.

Data subjects have four basic rights under the Data Protection legislation.

Firstly, a data subject can seek **compensation** through the courts for damage and any associated distress caused by the loss, destruction or unauthorised disclosure of data about that subject or inaccurate data about the subject.

Secondly, a data subject may apply to the courts **for inaccurate data to be put right** or even wiped off the data user's files altogether. Applications of this type may also be made to the Data Protection commissioner.

Thirdly, a data subject may **obtain access to personal data** of which he or she is the subject. So any data subject can use the right of subject access to see the personal data that the data user is holding.

Fourthly, a data subject can **sue a data user for any damage or distress** caused to him or her by personal data, which is incorrect or misleading as to matter of fact (rather than matter of opinion).

(ii) As the X Company will be holding personal data – that is data on a living individual – there are various actions that must be taken before the company starts trading.

The X Company will be a data user, that is X will hold personal data and will therefore need to **notify the Data Protection Registrar** of intention to hold and process data.

Data regarding opinions on the data subject, racial origin and health is classed as 'sensitive' under the DP Act. The express **permission of the data user** must be obtained before this information can be maintained on the computer system. The procedures for contacting customers must contain a reminder to sales representatives to ensure that permission is obtain to process this sensitive data.

The senior manager in the X Company will need to **obtain the appropriate notification forms from the Data Controller**. A Data Controller will have to be appointed, who will be responsible for maintaining and controlling the data within the company. The notification forms will have to be completed and returned to the Data Protection Commissioner, along with the £35 fee.

Upon request, data subjects must be provided with **a copy of the personal data relating to themselves**, and a reason for holding that data. Rights of access for data subjects will need to be established, with procedures being agreed to provide the appropriate information on receipt of a request for data.

(c) (i) **The 'V' model of software testing aims to show the relationship between system development, testing and quality assurance throughout the project lifecycle.** The model is in the shape of a 'V', with four main horizontal links between the two arms of the V representing quality control checks that take place during system development.

The four main sections of the model are outlined below.

1 **Requirements specification**

   The requirements specification explains the logical design of the software and will also form part of the Invitation To Tender (ITT) for the software. Following the issue of the ITT, the software will be developed. However, the specification itself forms the first control check, as the overall evaluation of the software will take place by comparing the final design to this specification.

From the scenario, it appears that the **specification has not been written**. It is important that the specification is accurate and contains information concerning usability criteria and departmental requirements. If these criteria are not stated correctly now, then the final software may not meet these requirements.

2   **Detailed requirements specification**

The detailed requirements specification will show exactly what users (external) and internal departments will expect from the software. This specification will provide the benchmark for user acceptance testing of the software prior to handover. As users will be accepting the software on the detailed criteria in this document, it is again essential that the detail is accurate.

Within the X Company, it is not clear who will be checking the software. While internal user departments are available, there are no third party users. Some staff that are not concerned with insurance sales may need to be involved at the specification and testing stages to provide realistic user input.

Testing at this stage may also include stress testing to ensure that the software will cope with more than the maximum number of transactions expected.

3   **Design**

Design of the software relates to the overview of how the logical specification will be translated into actual software. The design process will be carried out for the software overall, before is it split into modules for detailed programming.

From the scenario, the X Company will be following this software development route. From the point of view of testing, the overall design is tested by integrating the individual modules to provide the complete software package. At this stage, any errors in data transfer between the modules will be identified, and amendments made to the software to overcome these errors. Regression testing may be required to ensure that any amendments do not adversely affect other parts of each module.

The detailed testing at this stage is also called unit integration testing.

4   **Module design**

This stage of software development concerns the individual programme module; each large software development is likely to consist of a number of individual modules. This module will be specified regarding the inputs and outputs required, and the processing to take place. The module is then written and tested in isolation to ensure that these criteria are met.

Within the V module, unit testing is used to check the accuracy of processing within each module. While is it not clear from the scenario what the modules will be, they are being used and so unit testing will be necessary. When a module has completed unit testing, then it moves onto unit integration testing, as outlined in part 3 above.

(ii) **Possible weaknesses in the 'V' model regarding the situation in the X Company include the points below.**

There is a potential lack of user involvement in the system design. The model assumes that users will be involved in the development process, and specifically that they will test the completed software. However, as the company will not be trading at this time, there will be no end users, specifically for the web site. As an alternative, staff can test the site, although they should not have been involved in system design prior to this testing.

Integration testing may be difficult because the new software will need to be tested with the existing live systems; availability of these systems appears to be limited. However, testing may take place backup with copies of the software, limiting both disturbance of the on-line systems and the possibility of errors being introduced into the live software. However, full integration testing will be necessary at some stage, and an appropriate time must be found for this.

There is a high risk of testing not identifying all the errors in the software. The limited budgets indicate that this testing may not be completed correctly, increasing the risk of internal failure of the software. Additional time needs to be made available to ensure that the software is as error-free as possible.

52 HB MANUFACTURING

(a)   MEMO

To: Board of HB
From: Accountant
Subject: Reasons for an IT strategy
Date: July 20X7

Reasons for having an IT strategy

IT involves significant cost

IT systems in general and the proposed new system in HB involve a significant amount of expenditure. 4% of turnover appears to be a large figure, although given the different systems currently in use, there appears to be a requirement for a large IT expenditure. Preparing a budget is part of the overall strategy to ensure that expenditure is properly controlled and co-ordinated across the whole company.

Competitive advantage

The use of IT can result in competitive advantage. This is specifically the case where IT presents new or improved methods of presenting information or manufacturing products. HB has a web site under development.

It is not clear from the question whether this will provide any advantage to HB, although diversifying the method of sales will hopefully provide an increase in revenue.

IT affects all levels of management

Within an organisation, all managers will use the IT systems, and will therefore be affected by any changes made to those systems.

The new systems within HB present problems including changes to the infrastructure and lack of control from the point of view of divisional managers, over those changes. Care must be taken to involve managers in the change or they may reject the new systems.

IT affects the information systems

In almost any organisation, IT is used to process and transfer information around the organisation. The structure of the IT system affects to a large extent the information that can be provided. For example, a company without a WAN will not be able to transfer information easily between the different branches.

Implementing a WAN in HB will provide an enhanced information system with details from all branches being available at head office. A more significant change is the move to centralised accounting systems and additional planning and training may be required to accommodate this change.

IT requires effective management to obtain benefits from the system

Lack of management of IT can result in incompatible systems, limiting the benefits that can be obtained from integrated systems. These benefits may be in terms of lack of discounts from the purchase of IT equipment, or incomplete information concerning the activities of the organisation.

Within HB, there appears to be incompatible systems, while the lack of integration mean that directors will not have a complete picture of the company. Providing a new IT system will help obtain these benefits.

IT involves many stakeholders

Not having an IT strategy will have some positive and negative effects. For example, IT will affect suppliers, customers and employees, to take three stakeholders in the company. An integrated IT policy will provide suppliers with a definite list of hardware and software.

Having an IT strategy will help customers, possibly by providing better or more up-to-date information.

Employees may benefit from an IT strategy because systems will be compatible across the whole organisation, improving employee mobility.

(b) (i)   A **Local Area Network** is a network of computers based in a single building or on a single site. Computer cables link the parts of the network rather than via telecommunication lines, so a LAN does not need modems. A LAN provides easy access to shared resources such as printers and file servers, and also enables e-mail to operate between the different computers on the network.

Within factory A, the PC's, database and other devices such as printers will all be attached to the LAN. However, within factory B, there appears to be no LAN, which will make sharing of information and communication difficult.

Wide Area Networks (WAN) are networks on a number of sites, perhaps on a wide geographical scale. WAN's normally have the following features compared to LAN's.

• They cover a larger geographical area, and are not limited to a single site or building.

• Communication is via telecommunication links, using modems or ISDN links as necessary.

• They normally link two or more LAN's so that resources within each LAN can be shared over the WAN.

Within HB, the proposed WAN will link the four different LAN's together. This configuration will allow data to be shared as well as group wide communication using e-mail to be implemented. Using a VPN to link the LAN's means that HB

157

will not actually own the WAN links. However, communication links should still be secure as access to the VPN is limited.

The term 'client server' is a way of describing the relationship between the devices in a network. With client-server computing, different tasks are distributed between the machines on the network.

A **client** is a computer with requests a service, for example a PC running a spreadsheet application will request access to a printer to produce a hard copy of the spreadsheet.

A **server** is a machine, which is dedicated to providing a particular function or service requested by a client. Servers will include file servers, print servers and e-mail servers.

Within HB, client server computing implies that PC's will have the processing power required for local processing. However, other resources, such as databases, will be shared and accessible over the WAN by all users. This system will benefit HB by retaining computing power at the local level where it is required (and has been the custom in previous years) while providing access to shared resources required by the company.

(ii)   **Advantages for HB of centralising the accounting system at Head Office**

There will be **one set of files,** rather than individual files being duplicated across the different sites. This will help to ensure that all staff use the same information. For example, supplier information will be duplicated where different factories use the same supplier. Not only will duplication be eliminated, quantity discounts may also be obtained where bulk orders can be processed.

Aggregated company information will be easier to obtain. It is likely to be difficult to produce summary information across all factories for the whole company due to the different accounting systems in use. Using one centralised system will help to ensure common systems are available making the production of aggregated reports easier.

Data can be transferred to Head Office quickly and easily. With the present system, data has to be sent via post, fax etc. With a centralised system using a WAN, data can be sent using the computer system, either by e-mail or via centralised computer applications.

HB does need to purchase computer equipment to standardise systems across all locations. Implementing common systems may provide economies of scale for both hardware and software purchased.

(c) (i)   **The new accounting system can be made more user-friendly using some or all of the ideas given below.**

The data entry screens can be designed so that the order of input of data is the same as any manual documents, or follows a similar sequence to any existing computer systems. Taking this approach will enable staff to relate to the new system quickly as well as help check the accuracy of transcription from manual documents to the computer system. Comparisons will be relatively easy because fields will be in the same place.

The data entry screens should be **clearly designed**; for example, the input field currently in use being highlighted in some way, possibly using different colours. This will draw attention to the appropriate area of screen rather than waste the time of input clerks trying to find the correct field.

Default entries can be provided to save input time. For example, VAT rates, unique invoice numbers and dates can all be entered using system information (date), accumulators build into the accounting programme (invoice number) or look up tables in databases (VAT rate). As well as saving input time, this will also increase the accuracy of input.

The screen should contain **clear icons and menus**, so that users can make a reasonable guess concerning what they have to do at any stage of the program. This will again decrease input time and help staff to accept the new program.

Where possible, the different programs in the accounting software should have the same 'look and feel'. In other words, the location of various commands such as saving or printing, and the layout of toolbars should be identical in the sales, purchasing, cash and any other modules. Taking this approach will help staff learn the systems quickly.

The package should contain appropriate help systems accessible using a single key (eg F1) or common menu. This will provide staff with any easy source of reference; some help systems also incorporate 'assistants' or 'wizards' to help users locate the appropriate part of the help system using queries expressed in English terms.

(ii) One of the major reasons that systems projects fail is **lack of user involvement**. Obtaining involvement via structured walkthroughs and other techniques is therefore essential to the success of the project.

Structured walkthroughs are used to present designs of new systems to interested user groups. The walkthrough is a formal meeting where the documentation produced for development is reviewed and checked for errors or omissions. Benefits of having the walkthrough are noted below.

By being involved in the overall system development process, they will take ownership of the new systems and be more inclined to accept them.

By offering **constructive criticism** of the proposed system and making suggestions for amendments and improvements. The amendments may arise because the system does not meet the initial specification, or because precise detail of user requirements (eg fields appearing on one screen) were not catered for in the specification.

The walkthrough provides the opportunity for users to validate the system design. This is particularly helpful to systems development personnel because it provides re-assurance that the detailed systems design is correct.

(iii) Another method of helping users **understand the layout of any new system is prototyping**. A prototype is a model of part or all of a system, built to show users early in the design process how that system will appear.

The **prototype** helps users understand the layout of the system by providing example screens with the different fields located in the same way as the final design. This provides users with the opportunity to comment on overall design as well as specifics of how the screens should be laid out. Any amendments can be made by programmers prior to the 'real' software being written.

53 M-E-QUIP

(a) (i) **Distributed processing** is a combination of processing hardware located at a central place (such as the Head Office of an organisation), with other small computers located at different sites or branches. A communications network links all the computers. This system allows for the processing of individual transactions at the local level, with the communications links providing for access to individual files from any location on the network.

(ii) **Advantages of distributed processing for M-E-Quip Ltd**

The design of the system can be amended to provide for the specific requirements of each branch, while maintaining the important company specific 'core' of the system. For example, details on individual stock balances can be maintained for local and distributed access. However, the request for producing specific promotional letters for customers of specific branches can now be met as appropriate processing facilities are provided locally.

The amount of data transmission over the network can be restricted because there is no longer the need to access the stock files at head office. Given that the WAN was unreliable, this should help to provide a more reliable processing environment at each branch.

Assuming that the WAN is working then **stock balances at other branches can be viewed on-line**. This will remove the need to telephone other branches to determine stock levels, saving time for the stock managers in each location.

The **effect of computer or WAN breakdowns** is minimised because each branch can continue processing, even if the WAN is not available. Similarly, should the Head Office computer fail, then processing can still continue at the branch because stock balances are held locally.

Users can be more involved in the design and use of the computer systems. This will help to overcome the problems of some managers leaving because they could not amend computer systems.

(iii) **There are various options for backup using the new system.**

Each branch **could take an individual backup** and store this in an off-site location. Appropriate media include tapes and removable hard disks.

Alternatively, backup can be carried out over the WAN, with data and program files being transferred to another branch or Head Office after processing is complete for that day. However, on-site backup would also be needed in case the WAN is unavailable on any particular day.

During the day, **transactions could also be 'mirrored' to another site**, ensuring that all data is kept in two locations at any time. Even if one branch suffered a systems failure, copy data could still be recovered from another location. Again, the reliability of the WAN may limit the use of this option.

Alternatively, daily backups during the day are possible using dual servers and hard disks at each branch.

(b) (i) **The disadvantages with the outsourcing contract include the issues discussed below.**

There is a lack of capacity on the WAN itself. M-E-Quip should have discussed with the supplier its network requirements in more detail, although the significant increase in traffic could not necessarily have been planned for.

Similarly, the overall provision of bandwidth on the WAN needs to be discussed. It is unlikely that the WAN is failing simply from M-E-Quip's increased use. Plans to extend the WAN's bandwidth need to be discussed with the supplier.

Provision of computer services is not a core activity for M-E-Quip, so outsourcing appeared to be an appropriate action. The problem now appears to be that M-E-Quip is locked into the contract for a further three years. Given the importance of maintaining the WAN to M-E-Quip, then alternative suppliers may still have to be investigated. M-E-Quip can ask its solicitors to see if there is any way of terminating the agreement on the grounds of poor service while alternative WAN suppliers are located. Setting up a WAN in-house may be too expensive to consider at this time.

M-E-Quip may lose some competitive advantage because the WAN supplier does not allow links to 'unrecognised' third parties. In particular, M-E-Quip may require the ability to link to customers so that parts can be ordered over the Internet using e-mail. This facility will not be available with the present supplier, so a change of contract may be beneficial in this area.

(ii) The cost of upgrading the existing system at M-E-Quip to a distributed network is likely to include the items set out below.

Equipment costs

Each branch will need a more powerful CPU to process the stock and other branch transactions locally.

Local processing may also mean that more printers and similar peripheral devices are required to provide appropriate hard copies of documents (eg invoices or delivery notes).

There will also be a knock-on effect of requiring more consumables such as paper, printer cartridges etc.

New backup units will be required for each location to provide backup in case of WAN failure.

Installation costs

Any new equipment will have to be installed. The new computer may need environmental control (protection from humidity and extremes of temperature). Similarly, additional network cabling and power supplies may be required.

Development costs

The provision of a distributed processing system will result in a systems change for M-E-Quip. A systems consultant may be required to oversee the entire change process.

Other costs will include setting up new programs at each branch for stock control etc. and interfacing these programs via the WAN for general access by all users.

There will be system changeover costs including setting up new master file records and balances and finally transferring the current stock, debtor and other balances from Head Office to the individual branch.

Personnel costs

Staff will have to be trained on the new system, especially in respect of how that system interacts with the WAN and how stock balances at other branches are obtained.

New staff may be needed, for example, in the systems department, to monitor and repair the system when needed. A database administrator may also be required to control the distributed database.

There will also be an increase in pension contributions and other 'on-costs' for any staff hired.

Operating costs

One effect of the new system will be requiring more consumables such as paper, printer cartridges etc.

Heating, lighting and insurance will also increase because there will be more computer hardware in the company.

(c) (i) **An Invitation to Tender (ITT) sets out the specification for a computer system**. It is produced by the company requiring the new system and then sent to suppliers either on request or as part of a specific mail shot. It generally explains how the system will be used and the timescale for the implementation of that system. The performance criteria for the new system will also be outlined in the document. As a result of obtaining the ITT, suppliers are requested to make a proposal for implementing the new system.

(ii) The Invitation to Tender will generally contain the information outlined below.

(1) **Details of the background of the company**

In this situation, the ITT will mention M-E-Quip's business, number of branches and existing systems.

(2) **Purpose of the new system**

The ITT will provide some guidance on:

The need for a distributed processing system, identifying the requirement to maintain data at each branch, but for access to the data to be available throughout the whole company.

The volume of data to be processed in terms of number of transactions. This information will be available from the existing system.

Confirmation of the number of branches, possibly including the need to add more branches should the company expand.

Response times required from the system. Response times may be broken down between response from the local database and response from the distributed databases in other locations.

The different inputs and outputs required.

Confirmation that this will be an on-line real-time system.

Estimated life of the system.

The upgrades or expansion required in the new few years. The ability for customers to send orders directly via the Internet would be a relevant requirement of the system.

(3) **General information**

Other relevant information including:

- Contact person within M-E-Quip.
- Any financial constraints
- Form that submissions will take.
- Closing date for submission of tenders.
- Address to which tenders should be sent.

(iii) There are various methods for choosing between tenders submitted as a result of receiving the ITT. Whichever method is chosen, it is important to decide on this method prior to obtaining the tenders; this will help to avoid any bias (real or perceived) in checking the Tender details.

Where suppliers provide examples of the required systems, then these can be evaluated using benchmark or simulation tests. These tests measure how long it takes for a computer to run through a particular routine or set of routines.

If models of the system are not available, then the proposal document itself will be checked against some specific criteria for the system. The criteria (eg meeting system specifications or confidence in the supplier) are ranked and a value assigned to each potential supplier for that criteria. The supplier with the highest ranking overall is normally asked to complete the project.

54 MALTOVIA

(a) (i) **The aim of physical access controls over computer and other systems is to prevent intruders getting near to the computer equipment or other storage media.** The controls range from providing methods of recognising specific individuals through to more general controls of locking doors, which tend to be less discriminatory in providing access (if you have the key then you can open the door).

The actual controls used in any situation will depend partly on the sensitivity of the data being controlled, and also on the budget available to implement the controls.

(ii) **As the data itself is sensitive, there needs to be appropriate physical access controls over the system.**

Entry to the building should be controlled so only recognised individuals are allowed to enter. Security controls include fingerprint or retinal scanners, although these are relatively expensive. Alternatively, security guards can be employed to compare people to a list of authorised photographs, or simply to a security card carried by the employee with their photo on it.

Entry should also be limited to a few doors, each with its own security guard on duty.

Inside the building, entry to specific areas may be further limited by **security codes on doors,** or by the employee's magnetic badge being read at each door and only allowing access to certain areas. Security may also be implemented using Personal Identification Numbers, which are entered onto a keypad beside each door. Alternatively, each door may have a unique number; access to more secure areas will only by having the appropriate door PIN number.

The computers and filing cabinets themselves may be **protected by security chains to prevent unauthorised removal**. Access to computers can also be limited by use of hierarchical passwords. These passwords will allow any user to log onto the system, but only users with appropriate passwords will be able to access the more sensitive data on the computer.

(iii) **Password controls** are appropriate in some situations; without knowledge of the password, the computer system cannot be accessed. Passwords themselves are a set of characters, which may be allocated to a person, terminal or facility which are required to be keyed into the system before further access is permitted.

However, password systems do have some weaknesses.

Allowing users to choose their own passwords may mean that the password becomes easily '**guessable**'. Certainly, amending the password each week lends itself to passwords in the form FRED01 for week 1, FRED02 for week 2 and so on simply to help users remember what their password is this week. Using a sequence in this way makes the password easier to guess.

Similarly, many passwords are chosen because they relate to the user in some way. For example, passwords are likely to contain **familiar names**, such as family or pets, or relate to the users hobbies or interests, eg Golf23. Again, allowing the user to choose their password may make the password easier to guess.

A more secure system may be to provide the user with **randomly generated passwords and to use these only**. However, this system also has disadvantage in that the user will normally need to write the password down so as not to forget it.

(b) (i) The steps in producing and agreeing a suitable prototype are outlined below.

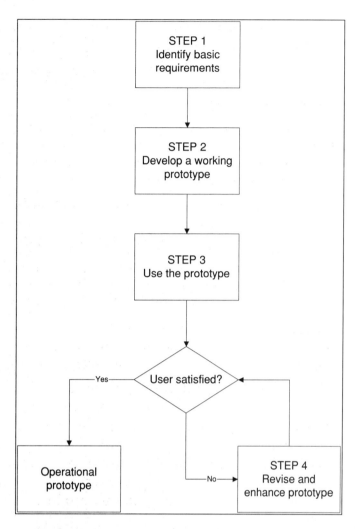

Step 1.   Identify the **system requirements** from other documentation produced for the new system, such as DFD's and narrative notes.

Step 2.   **Develop a working prototype** by using appropriate prototype writing tools. The analyst may produce the prototype, or this may be delegated to a programmer. In this case the analyst will need to review the prototype to ensure that it meets the system requirements.

Step 3.   **Use the prototype**. The prototype is presented to the users, and tested to show the functionality of the new system. If the users are satisfied with the system, then an operational prototype, which links to the main data used in the system, can be produced. However, if the user is not satisfied, then step 4 must be undertaken.

Step 4.   Where the user is not satisfied with the prototype, then it will have to be **revised and enhanced**. Revisions may take the form of small amendments, eg moving the position of some controls on screen, to more detailed amendments incorporating more radical screen designs or making entirely new screens. After a number of iterations the prototype will be agreed and the operational prototype developed.

(ii)   **Disadvantages of prototyping in this situation**

Some prototyping systems are tied to a specific make or model of computer. Given that the hardware for the new software system is not going to be amended, this may give some problems in either running the prototype, or using the prototype to produce the operational system.

BPP
PUBLISHING

Prototyping may steer users back towards their existing system, especially where they do not like the format or design of the new system. There may also be a problem in that users appear to have a lack of vision concerning the system that they require. They will therefore be more likely to accept small amendments to the existing system, rather than think about what they would like from a brand new software system. This will limit the effectiveness of prototyping.

The possible lack of information about the requirements of users may result in a prototype being developed that is a long way from meeting user requirements. The prototype will therefore tend to undermine the integrity of the development process, decreasing users' trust in the new system. The analyst is therefore taking a considerable risk in producing a prototype on incomplete information. However, this has to be done to ensure that users are getting the system they expect.

(c) (i) A framework that can be used to help obtain agreement to project objectives is SMART. The SMART implies that project objectives must be:

- Specific
- Measurable
- Agreed upon
- Realistic, and
- Time-bound

Objectives must **be specific** so that all people involved in the project realise that they are working to the same end. The analyst will find this objective difficult because the focus of many of the workers in the centre appears to be in maintaining the current system, rather than planning for a new system. There is a danger that staff will simply accept what is proposed to them now, and then reject any system at a later stage on the grounds that they were not fully involved.

Objectives need **to be measurable** so all people involved in the project know how success will be measured. In this situation, where it is difficult to agree the objectives, agreeing measurable success criteria will also be difficult. There is a danger that the project will 'fail' simply because there was no definite indicator of success.

Objectives must be **agreed on by all team members and stakeholders**. The objectives therefore provide a shared vision concerning what the project will do. Agreement may be difficult to obtain from staff in the information centre due to lack of time or interest in the project.

Objectives need to **be realistic** to provide motivation for the users and project team. The danger here is that the indifferent attitude of the users may result in the project team being poorly motivated. If users are not interested in the system under development, then the project team may wonder why they are undertaking the work; quality of work as well as motivation may suffer.

Finally, objectives **are time bound**. Dates are allocated for the achievement of objectives to provide focus and aid priority setting. Given the lack of agreement of objectives, there is a risk that the project will overrun. This may result from an excessive amount of remedial work to ensure that the project meets user requirements, or lack of motivation of project staff, as already discussed above.

(ii)   **The analyst can try and get users more involved in the system project in various ways.**

One of the most important tasks in a system project, at least in respect of users, is **sitting on project group meetings**. These measures enable users to have a voice in the development of the new system, as well as being responsible for signing off the different stages of the project. As well as the need to be involved, the analyst could warn users that lack of involvement may mean that the system developed will not meet their requirements. If the users have not been involved with the project then it will be very difficult to complain about the final system.

Users can take responsibility for design and sign-off of the user interface. As this is the part of the system that users see, it is important that the interface is correct. Delegating responsibility in this area will stress this importance and help users feel part of the overall project.

Management can provide information on the importance of the systems change. This provision can be via notices, meetings or specific e-mails to the staff at the information centre. However, management taking time to be involved with the project will provide a good example and help to involve users more.

The analyst can also provide information on the benefits of the new system. This will hopefully encourage staff to take more time to investigate the system and make their requirements known.

However, if staff do not want to be involved, they cannot be forced. At the end of the day, it is their loss if they ignore the system development, as the final system may not be exactly what they required.

Information Systems
BPP Mock Exam 1:
December 2001

Question Paper:	
Time allowed	**3 hours**
This paper is divided into two sections	
Section A	These THREE questions are compulsory and MUST be attempted
Section B	TWO questions ONLY to be answered

Disclaimer of liability

Please note that we have based our predictions of the content of the December 2001 exam on our long experience of the ACCA exams. We do not claim to have any endorsement of the predictions from either the examiner or the ACCA and we do not guarantee that either the specific questions, or the general areas, that are forecast will necessarily be included in the exams, in part or in whole.

We do not accept any liability or responsibility to any person who takes, or does not take, any action based (either in whole or in part and either directly or indirectly) upon any statement or omission made in this book. We encourage students to study all topics in the ACCA syllabus and the mock exam in this book is intended as an aid to revision only.

paper 2.1

DO NOT OPEN THIS PAPER UNTIL YOU ARE READY TO START

UNDER EXAMINATION CONDITIONS

Section A – ALL questions are compulsory and MUST be attempted

SCENARIO

You work for a firm of accountants involved in implementing information systems. The latest assignment is to implement new systems at a small chain of ten shops managed by FRS Ltd and to integrate these into the systems of a multinational retail organisation (MRO Inc) that has recently acquired them. FRS Ltd sells a range of wines, spirits and groceries.

The chief executive of FRS Ltd is not particularly happy about the fact that, as part of the acquisition, FRS Ltd will be required to introduce new technology and be linked to the systems of MRO Inc. One of his favourite comments is to tap his head and say, 'That's the best computer, you don't need all this new technology.'
You have been provided with the following information.

Extracts from notes of a meeting with the chief executive of FRS Ltd

Based upon previous experience the chief executive stated his fears about information systems (IS) projects. He gave the following as specific examples:

- Information systems staff do not talk to users

- Systems are always late, cost more than the original estimates and usually fall a long way short of user expectations

- Programs invariably contain errors

- Programmers do not always think about the practicality of their programs. One system he had experienced in the past utilised function key F3 to produce a look-up table in the sales-ledger program, but on the purchase-ledger program the F3 key was used to quit (exit) the program. The IS department refused to change it, saying that it was too late and too expensive to do

- Reporting facilities are often not flexible enough. At FRS Ltd they use a spreadsheet for management reporting

The organisation and information systems at MRO Inc

Management of staff

Each department has its own manager with a structure of support staff below, comprising supervisors and clerks. The operations department is split into three distinct areas of operation as indicated by the chart, each with its own supervisor and staff who work exclusively within that section.

Information systems

Each shop has a local area network (LAN). Customer service/payment points are connected to the LAN and update a database which holds stock and sales details. The members of staff in each department utilise personal computers (PCs) with access to office software such as spreadsheets and word processing. They can also access database via the LAN. Stock and sales data are updated in real time.

All shops are connected to the head office computer network over a wide area network (WAN); they send a copy of the daily transactions to head office at close of business each day. This provides them with an additional copy for security purposes and enables members of the senior management team, who have access to an executive support system (ESS), to monitor the performance of the group as a whole and to investigate performance of individual shops if they wish.

There is an information systems department at head office, which provides support services to the shops and manages the wide area network (WAN). Email facilities are also provided between members of the group over the WAN.

The organisation and information systems at FRS Ltd

Management of staff

A manager and an assistant manage each shop with support from an operations supervisor and an administration supervisor. The operations supervisor is in charge of goods inwards, shelf stock and payment points. The administration supervisor is in charge of accounts and purchasing

Information systems

Head office has a computer system that is used for accounting transactions, and a PC that is used by the accountant to analyse the sales figures and to consolidate the data from each shop.

Information from the other shops in the group arrives in a variety of formats. Some shops use floppy disks, others end a hard copy from which the accountant enters manually. One shop sends the data via a dial-up link, which the manager had established from within his own budget.

Two shops do not use a computer at all. At the end of each month, they send to head office a copy of the cashbook, from which the data is extracted and entered into the PC.

The accountant at FRS Ltd, Mr Black, provides a summary of the profit and loss account for all shops at the end of each month. This is usually produced by about the twenty-first day of the following month, as he has to wait until all shops have sent the information.

Mr Black has been suggesting for some time that FRS Ltd should install computer terminals at each shop and connect them to a centralised mainframe computer at the head office. His argument is that all the information would be in the same format and it would make controlling it very simple. The chief executive is now keen to accept this idea to enable him to retain control over the individual shops.

Problems at FRS Ltd
A recent audit report from the auditors of FRS Ltd indicated problems in several key areas of the business.

Stock control was reported as being weak:

- Stock discrepancies of high value items such as wines and spirits had been found, resulting in stock losses being recorded in the accounts

- Perishable items had been written off on a number of occasions

- The local government health department had warned one shop that goods were still on the shelf after the 'sell by' date. This had resulted in a warning that legal action could result if additional infringements are discovered

Required:

1   Prepare a report for the chief executive of FRS Ltd that:

   (a) Explains the difference between distributed processing and centralised, multi-user processing. *(5 marks)*

   (b) Explains the relative merits of adopting the information systems utilised by MRO Inc. *(5 marks)*

   (c) Illustrates how information could be utilised for decision-making at the various levels of an organisation such as MRO Inc and the types of information system which support those decisions. *(10 marks)*

   (20 marks)

2

   (a) Explain the benefits of using a structured methodology to develop and implement new systems at FRS Ltd, indicating how this methodology will overcome the types of problems the chief executive has experienced in the past. *(10 marks)*

   (b) Explain how the concept of quality can be applied to information systems and how quality can be assessed and measured. *(10 marks)*

   (20 marks)

3

   (a) Evaluate the range of project management tools and techniques that can be used to justify and control the implementation of the information systems used by MRO Inc at FRS Ltd. *(10 marks)*

   (b) The information systems department of MRO Inc has drawn up an outline timetable for the introduction of the new system to FRS Ltd. The first draft of this is shown below.

Task	Description	Planned duration (weeks)	Preceding activities
A	Communication – inform staff at each FRS shop and indicate how it will affect them	1	-
B	Carry out systems audit at each FRS shop	2	A
C	Agree detailed implementation plan with board of directors	1	B
D	Order and receive hardware requirements	4	C
E	Install hardware at all FRS shops	4	D
F	Install software at all FRS shops	2	D
G	Arrange training at premises of MRO Inc	3	D
H	Test systems at all FRS shops	4	E and F
I	Implement changeover at all shops	10	G and H

   Produce a critical path analysis of the draft implementation plan suggested by the IS department manager. (This should identify the critical path and the total elapsed time.) *(10 marks)*

   (20 marks)

SECTION B - TWO questions only to be attempted

4   The directors of DS are not satisfied with the GDC Ltd facilities management company. The appointment of GDC Ltd was relatively rushed and although an outline contract was agreed, no detailed Service Level Agreement was produced. Details of the contract are shown below.

The contract can be terminated by either party with three months' notice

GDC Ltd will provide IT services for DS, the services to include:

- Purchase of all hardware and software
- Repair and maintenance of all IT equipment
- Help desk and other support services for users
- Writing and maintenance of in-house software
- Provision of management information

Price charged to be renegotiated each year but any increase must not exceed inflation, plus 10%.

Required:

(a) **Explain, from the point of view of DS, why it might have received poor service from GDC Ltd, even though GDC Ltd has met the requirements of the contract.**
(12 marks)

(b) **Explain the courses of action now available to DS relating to the provision of IT services. Comment on the problems involved in each course of action.**
(8 marks)

(20 marks)

5   CP Ltd is a small but successful company which specialises in selling car and home insurance to individuals. All sales are made over the telephone. The company employs 25 staff, 22 in the telephone sales department and the remaining three in accounts and administration. CP Ltd is planning to expand its operations.

CP Ltd's accountant has calculated that 90% of office costs can be avoided if the telephone sales staff worked from their homes.

At present, employees appear to enjoy working in the office. Coffee and lunch breaks are normally spent in the rest area where staff also compare some notes and queries concerning their jobs. All the data that they need to perform their job is otherwise available on the computer system. This data includes:

(a) Records on each customer.

(b) Access to a value added network (VAN) providing costs of insurance from other companies which sell insurance.

(c) Word-processing and other systems for producing letters and insurance quotes to customers.

The proposal to work from home was put to staff last week and this has met with some initial resistance.

Required:

(a) From the viewpoint of the staff, explain the potential benefits that will be gained by homeworking. Explain the concerns that staff may have over homeworking and whether the IT infrastructure can help alleviate these concerns. (12 marks)

(b) Explain what can be done to encourage staff to accept the proposed change. (8 marks)

(20 marks)

6   JH Ltd has established a working group to produce an outline IT strategy. The group members are as follows.

Senior manager	• Does not have much knowledge of IT because he does not believe IT provides benefits for his job
	• Fearful of IT
	• Task-orientated
	• Good at producing overall policy directives
IT professional	• She has an excellent knowledge of mainframe computers
	• Enjoys being in charge of a large IT department
	• 20 years in computing
	• Has ignored the recent shift towards end-user computing
	• Some knowledge of PCs
	• Little contact with the users of the information that the IT department produces
IT user: trainee accountant	• An ACCA Professional Level 3 student
	• This is his first major assignment
	• Favours PC applications
	• Looking to advance rapidly in the company by being the IT 'champion'

Required:

(a) Comment on the disadvantages that could arise for JH Ltd by not having an overall IT strategy in place. (8 marks)

(b) Explain how the background of each individual in the working group may present barriers to the production of an IT strategy. Also, suggest how these barriers may be overcome. (12 marks)

(20 marks)

MOCK EXAM 1 ANSWERS

DO NOT TURN THIS PAGE UNTIL YOU
HAVE COMPLETED MOCK EXAM 1

WARNING! APPLYING THE BPP MARKING SCHEME

If you decide to mark your paper using the BPP marking scheme, you should bear in mind the following points.

1   The BPP solutions are not definitive: we have applied the marking scheme to our solutions to show how answers should gain marks, but there may be more than one way to answer the question. Try to judge whether different points made in your answers are correct and relevant and therefore worth marks.

2   If you have a friend or colleague who is studying or has studied this paper, you might ask him or her to mark your paper for you, thus gaining a more objective assessment. Remember you and your friend are not trained or objective markers, so try to avoid complacency or pessimism if you appear to have done very well or very badly.

3   In some instances, BPP's answers are longer than you would be expected to write. Sometimes, therefore, you would gain the same number of marks for making the basic point as we have shown as being available for a slightly more detailed solution.

A PLAN OF ATTACK

Tackling scenario questions

Section A of the examination for Paper 2.1 comprises a written scenario with three compulsory questions from across the syllabus **linked** to the narrative scenario. The information provided usually includes some discussion of the organisation's current situation, and there is often one or more central characters charged with the task of resolving the problem, or exploiting the opportunity.

The function of this type of question is to test a candidate's ability to tackle unstructured problems, and to **apply** what they know to 'real' situations. There **may be several feasible solutions** and candidates should not necessarily expect there to be a single definitive answer. The solution will involve the use of techniques which have been learned, but usually also requires the exercise of judgement. Preparation to scenario-based questions cannot rely on reading alone, but must be supplemented **by question practice under examination conditions**.

The **ability to structure a coherent answer** which leads logically to its conclusion is essential. Recommendations are often required. Acceptable recommendations may vary, but must be sensible and justified.

Key points to remember when tackling scenario questions:
- Answer the question asked – tailor what you know to fit the scenario
- Prepare a rough plan – this will help clarify your thoughts
- Structure longer answers eg introduction, body of answer, conclusion
- Justify any recommendations

Mock exam 1

If this were the actual exam paper in front of you right now, how would you react? Having read the scenario and three compulsory questions, would you be panicking or feeling relieved because a favourite topic had been emphasised?

Start by spending 5 minutes looking through the paper, gaining an understanding of the scenario.

Option 1 (if you're thinking 'Help!')

If you don't feel confident about the scenario questions, you may find it helpful to choose and complete one or both of the two questions you are required to answer from Section B. For example, if you feel Facilities Management and Outsourcing is an area you can score well in, you could start with **Question 4**.

Starting with a question you find 'easier' should **build your confidence** before you attempt the questions you expect to prove more difficult. At the start of the exam you will be fresh - you should be in the best frame of mind to **apply the knowledge** you possess to the specific **requirements of the question**.

Starting with a question you feel confident with should help you 'get into' the exam. After completing your first question you should be mentally tuned in and ready to attempt the more difficult questions.

Attempting a question you find difficult at the start of an exam can result in some candidates **losing confidence**. As a consequence of this lack of composure, these candidates often go on to score poorly on later questions that they would ordinarily score well on. But remember, you will have to answer the scenario questions

Option 2 (if you are thinking 'No problem!')

Try not to be overconfident, but if you are feeling fairly comfortable, then tackle the scenario questions first, then move on to your selected questions from Section B.

Comments on questions from Mock Exam 1

- After reading and re-reading the scenario take a calm look at **Question 1** and break down the requirements. There are three components – all to be included in one report. Ensure you head up the report correctly, and **structure the report around the question requirements**.

  - ° Part (a) is a straightforward question related to types of processing. Remember to relate your knowledge to the scenario – you are writing a report for the chief executive of FRS not simply reproducing a text book.

  - ° Part (b) refers to 'the information systems utilised by MRO Inc.'. The systems mentioned in the scenario are a LAN and database at each shop, and an ESS and WAN based at head office. How networks help the sharing of information is relevant here.

  - ° A well prepared candidate should find Part (c) fairly straight-forward.

- **Question 2** contains two parts – part (a) requires you to apply your knowledge of structured methodologies to the scenario. In Part (b), start by defining quality in general, then apply this definition to information systems.

- **Question 3** part (a), a **quick answer plan** may start with a list of all the main project management tools and techniques you are aware of. As a **guide to answer length** remember that this part of the question is 10 marks and should take 17 minutes. Candidates that have practised producing Critical Path Analysis should score well in part (b).

- **Question 4** should prove simple for students who have revised the key features of Service Level Contracts. Part (b) provides an opportunity to include a wide range of material (eg information centre, new outsourced supplier, insourcing, software package purchase etc.).

- **Question 5.** In part (a), ensure you answer from the viewpoint of the **staff** – not from the viewpoint of CP Ltd (reading the question carefully is vital). IT may be able to play a role in reducing feelings of isolation. General issues related to change and communication should be sufficient to score well in part (b).

- **Question 6.** Part (a) provides an opportunity to include a wide range of material – ranging from the cost of IT and the need for compatibility across systems to the need for an IT strategy that compliments the overall business strategy.

Time allocation...

Allocate your time according to the marks for the question. Each 20 mark question should take you 36 minutes. If you have allocated your time properly then you shouldn't have time on your hands before the full three hours is up. But if you do find yourself with a spare ten minutes check that you have answered all questions **fully**.

Finally...

After sitting the 'real' exam, do not worry if you found the paper difficult. Chances are, others will have too. Forget about that exam and prepare for the next one!

1   REPORT

To: Chief Executive FRS Ltd
From: Management Consultant
Date: 29 April 200X
Subject: Introduction of IT systems

(a)   The new Information system at FRS could be set up to process data using either distributed or centralised multi-user processing. An outline of the differences between the two follows.

Distributed processing utilises multiple processing units distributed around the system. The processors are linked (preferably via dedicated ISDN lines), enabling the transfer and utilisation of data held at different locations. Distributed processing is characterised by:

- Computers spread over a wide geographical area
- Shared data files
- The processing of data at more than one location

MRO Inc operates a form of distributed processing. Each local shop has its own processing capability (usually a PC). These processors are linked together with neighbouring outlets forming a Local Area Network (LAN). Each LAN is linked to MRO head office, forming a Wide Area Network (WAN). This network provides a means of communication between all shops and each other, as well as with head office.

Centralised multi-user processing describes the situation where all data is processed in a central location, such as head office. At the head office there will be a reasonably powerful computer (probably a mainframe) holding all the program and data files utilised by the system.

The hardware at individual shops would therefore not require processing or data storage capability. This would enable the installation of 'dumb terminals' – essentially a keyboard and screen linked to the central computer.

Many users are able to access the central processing unit at the same time, and process data simultaneously. If FRS Ltd adopted a multi-user system the terminals would be located in individual shops, and connected by an external data link.

(b)   The **relative merits** of implementing the type of information system used by MRO Inc:

Sharing of information

The MRO network solution would enable the sharing of information through the use of e-mail, bulletin boards and if justified the setting up of a group intranet. The IT infrastructure could be used as a tool to provide cohesion to the group, and encourage communication between individual shops.

Enhanced management information

Head office will be able to view summary level information using the Executive Support System (ESS). If further detail is required, management would be able to 'drill down' to view underlying data, such as the performance of individual shops.

More relevant information

Under the MRO system, each shop would have access to its own data and information, allowing more informed decisions to be made. The EPOS and EFTPOS systems would allow each shop to capture sales and customer data, which could be used in stock management and marketing promotions.

Less risk of complete system failure

Each shop has its own processing capability, so a problem in a single location will not prevent operations continuing as normal elsewhere. If centralised processing as suggested by Mr. Black was adopted, a problem with the central computer would affect all shops.

Greater flexibility

Distributed processing allows for greater flexibility in systems design. If an individual shop has a specific requirement this can be built into the system. For example, an individual shop manager may have the ability and inclination to use spreadsheet software as a management tool. Office software could be purchased and offered to be installed on the shop PC. Greater flexibility is also provided regarding possible future changes to the system.

(c) **Information for decision making.**

There are three levels of information within an organisation, strategic, tactical and operational.

Strategic information is 'high level' information relating to the organisation as a whole. It is used to plan the medium to long term objectives of the organisation to monitor and control progress towards those objectives. Strategic information should include external as well as internal data, as the external environment is a major influence on organisation performance. Some strategic reports should be produced on a regular basis, eg a monthly summary of group performance each month or quarter.

Strategic decisions have to take into account a wide range of variables. A system that gathers and analyses information relating to those variables is required to support strategic decision making. An **Executive Support System (ESS)** is used for this task. The ESS is in effect a corporate model, which enables key information to be analysed.

At the other end of the information spectrum is **operational information**. Operational information is:

- Related to day to day operations
- Derived from internal sources
- Detailed
- Prepared regularly, preferably in a standard format
- Transaction-based

For FRS Ltd this would include the daily recording of (for each shop):

- Employee hours
- Stock levels
- Daily sales
- Banking and cash 'float' details

The majority of operational information would be recorded on transaction based systems. In FRS Ltd sales transactions would be captured electronically at the point of sale, while other data such as employee hours would require manual input. The data would feed into the relevant modules of an **integrated accounting system.** (eg sales ledger, purchase ledger, cashbook and payroll).

A real-time integrated accounting system such as that used by MRO provides the advantages of easy posting and reconciliation between modules and constantly up to date information on which to base decisions on eg stock items that require re-ordering, quick or slow moving product lines.

Between strategic and operational information is **tactical information**. Tactical information is:

- Wider in scope than operational data - but still mainly internal

- Short to medium term based

- Usually summarised (eg monthly sales of a singe shop, delicatessen profitability over a range of shops)

- Often presented in the form of a comparison (eg actual against plan

Tactical decisions are often based on data that is summarised and processed in such a way that will aid decision making eg a **spreadsheet** model utilising 'what if' functionality could quickly calculate profitability based on various sales mixes. A package such as Microsoft Office provides spreadsheet (Excel), database, and word-processing facilities, and a user-friendly e-mail interface (Outlook).

Marking guide				Marks
1				
	(a)	Award up to 2 marks for each valid difference and explanation, maximum available 5 marks		5
	(b)	Award up to 2 marks for each valid point and explanation, maximum available 5 marks		5
	(c)	Award up to 2 marks for each valid use of information and explanation, maximum available 5 marks	5	-
		Award up to 2 marks for each valid system and explanation, maximum available 5 marks	5	-
				10
				20

2

(a) There are a wide range of **structured methodologies** that can be applied to systems development and implementation. Each methodology recommends a logical step by step approach. Structured Systems Analysis and Design Methodology (SSADM) is a methodology that distinguishes between logical and physical design.

- Logical design refers to how the system is designed to meet user needs eg screen layout, menu structure

- Technical design refers to the 'hidden' aspects of the system that enable the logical design to operate eg file structures

The type of problems experienced in the past should either be avoided or their impact minimised through the use of a structured methodology.

Problem: Information staff do not talk to users

Solution: A structured methodology involves users at all stages of design and implementation. Users are the 'customer' the methodology aims to satisfy. ('Users' means just that - the people who use the system hands-on. It is not good enough to include only the managers of users). User sign off is required at key stages of development, before further work commences. Communication between developers and users is key, and encourages the development of good working relationships. The relationship should be formalised through user-representation on the project implementation team.

Problem: Systems are late, over budget and under-perform

Solution: A structured methodology acts as a form of project control. Key milestones in development are highlighted and scheduled with the participation and agreement of all involved. Unrealistic timetables should not be accepted.

A major reason systems are often delivered over-budget is that they are late (ie more staff time is required than budgeted for). A realistic timetable that is agreed to by all should prevent this. User involvement at all stages should prevent should prevent costly reworking being required as a result of something being overlooked.

Systems often give the perception of under-performing due to unrealistic expectations. These expectations may be built up by systems personnel making unrealistic promises, or may be due to a lack of user knowledge regarding what computer systems are capable of. User involvement in the process at every stage should ensue expectations are realistic, and discourage unrealistic statements being made.

Problem: Programs contain errors

Solution: Structured methodologies include comprehensive testing procedures in conditions designed to replicate the actual operating environment. Users are heavily involved in testing, and user authorisation is required before implementation. Even with this emphasis on testing, some errors may only be discovered after the system 'goes-live' - when a unique set of circumstances occur. Post implementation testing should locate these errors enabling them to be corrected with minimum disruption.

Problem: Inconsistency

Solution: The inconsistent application of function keys is a basic error. The standardisation of function keys across modules is accepted practice in accounting packages, and would be developed in consultation with users if a structured methodology were used.

Problem: Inflexibility in reporting

Solution: A combination of user involvement and a flexible report writer should ensure the information required can be obtained from the system direct – without the need for further manipulation in a spreadsheet.

(b) **Quality and Information Systems**

Quality can be defined as 'fitness for purpose'. The purpose of an information system should be defined by developers and users before development work begins. Quality can then be measured against this agreed purpose.

Quality can be split into two components; design quality and conformance quality.

- In relation to an information system design quality relates to the user-friendliness of the system. Not only should the system be capable of doing what is required, operation of the system should be logical, consistent and easy to learn.

- Conformance quality means the ability of the system to do what is required of it, for example the absence of any major bugs.

The concept of quality can be applied to information systems in three steps.

Step 1 - Set measurable objectives

Realistic objectives must set that are measurable in terms of time, cost and performance. Objectives for system reliability and speed can be developed fairly easily. Qualitative factors such as user-friendliness and customer satisfaction also require objectives to be set.

184

Step 2 - **Monitor progress**

Hardware quality can be assessed by monitoring response times, number of system crashes, downtime and network traffic.

Programming quality can be measured via monitoring error reports during testing and the faults reported by users.

The use of the features within the package can be monitored to establish how often users utilise them. For example, if the main customer enquiry screen is rarely accessed it is likely that either users don't know how to use it or are unaware of it, and require further training, or that it is faulty. Both illustrate a reduction in quality of the system and should be rectified.

Software user-friendliness can be monitored through contact with users, and the tracking of customer support calls to helpdesks.

Overall **customer satisfaction** could be monitored using a user-satisfaction scale.

Step 3 - **Monitor the overall effect of the system**

Systems are not produced for their own ends. In the case of FRS, the overall aim of the new information system is to improve shop productivity, through the provision of more accurate and timely information. For example, if a reduction in inventory holding costs is noted, this could be a result of more accurate and timely stock information. Although the establishment of a direct relationship between a new system and improved business performance can be difficult to establish, an educated attempt should be made as that is the true indicator of system quality.

Marking guide				**Marks**
2	(a)	Award up to 2 marks for each valid benefit and explanation, maximum available 5 marks		5
		Award up to 2 marks for each example of how problems could be avoided/overcome, maximum available 5 marks		5
				10
	(b)	Award up to 2 marks for each valid explanation of the application of quality - to a maximum of 5 marks		5
		Award up to 2 marks for each valid suggestion to assess/measure quality - to a maximum of 5 marks		5
				10
				20

3

(a) There are a range of project management tools and techniques available to manage the implementation project. The major tools that would be applicable are outlined below.

A **Strengths, Weaknesses, Opportunities and Threats** analysis could be undertaken to assess whether the implementation fits with FRS Ltd's overall business objectives. A cost-benefit analysis could be included in this process to establish the economic feasibility of the project. The technical aspects of the project should also be evaluated as to its practicality and suitability to the businesses operations. A **contingency plan** should exist containing strategies for those risks identified as posing a material threat to the project. It may be necessary to transfer some risk via insurance.

The process of project selection and the measuring of the financial performance of a project can be achieved through **investment appraisal** techniques. Techniques such as Net Present Value, Internal Rate of Return, Accounting Rate of Return and PayBack can be used to evaluate whether the project should be undertaken. Expected costs and returns should be able to be estimated reasonably accurately based on the experience of MRO Inc.

Control over the implementation can he helped through the use of a **structured methodology** and a close relationship with users. An **external quality management** system, such as ISO 9001 can help maintain control and quality.

The project planning can be carried out with the aid of **project management software** such as Microsoft Project. The project should be broken down into individual tasks using **Work Breakdown Structure**. These tasks and projected completion dates together wit available resources form the major input into the software package. The package is then able to produce a **Critical Path Analysis** detailing the sequence and inter-relationship of tasks and **Gantt Charts** highlighting the resources required and the activities for which team members are involved in. Actual progress can then be reported against the plan as a means of control.

The tasks identified during Work Breakdown Structure also form the building blocks for the construction of the **project budget**. Financial control should be exercised through the budget using variance analysis and exception reporting.

(b) Critical path analysis

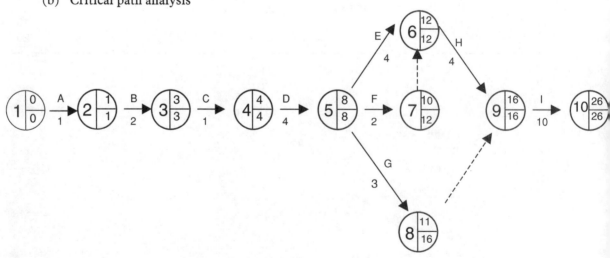

The critical path is A, B, C, D, E, H, I. The total elapsed time is 26 weeks.

Marking guide			
			Marks
3			
	(a)	Award up to 2.5 marks for each valid tool/technique and explanation	10
	(b)	Award up to 3 marks for clear/logical diagram style	3
		Award up to 3 marks for logical sequencing of tasks	3
		Award up to 2 marks for the logical identification of the critical path	2
		Award up to 2 marks for the logical identification of the total elapsed time	2
			10
			20

4

(a) GDC Ltd appears to have met its legal obligations even though the level of service it has provided to DS has been poor. There are a number of reasons for this.

DS rushed the appointment of GDC and did not insist on a **detailed Service Level Agreement (SLA)**. The contract does not specify the level of service that GDC will provide.

For example, GDC is obligated to provide 'management information', but there is no detailed definition of what this information will entail, and no deadline for the provision of the information. (eg '...within 5 working days of month-end').

DS handed **complete control** of its IT systems to GDC Ltd. The absence of IT expertise within DS puts it at a **disadvantage** when arguing its case with GDC Ltd.

For example, GDC could spend significant amounts of DS money on sub-standard hardware and software. DC Ltd would **not have the expertise to question** or challenge this purchase, resulting in poor use of DS funds and a poor level of service. However, even when purchasing sub-standard hardware GDC would not have breached the requirement of the contract to 'purchase all hardware and software'.

GDC Ltd is also responsible for the writing and maintenance of in-house software. **Unless GDC has a detailed understanding of DS the software written may not be suitable**. As GDC receives a set annual fee, it may be tempted to produce software as quickly and cheaply as possible. As the contract has no mention of software standards, GDC would be meeting its legal obligations.

Another reason that could be contributing DS receiving poor service is that **the agreement is now two years old**. Changes could have taken place inside DS within the past two years that an outside organisation such as GDC does not understand. The nature of management information required now may be different to that required two years ago.

Service levels could also be suffering because **GDC has no financial incentive to provide a good standard of service**. GDC Ltd has the right under the contract to increase the annual fee, above the rate of inflation, without any consultation and with no reference to the satisfaction of DS.

(b) The courses of action now available to DS relating to the provision of IT services, and the problems involved in each, are outlined below.

    (i) **DS could carry on under the existing agreement**, protecting the knowledge that GDC has built up on the provision of IT services to DS, **but applying 'moral' pressure** (in the form of complaints and meetings with GDC management) to obtain a better level of service. The main problem with this course of action is that the level of service may not improve at all.

(ii)   DS could terminate the existing contract by giving three months' notice, and **negotiate a new contract with GDC with a well-defined SLA**. Possible problems include the fact that GDC may not wish to negotiate a new SLA leaving DS with no IT services, or GDC may agree a new SLA but still provide the old shoddy service.

(iii)   DS could terminate the existing contract by giving three months' notice and **look for a new supplier** of all its IT services. However, this would mean 'starting from scratch'. Even an efficient provider would take time to develop a feel for the requirements at DS, and build up their expertise. There is no guarantee the new service provider would be better than GDC, although a more detailed SLA would help.

(iv)   **DS could establish its own in-house IT team**, probably using a combination of contractors and 'permanent' employees. The main problems with this option are the time and cost of finding setting up the team and that the team would be 'starting from scratch' and may only receive limited help from GDC during the hand-over.

Marking guide

			Marks
4			
	(a)	Award up to 3 marks for each valid point and explanation	12
	(b)	Award up to 3 marks for each valid course and associated problems - to a maximum of 8 marks	8
			20

5

(a) **Potential benefits**

1   **Savings in travel time and cost**

The staff will not have to travel to work, which could be a significant advantage to those who have long or difficult journeys. They will also save the cost of travel to and from work.

2   **Flexibility**

Staff can be more flexible about the hours they work (eg 7 to 3, 8 to 4, 9 to 5, or whatever suits them) and about the timing of breaks. It would also make it easier for them to **contact customers outside normal office hours**, giving them the satisfaction of providing a **better service** and increasing their potential **sales bonuses** (this is, of course, a benefit to the company too).

3   **Work environment**

There are many **disruptions** at work which can hinder or distract employees: examples are constantly ringing telephones, printer noise, loud conversations. These would not be present at home, and although there may be **other distractions** these are less likely to be stressful ones.

4   **Quality of life**

More generally, homeworking should provide a better quality of life for the individual working at home. The home is likely to be **better lit, heated** to suit individual taste, more **comfortable**, and have **more facilities**. It will not be necessary to cram domestic chores such as shopping, cleaning, washing into evenings and weekends. It may be possible to adapt working hours to accommodate **family commitments**, such as taking and collecting children from school.

Staff concerns

1   **Employment relationship and legal implications**

Staff may be concerned about their **employment rights** if they work from home and whether there are any implications in terms of **health and safety** regulations, **insurance and tax**, mortgage and council tax.

A further concern in this area is whether they will have enough **space** to work effectively at home.

I suggest we clarify these matters and then **brief the staff** about any potential implications on an individual basis if necessary.

2   **Isolation**

Staff currently have a great deal of interaction in the office, so a concern of staff could be that they become **cut off from their colleagues** and will miss the social contact. This could engender a feeling of uncertainty in staff which could affect their ability to provide an efficient service. They may also fear that being out of sight and out of mind will damage any **prospects of being considered for advancement** within the organisation.

3   **Exchange of information**

Staff help each other by **exchanging information** about work-related matters and **sharing the problems** they have experienced. There may be fears that they will lose this mutual support if working at home.

How the IT infrastructure can help

1   Much of the information that is required for the staff to carry out their jobs is on the computer system. It is fairly straightforward to provide a connection to the computer system to each employee in their homes and provide them with the necessary hardware.

There will obviously be an associated **cost** to this which we will need to quantify to ensure that it is not prohibitive.

The link could be a permanent link or a dial up facility. The **dial-up facility** may be more appropriate if it is possible to download the files staff need to access onto a local PC. This could then be updated at intervals avoiding the need to be permanently connected.

2   The same link could also be used to provide **e-mail** and **bulletin board** facilities to enable the staff to keep in contact and exchange information.

3   Access to the **VAN** would also be possible using the same link, but again the **cost implications** would need to be investigated in more detail.

4   Local copies of **software** such as word-processing packages and spreadsheets can be provided to produce the necessary documents and letters.

5   IT is only part of the answer, however: telecommunications links are a poor substitute for the actual **direct social contact** currently enjoyed. A carelessly worded e-mail, for instance, can easily be misunderstood.

Overcoming the concerns of staff

1   It will be important for us to ensure that the staff are **kept informed** of developments and that we consult with them to **identify any worries** they may

have. This will enable us to prepare them for the change and to alleviate their key concerns. The key **benefits** to them and the organisation should be **stressed**. It is important that they realise that the individual and not just the organisation will benefit. This will hopefully enable them to **own** the change and buy into it.

2   Consideration could be given to **piloting** the method of working with a few individuals who are already pro-homeworking. They will **champion the change** later if we decide to implement it throughout the sales staff. Asking for volunteers and for suggestions on implementation will ensure that staff feel that they have been properly consulted.

3   Consideration could also be given to setting up a **demonstration** to impress upon them that they will still be able to perform their jobs and keep in touch with each other. A visit to (home and office) sites of an organisation that already uses this method of working may also help staff to realise its benefits and its operability as well as its ease of use. It will also help us to assess the **level of training** necessary which must be given to support the staff.

4   **Social contact** could be retained to a limited extent by providing **regular meetings** at a convenient place. This could be used to update staff collectively of developments, organisational matters and reinforce the commitment and cultural aspects of the organisation whilst providing the opportunity for social contact.

5   The company will **save** a considerable amount of money (90% of £3,500 to £4,000 per employee per annum). Part of this could be **offered to staff** as an incentive to work at home.

Marking guide

			Marks
5			
	(a)	Award up to 2 marks for each valid benefit	4
		Award up to 2 marks for each valid concern	4
		Award up to 2 marks for each valid point relating to the IT infrastructure	4
			12
	(b)	Award up to 2 marks for each valid point	8
			20

6

(a) **Disadvantages of not having an overall IT strategy**

(i)   One of the important aspects of the IS/IT strategy is that it **supports the business strategy** by fulfilling the information needs of the organisation. An important element of this is that the **information needs** are clearly identified before the actual IT (hardware and software) is decided upon. If the organisation has no strategy for its IT there is the danger that it can **spend a large amount of money** and yet **still not meet** managements' **key information requirements**.

(ii)   As IT can involve high costs there is usually a **high risk** associated with the IT spend. This in part relates to the technical issues to be dealt with and the need to ensure that current IT and future IT is **compatible**. Without a strategy it is possible to invest in incompatible systems that increase the cost and complexity of working in the future.

(iii)   Many companies are able to use IT to gain a competitive advantage, either by exploiting IT in their operations or by managing their information far better. It therefore follows that not having a strategy can lead to the company **losing advantage to its competitors** and falling behind in terms of technology used.

(iv)   Not only do organisations rely on IT far more than they used to but **IT is changing the way many industries work**. For example the availability of information over the Internet is changing the way information is gathered and managed in many industries that are information-driven. Companies need to **build this into their future plans** and therefore plan IT to help them cope with the changes and remain competitive in the industry.

For example, retailing is becoming much more information-driven and many aspects of service industries such as travel agencies can do business over computer networks. The absence of an IT strategy will mean that the organisation is **not matching its future information needs** and **retaining its ability to compete** in a changing environment.

(v)   IT is changing the **way** information is **collected**, the **amount** of information **collected** and **what is done with information** once it has been collected. For example, in retailing, EPOS systems and loyalty card schemes are allowing supermarket chains to build up vast databases of individual consumer preferences.

Companies that do not take advantage of this are liable to **fall behind the competition** and find it impossible to **reap the benefits** of using information as a strategic resource.

(vi)   **Exchange of information** between various **stakeholders** is facilitated via IT and is also having an impact upon the **structure** of organisations making them more flexible, or softening the organisational boundaries. Where an organisation does not plan for this, it will **limit its ability to react quickly to changes.**

(vii)   It is important for organisations to ensure they provide their **employees** with the resources (including IT) they need to do their jobs well and to keep morale high. Employees may see other organisations utilising the latest technology and become **demotivated**: the older technology will limit their own effectiveness and harm their career prospects.

(b)   **Barriers presented by individuals**

(i)   **The senior manager**

The senior manager has **little knowledge** of IT and is also **fearful** of it. Underlying his dismissive attitude may be a fear of losing face in front of his more IT-literate colleagues. He will therefore have little appreciation of the potential business benefits of IT.

He will also **fail to see the relevance of IT** to the industry in a wider sense, which could result in **missing a strategic advantage.** The fact that he is good at producing overall policy may mean that he produces a general policy that skims the surface of the issues. His being task-orientated may also mean that insufficient time is taken to consider the issues fully. He is more likely to try and **push through his ideas** as fast as possible.

The first thing that needs to be done is to **increase his general awareness** of IT and its capabilities and relevance. He will then be much better able to focus on the benefits of IT for the company. Providing him with copies of **relevant, well-written articles** from non-technical journals (for example the FT's regular IT articles and supplements) should open his eyes to what his company may be missing.

Provided he is not totally resistant, the senior manager could be provided with a **desktop PC** and be shown how to use some **simple but useful applications** that will save him time from day to day. This may assist his confidence, kindle some enthusiasm and help to overcome his fear of IT.

(ii) **The IT professional**

The IT professional is probably **too close to IT**. She says she believes that IT is best left to specialists, yet her knowledge is **not as up to date** as one would expect a specialist's knowledge to be.

This may mean that she does not pay enough consideration to **user needs**. Many of the users may be familiar with PCs but she is unlikely to recommend devolving computing power into the hands of the user as she neither **understands** their needs nor **believes** they should be involved.

Her natural tendency will be to suggest an IT strategy that **preserves her empire** and revolves around the technical **IT department** rather than the **business needs**. There is also the danger that she will suggest continued use of technology within her own current knowledge, **ignoring current trends and developments**. Given that the Senior Manager may wish to rely on her knowledge to produce a quick solution, this could result in an inappropriate strategy.

These barriers may be overcome in a variety of ways.

(1) She needs to **update her knowledge** by reading computer journals and business press.

(2) She will probably need **further training** in topics such as client/server systems.

(3) She must be given top-level encouragement to look at the benefits of IT from the **business needs** viewpoint, rather than seeing IT as an end in itself.

(4) She must spend time with the **users** to realise that they have different needs and that their input can be valid in the development of the strategy.

(5) Visits to **other organisations** that are technically well advanced may also assist in overcoming her resistance to modern technology.

(iii) The trainee accountant may bring a lot of enthusiasm to the project, wishing to **prove himself** and bring all his knowledge to bear, but his desire to be the **IT champion** may well mean that he has a **private agenda** which could be **sub-optimal**.

He may have a **short-term focus** to the problem, as it will complement his studies.

His **limited experience** and position in the firm may limit his ability to see the **wider picture** effectively. However, being a user of IT, he will bring a valuable perspective to the project if his enthusiasm can be contained.

His input could also be **resented by the IT manager** who may try to blind him with science, especially as he is pushing for more end-user computing and less reliance upon her department. This could be a significant source of conflict within the group.

It will be important to **overcome any conflict** between the group arising from personal differences and background. This could be achieved by a careful **brief and initial discussion** by a board member ensuring that they all know why they have been included and **what their respective roles will be** expected to bring to the process. They all have a **valuable contribution** to make and making that clear to the group will help to understand the **objectives** of the group more clearly.

Marking guide

			Marks
6			
	(a)	Award up to 2 marks for each valid point	8
	(b)	Award up to 2 marks for each valid point relating to barriers	6
		Award up to 2 marks for each valid suggestion to overcome the barriers	6
			12
			20

Information Systems

BPP Mock Exam 2: Pilot Paper

Question Paper:	
Time allowed	3 hours
This paper is divided into two sections	
Section A	These THREE questions are compulsory and MUST be attempted
Section B	TWO questions ONLY to be answered

paper 2.1

DO NOT OPEN THIS PAPER UNTIL YOU ARE READY TO START
UNDER EXAMINATION CONDITIONS

Section A – ALL questions are compulsory and MUST be attempted

SCENARIO

CAET Insurance offers motor, home, property and personal insurance. It has recently developed a holiday insurance product that it provides to the public. A potential customer is able to telephone a specially trained adviser who asks a number of pertinent questions. The answers to these questions are entered directly into a computer system that calculates and displays the premium. The adviser communicates the premium to the potential customer who may either accept or reject it. Accepted quotations are paid for by credit card and printed off and sent to the customer, along with the payment details.

The software to support the on-line holiday insurance quotation was developed in-house by the Information Systems (IS) department. It was developed in a GUI-based programming language and was the first system to be produced by the Information Systems department using this language. The project was delivered late and it exceeded its budget. The software has suffered many problems since it was installed. Some of these have been solved. However, there are still significant problems in the actual function that the advisers use to record the details of potential customers and produce the quotation.

In a recent meeting with the IS department, the advisers identified four main problems.

Illogical data entry

The advisers claim that the sequence is illogical. The questions jump from personal details, to holiday location, to travel details, back to personal details, to holiday location etc. There seems to have been little thought about logically grouping the questions and as a result potential customers become 'confused'.

Unclear field entry

Some of the information we ask for is mandatory and some is optional. Furthermore, the relevance of some questions depends on the answer to a previous question. For example, travel method is only relevant if the potential customer is travelling abroad. Unfortunately, the system does not show if a field is mandatory or optional and it shows all fields, whether they are relevant or not to a particular quotation.

Inconsistent cursor control

The information has to be entered very quickly. Many fields are filled completely during data entry. On some screens, the cursor jumps to the next field immediately after filing the previous field. In other screens, the cursor only moves after pressing the TAB key even when the field is filled. This inconsistency is very irritating, we often find ourselves over-typing completed fields and it is particular confusing for new advisers who are not used to the software.

Performance problems

One of the primary requirements of the system was the ability to process enquiries on-line and to produce instant quotations. However, at peak times the system is too slow to produce the quotation. Consequently, we have to promise to telephone the potential customer back and this destroys the immediate impact of the system. Hence the system is not fulfilling one of its primary requirements.

CAET Insurance has brought in a consultant to review the on-line holiday insurance system. The consultant has made a number of observations regarding the project and the developed software. Two summary paragraphs are repeated below.

197

Extract from the management summary

Project

The IS department failed to recognise that this was a very risky project. Three issues made it particularly risky.

- The users of the system had no experience in the holiday insurance industry hence they found it difficult to specify their requirements in advance.

- The decision to use a programming language that the department had not used before.

- The system had exacting performance requirements.

All projects at CAET Insurance are supposed to undergo a risk assessment as part of producing the Project Quality Plan (PQP). This risk assessment was omitted from this project for reasons that are still unclear. This was a serious omission.

The software

There is considerable evidence that the product is unstable and suffers from significant performance problems. My recommendation is that the bespoke system is abandoned and a suitable application software package is selected and installed. My research suggests that there are a number of possible solutions in the marketplace and these packages offer 'tried, tested, and error-free solutions'. It will be more cost-effective, in the long run, to adopt one of these packages rather than maintain the bespoke in-house software.

1   The consultant has pointed out that the project did not undergo the required risk assessment. This risk assessment would have required the project team to identify ways to avoid or reduce the chance of each risk occurring.

Required:

(a) **In retrospect what could have been suggested at the start of the project to avoid or reduce each of the following three risks identified in the consultant's report?**

   (i)   **The users of the system had no experience in the holiday insurance industry hence they found it difficult to specify their requirements in advance.**

   (ii)   **The decision to use a programming language that the department had not used before.**

   (iii) **The system had exacting performance requirements.**   (12 marks)

(b) **The risk assessment is an important part of the Project Quality Plant (PQP). Two other terms used in the CAET Insurance PQP are:**

   (i)   **Project Sponsor**
   (ii)   **Project Plan**

   Explain the meaning and significance of each of these items.   (8 marks)

                                                                        (20 marks)

2   One of the key requirements of the holiday insurance system was the need to speedily process requests for an insurance quotation over the telephone. The users have identified four specific problems with the on-line insurance quotation function.

(i) Illogical data entry
(ii) Unclear field entry
(iii) Inconsistent cursor control
(iv) Performance problems

The IS department still believes that these four problems can be solved and that there is no need to abandon the development of the bespoke system and use an application package solution.

Required:

(a) **Suggest how each of the following four problems could be solved, now that the system is live, and comment on the difficulty of implementing your solutions.**

(i)	**Illogical data entry**	(2 marks)
(ii)	**Unclear field entry**	(3 marks)
(iii)	**Inconsistent cursor control**	(2 marks)
(iv)	**Performance problems**	(4 marks)

(b) **Suggest how each of the following four problems could have been prevented or detected before the system went live.**

(i)	**Illogical data entry**	(2 marks)
(ii)	**Unclear field entry**	(2 marks)
(iii)	**Inconsistent cursor control**	(2 marks)
(iv)	**Performance problems**	(3 marks)

(20 marks)

3   The consultant has suggested that one of the main advantages of the application software package approach is that the software is tried and tested.

Required:

(a) **Bespoke application systems developed in the IS department has to pass through the following three stages.**

(i) **Requirements analysis**
(ii) **Systems design**
(iii) **Programming**

Describe the quality assurance and testing associated with each of these three stages of the IS development process. (12 marks)

(b) **Explain where quality assurance and testing should still be applied by the IS department when using an application software package approach and hence comment on the consultant's assertion that the software is 'tried, tested and error-free'.** (8 marks)

(20 marks)

SECTION B - TWO questions only to be attempted

4 A recently appointed financial director has reviewed how information systems are developed in a public sector authority. She has suggested that the information systems (IS) staff should concentrate on developing new systems, rather than maintaining the existing ones. She suggests that 'the maintenance of legacy systems should be outsourced to an external software house'.

Required:

(a) **Briefly explain what is meant by the term 'outsourced'.** (3 marks)

(b) **Briefly explain what is meant by the term 'legacy systems'.** (3 marks)

(c) **Describe two likely benefits of the financial director's recommendation to outsource the maintenance of legacy systems.** (4 marks)

She has also suggested that all systems development projects should use a project management software package to help plan, control, monitor and report progress in the proposed new development projects.

(d) **Explain what is meant by a project management software package.** (4 marks)

(e) **Briefly describe two advantages of using a project management software package.** (6 marks)

(20 marks)

5 A business analyst is preparing to interview a user about how insurance claims are handled by the business.

Required:

(a) **Briefly describe four specific activities the business analyst should undertake in preparation for the meeting.** (8 marks)

During the meeting, the user specifies the following requirements.

Insurance claims are received into the department. These are defined as Pending Claims until a Claims Inspector can review them. The result of the review is either an Accepted Claim or a Rejected Claim. Only Accepted Claims can be paid. After six months all Paid Claims are archived.

(b) **Construct an appropriate event model for this business requirement.** (8 marks)

(c) **Provide an explanatory key to this model so that the user can understand it.** (4 marks)

(20 marks)

6

Required:

(a) Describe the meaning and purpose of a post-implementation review.

(4 marks)

The Human Resources Directors of a large company wants to measure the success of the application software he has commissioned and implemented for a personnel system.

(b) Briefly describe three measures he could use to quantify the success of the application software and state what each of these three measures is attempting to assess. (9 marks)

It is expected that the user will define new requirements (and change old ones) throughout the life of the system.

(c) List the components of a procedure for recording, prioritising and implementing these changes. (7 marks)

(20 marks)

MOCK EXAM 2 ANSWERS

DO NOT TURN THIS PAGE UNTIL YOU
HAVE COMPLETED MOCK EXAM 2

WARNING! APPLYING THE BPP MARKING SCHEME

If you decide to mark your paper using the BPP marking scheme, you should bear in mind the following points.

1   The BPP solutions are not definitive: we have applied the marking scheme to our solutions to show how answers should gain marks, but there may be more than one way to answer the question. Try to judge whether different points made in your answers are correct and relevant and therefore worth marks.

2   If you have a friend or colleague who is studying or has studied this paper, you might ask him or her to mark your paper for you, thus gaining a more objective assessment. Remember you and your friend are not trained or objective markers, so try to avoid complacency or pessimism if you appear to have done very well or very badly.

3   In some instances, BPP's answers are longer than you would be expected to write. Sometimes, therefore, you would gain the same number of marks for making the basic point as we have shown as being available for a slightly more detailed solution.

A PLAN OF ATTACK

Tackling scenario questions

Section A of the examination for Paper 2.1 comprises a written scenario with three compulsory questions from across the syllabus **linked** to the narrative scenario. Refer to the 'Plan of Attack' for Mock Exam 1 for general advice regarding how to approach scenario questions - we repeat the key points below.

Key points to remember when tackling scenario questions:
- Answer the question asked – tailor what you know to fit the scenario
- Prepare a rough plan – this will help clarify your thoughts
- Structure longer answers eg introduction, body of answer, conclusion
- Justify any recommendations

Mock exam 2

This mock exam is the **pilot paper** put together by the examiner. While the real exam is not going to replicate this one, this is the best indication of topics and question styles favoured by the examiner.

Start by spending 5 minutes looking through the paper.

Option 1 (if you're thinking 'Help!')

If you don't feel confident about the scenario questions, but feel there is at least one question you are well prepared for in Section B, you may find it helpful to complete the two questions you are required to answer from Section B first. For example, if you feel confident drawing event models, you could start with **Question 5**.

Starting with a question you find 'easier' should **build your confidence** before you attempt the questions you expect to prove more difficult. At the start of the exam you will be fresh - you should be in the best frame of mind to **apply the knowledge** you possess to the specific **requirements of the question**.

Starting with a question you feel confident with should help you 'get into' the exam. After completing your first question you should be mentally 'tuned-in', which should help when you attempt the more difficult questions.

Attempting a question you find difficult at the start of an exam can result in some candidates **losing confidence**. As a consequence of this lack of composure, these candidates often go on to score poorly on later questions that they would ordinarily score well on.

But remember, you can not avoid the three scenario questions – you have to answer them.

Option 2 (if you are thinking 'No problem!')

Try not to be overconfident, but if you are feeling fairly comfortable, then tackle the scenario questions first, then move on to your selected questions from Section B.

Comments on questions from Mock Exam 2

- **Question 1**

    ○   In Part (a), your knowledge of how user involvement can be encouraged in systems development is relevant, as are issues relating to staff training and recruitment. You must address each of the three risks identified.

- ° Part (b) should provide well-prepared candidates with 'easy marks'. Ensure you explain both the meaning and **significance** of the two terms.

- **Question 2**

  - ° On first reading, you may not immediately identify solutions for the problems identified in part (a). However, if you are able to **apply** what you have learned regarding user-friendly computer interfaces, you should score well.

  - ° Apply your knowledge of user-involvement in system development to part (b).

- **Question 3**

  - ° Part (a) is worth 12 marks, and appears to be an 'essay style' question. However, you should ensure you answer the set of six 2 mark questions – ie 2 marks for quality assurance at the requirements analysis stage, 2 marks for testing at the requirements stage etc.

  - ° In part (b), remember that even packaged software should be tested in actual operating conditions, and that it is very unlikely that any software is completely 'error-free'.

- **Question 4**

  - ° Parts (a) and (b) should prove straightforward for well-prepared candidates.

  - ° Part (c) requires a little more thought. You do not need to restrict your answer to technical issues – for example staff morale could be relevant.

  - ° Part (d) should not prove difficult if you have revised your project management software material.

  - ° Ensure you provide an answer sufficient to justify 3 marks per advantage in part (e).

- **Question 5**

  - ° For part (a), keep it simple. Activities could include deciding where to meet and communicating the objectives of the meeting.

  - ° Apply your knowledge of user-involvement in system development to part (b).

- **Question 6**

  - ° Part (a) is able to be answered straight from 'book knowledge'. Ensure you pick all of these 'easy marks' by providing both the meaning and **purpose**.

  - ° Part (b) requires more thought. Remember that the amount a non-essential system is used can indicate how popular it is. Also think about user requests for help, and system amendments.

  - ° If you are initially unsure about your ability to answer part (c), think about the process logically. A method (eg a form) to request a change is a good starting point.

Time allocation...

Allocate your time according to the marks for the question. Each 20 mark question should take you 36 minutes. If you have allocated your time properly then you shouldn't have time on your hands before the full three hours is up. But if you do find yourself with a spare ten minutes check that you have answered all questions **fully**.

Finally...

After sitting the 'real' exam, do not worry if you found the paper difficult. Chances are, others will have too. Forget about that exam and prepare for the next one!

1

(a) (i) **Risk: lack of user experience in the holiday industry**

Avoiding risk

Experience in the holiday industry could be obtained by either recruiting new staff with the appropriate experience, or by helping existing staff obtain that experience, through their work and possibly by attendance on some appropriate training courses. However, using the latter option will almost certainly have delayed the systems project.

Reducing risk

Involving users throughout the design process could reduce the risk of implementing an incorrect or partly functional system. Specifically, system prototypes and pilot testing could be carried out to check the appropriateness of any system design.

Reviewing similar systems that may already be available on the market or at third parties may also reduce risk. The latter will be difficult to achieve where third parties do not want to share their knowledge although a review of propriety software will at least indicate the functionality that can be included in any new system.

(ii) **Decision to use a programming language with no experience of that language in-house**

Avoiding risk

This risk can be avoided, either gaining the appropriate experience in-house, or by using a different programming language that in-house already have experience in. The choice will depend on how important it is to use the functionality in the chosen language.

Reducing risk

If the unfamiliar language has to be used, then risk of failure can be reduced firstly, by allowing more time in the project plan for training or hiring of staff. Another alternative is to put back the project delivery time to recognise that problems may occur in writing and testing the software. These alternatives may be more appropriate than implementing software that fails or causes errors shortly after implementation.

(iii) **Exacting performance problems**

Avoiding risk

Performance problems can be avoided by decreasing the use of the computer system at busy times. This may mean storing customer telephone calls in a queue and only taking the number of calls that the system will process or promising to call customers back at a less busy time. As a last resort, CAET could stop giving quotes on-line, although this may not an acceptable option, given CAET's commitment to using the system.

Reducing risk

Checking that high specification hardware is installed to provide adequate processing power can reduce the risk of poor performance. Faster hardware will decrease the waiting time for response from the system.

Alternatively, prototypes can be produced during the design and build phase to test the system response times. If performance cannot be improved, then at least expectations of users and customers regarding performance can be managed.

(b) (i)   **Project sponsor**

The project sponsor is the customer for the system. This person is not necessarily the finance director, but the manager of the business unit or department where the new system will be implemented. The sponsor will have made the business case for any new or revised system, and will seek to ensure that those benefits are delivered in the final system.

As the project sponsor is responsible for delivering the benefits of the project, that person will also be promoting the project prior to implementation. Promotion in this case will mean ensuring that appropriate resources are allocated to the project as well as ensuring potential users are aware of the project and are briefed on the benefits of that project. Lack of a project sponsor will increase the risk of project failure, due to lack of co-ordination of the activities of the project and possible lack of priority for the project within the organisation.

(ii)   **Project plan**

The project plan provides an overall picture of the project showing the activities to be carried out, the time of those activities and how the different activities are related to each other. Most project plans are presented as some form of chart (eg GANTT chart) or network so that interconnections between the activities can be seen clearly.

The project plan is used to estimate the total time to complete the project and identify those activities, which must be completed on time to avoid the whole project being finished late. The effect on total project duration from changes in activities can also be estimated by entering revised times for activities into the plan. If no plan is produced, then the overall project time and critical activities will be difficult to predict. There will also be an increased risk of late completion due to overall lack of control.

Marking guide

			Marks
1	(a)	One mark for each valid point up to a maximum of four marks for each risk. Three risks required giving a total of twelve marks.	12
	(b)	One mark for each valid point up to a maximum of four marks for each section. Two sections are required giving a total of eight marks.	4 4 — 8 20

2

(a) (i)   **Illogical data entry**

The logical order to input data into the system needs to be ascertained from the users of the system. This error could have been identified in a prototype and the screen design amended at this time. However, given that the correct fields appear to be available, rather than some fields actually missing, the screen should be fairly easy to amend. Within the GUI interface, each field will have its own placeholder (similar to those in Microsoft Access), so these can be dragged to a new location and the order of using the fields amended to reflect the user requirement.

(ii) **Unclear field entry**

Mandatory fields should be easy to identify, possibly by using a different colour to shade the field or providing a darker boarder around the input box. Similarly, displaying some fields should be made dependent on entries actually made in previous fields. Again, using the GUI interface tools, amendments to field properties should be fairly easy to accomplish.

(iii) **Inconsistent cursor control**

Inconsistent cursor control is difficult for the user as the action of the cursor is difficult to predict, as the case study shows. A survey of users will help to identify which action on the completion of each field is actually appropriate. Pressing the tab key may be the easiest option because the software may not always identify when a field is complete (eg when does an address end?). However, as long as the action is consistent and logical, then the actual alternative chosen is irrelevant.

The change should again be easy to implement by ensuring that the properties for completion of input in each field are the same.

(iv) **Performance problems**

Performance problems are more difficult to remedy as they may require amendments to hardware or software, which are simply not possible post-implementation. However, it may be possible to:

Add additional disk space, RAM memory or upgrade network cards to a higher specification or install a more recent processor to try and improve overall system performance. All of these alternatives should help to reduce the response time.

Alternatively, the actual use of system resources in terms of which programs are being run at specific times can also be reviewed. If resource-intensive programs, such as file re-organisation, are being run during the day, then these can be deferred to a less busy time. This will free up system resources for more important programs such as the on-line insurance system.

(b) (i) **Illogical data entry**

Ensuring that the screen correctly reflects the method of work would normally be checked during the design stage of a system, specifically by using a prototype of the screen layout. At this time, amendments to the screen design could be made prior to the final system being built, avoiding these errors at the user acceptance test. However, given that this is a new system, even a prototype may have been of limited use because users could still have been uncertain about how they wanted to input data.

(ii) **Unclear field entry**

The issue of some fields being optional could again have been detected at the build stage using a prototype to check which fields actually needed to be completed for each data record. Alternatively, data collection during the building of a logical model during system design may also have detected that some fields were optional.

However, in the current situation, some design standard is required to distinguish optional from mandatory fields. This will ensure that optional fields will only be shown when they are required.

(iii) **Inconsistent cursor control**

The lack of consist use of the cursor again implies a lack of standards during the design phase of the software. Stating the action to take on completion of a field in a style manual would help to ensure this error did not occur, or if it did, the manual would show which style should be applied.

Design errors would be detected during systems testing, as this is now a systems standard.

(iv) **Performance problems**

The performance of the system should be checked during system testing; specifically when the response times to processing increasing large amounts of data were checked. It is possible that this load testing was not carried out, or that the system was inadequately tested at this time, with only a small number of transactions being processed. If the problem had been detected during testing, then the software could have been amended to try and enhance performance prior to going live.

Marking guide		Marks
2	(a) One mark for each valid point up to a maximum of two marks.	2
	(b) One mark for each valid point up to a maximum of three marks.	3
	(c) One mark for each valid point up to a maximum of two marks.	2
	(d) One mark for each valid point up to a maximum of four marks.	4
	(e) One mark for each valid point up to a maximum of two marks.	2
	(f) One mark for each valid point up to a maximum of two marks.	2
	(g) One mark for each valid point up to a maximum of two marks.	2
	(h) One mark for each valid point up to a maximum of three marks.	3
		20

3

(a) The three areas of application development mentioned in the question relate to the three stages of testing outlined in the 'V' model of system development. In this model, analysis and testing are linked at three specific points:

1.   Requirements analysis and user acceptance testing
2.   Systems design and systems testing
3.   Program design and unit or module testing

This format is followed in the answer.

(i) **Requirements analysis**

In the requirements analysis stage, documentation is produced to show what the system is required to do in terms of input, output and processing. The documentation will be produced in text or graphical form, and then checked to ensure that it is complete and adheres to appropriate design standards.

In user acceptance testing, the requirements analysis is re-visited and checked against the new system. The new system should fulfil the requirements previously defined in the requirements analysis; if it does not, then further amendments may be required before the users sign-off the system.

(ii) **Systems design**

During system design, the architectural software design is produced from the business requirements and technical specification for the software.

Documentation is produced to specific design standards so it can be checked using formal walkthroughs.

In systems testing, all of the individual programs are tested together as one integrated suite of software. The integrated software is compared back to the original design specification to check that the programs work as outlined in this design. If the design is not met then the systems testing fails and amendments to the overall design of the software may still be required. When the systems testing is complete, the integrated software is forwarded for user acceptance testing.

(iii) **Programming**

At this stage, the individual programs or modules of the software are designed. The actual designs will again be produced in accordance with specific design standards and tested prior to the program itself being written.

After the program is written, it is checked back to the program specification to ensure that this has been met. This testing is normally called unit testing. Any errors in the program modules are corrected or debugged before the individual programs are sent for systems testing.

(b) **Using an application software package approach means that software is purchased from a third party supplier ready for use within the organisation.** This means that systems design and program design and their associated testing phases are not required because the software house will have already performed this testing.

However, a specification of requirements will still be required, and therefore user acceptance testing will also be required. The specification of requirements is necessary because the software must still meet the business needs of the organisation. The requirements must therefore be listed and compared to the specification for the program. It will be very difficult to amend the application software after it has been implemented, so checking requirements is essential.

User acceptance testing is also necessary to ensure that the requirement specification is met, and that the software adequately supports the business needs of the users as well as the volume of transactions.

The comment concerning 'tried, tested and error free' may be incorrect.

Firstly, the software has not been tested in the organisation, so it may not meet the specific requirements of users. The testing to date has been against the requirements of designers in the software house, not the organisation where the software is being implemented.

Secondly, the software is unlikely to be 100% error free. The software house may not have been able to test all combinations of the different software modules or with the specific transactions that will be used in the organisation in a live situation. Errors may still occur.

Marking guide			**Marks**
3	(a)	One mark for each valid point up to a maximum of four marks for each stage.	4
		Three stages required giving a total of twelve marks.	4
			12
	(b)	One mark for each valid point up to a maximum of eight marks.	8
			8
			20

BPP
PUBLISHING

4

(a) **Outsourcing** means that the part of all of or the IT systems within an organisation are provided or maintained by a **third party supplier**. In this situation, it is the legacy systems that are to be outsourced.

The terms of the outsourcing contract will include number of years and cost of the service, as well as precise details of the service such as changes to be made to the systems or any new reports that will be generated.

(b) The term **legacy systems** in an organisation relates to the **old systems**, implemented some time ago, **which are no longer updated**. Legacy systems are likely to have been written in older languages such as COBOL or FORTRAN, which are rarely used. So it is possible that the software cannot communicate with more recent systems, and the data is only accessible from within the legacy system.

However, the systems are generally reliable, and the users see very little need to amend or upgrade. Similarly, it may be difficult to present a business case to replace the systems.

(c) Outsourcing of the legacy systems may provide the following **benefits** to the organisation. [Only two required – three are provided here for study purposes]

(i) **Access to programming expertise**

Most new software systems are written in more modern computer languages, so it is not necessary to maintain expertise in relatively old languages in-house. It may even be difficult to find programmers with appropriate experience to maintain the programmes, as the computer language is old.

However, an outsourcing company may still employ COBOL programmers, because the costs can be shared across a wider client base. The company can continue to obtain access to this expertise as required.

(ii) **Cost savings**

Outsourcing may provide a cheaper alternative to employing staff to maintain the legacy systems. Very few changes are likely to be required to the systems, so it is unlikely that in-house staff would be fully employed maintaining them. Purchasing the expertise as and when required is likely to be a cheaper option.

Cost may also be saved because all changes to the legacy systems will need a business case to justify the expenditure. As this is now an external cost, very good business cases will be required to justify the amendments.

(iii) **Morale**

If a third party provides maintenance of the legacy systems, then programming staff can concentrate on new in-house projects. This is likely to enhance employee morale, as producing new systems is normally more enjoyable than maintaining old systems.

(d) **Project management software is a specific program which is design to help plan and control a project.** Popular examples include Microsoft Project and Project Manager Workbench.

These packages allow managers to plan projects by constructing network diagrams or GANTT charts along with budgets when costs are allocated to individual activities within each project. Network diagrams will also allow the critical path of the project to be highlighted. The cost effect of amendments to a project may also be determined.

Inputting completed activities can help monitor the progress of a project, and a variety of reports are normally available to help monitor the progress of the project.

(e) **Advantages of using project management software**

(i) **Allocation of resources across projects**

Project management software will identify the critical path for a project. This will help to ensure that appropriate resources are allocated to the activities on the critical path to ensure that they are not delayed. The software can also be used to allocate resources over several projects running at the same time. Updating several manual project plans and keeping these concurrent with each other will be quite difficult; however, this activity will be relatively simple using project management software.

(ii) **Changes to projects**

Amendments to projects can be input into project management software to quickly identify the effects on the timescale and resources needed for the project. The effect of making different amendments could also be compared so that amendments causing the smallest change to the project can be selected. The effect of amending resource allocation over all projects can easily be seen by reviewing outputs from the software.

Marking guide

			Marks	
4	(a)	One mark for each valid point up to a maximum of three marks.		3
	(b)	One mark for each valid point up to a maximum of three marks.		3
	(c)	One mark for each valid point up to a maximum of two marks for each benefit. Two benefits required giving a total of four marks.	2 2	4
	(d)	One mark for each valid point up to a maximum of four marks.		4
	(e)	One mark for each valid point up to a maximum of three marks for each advantage. Two advantages required giving a total of six marks	3 3	6
				20

5

Tutor's hint. In part (b) we have produced a simple flowchart type model as this suits the circumstances outlined. Other types of model could have been used. The Key should enable an 'outsider' to understand the conventions used in the model.

(a) To prepare for the meeting with the user, the analyst will need to carry out the activities below.

Confirm the time and location of the meeting. All attendees will need to know where the meeting is held, and the analyst may need to ensure sufficient chairs tables etc. are available and book refreshments.

Confirm the objectives of the meeting. The user will need to know why the meeting is being held; a list of objectives should be circulated to all attendees prior to the meeting.

Prepare for the meeting – background information. The analyst will need to research the history of the company, check current procedure manuals and clarify any technical terms that may be used. This will help the analyst identify the situation of the user and 'talk the user's language'.

Prepare for the meeting – questions to ask. The analyst will need to plan and write out the questions to be asked during the meeting. A checklist of points to be covered may also be required to ensure that all the information required is actually obtained.

(b)   **Event model for Insurance claim**

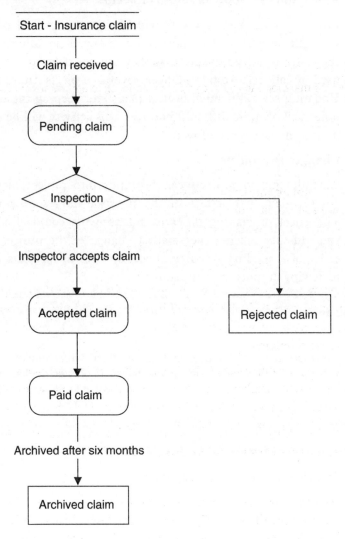

(c)   **Key for event model**

Symbol	Explanation
————————————	The start of the model stating the event being modelled.
↓	Possible transitions between different states of an object.
◇	An activity, the outcome of which decides the next transition.
	A state of an object awaiting further transition.
	The final state of an object.

Marking guide

			Marks
5	(a)	One mark for each valid point up to a maximum of two marks for each item.	2
		Four items required giving a total of eight marks	2
			2
			2
			8
	(b)	One mark for each valid part of the model up to a maximum of eight marks.	8
	(c)	One mark for each valid part of the model up to a maximum of four marks.	4
			20

6

(a) **A post-implementation review takes place a few months after system implementation is complete**. The review is to receive feedback from users on how well the system is working and to check that the objectives of the project have been met. The review normally takes the form of a meeting between the project sponsor, systems analyst, developers and users.

The review will investigate both the procedures used throughout the project and the systems that have been produced. The purpose of doing this is to identify what features of the project went well, and what went wrong or badly, so that future projects will avoid these problems.

In reviewing the objectives of the project, the review will also check whether or not the business benefits expected from the project have been achieved. Where benefits have not been achieved, or other objectives of the project have not been met, the review may also recommend remedial action to ensure that the required benefits are obtained.

(b) **Measures of success for application software**

(i) **Number of calls to the help desk**

Ascertaining the number of help desk calls per 100 employees (or some other useful number) will help to determine how useable and user-friendly the system is. The number of calls may also give an indication of the effectiveness of the training provided.

(ii) **Number of errors reported**

A log can be maintained, either by individual users or the help desk, of the number and type of errors found in the system. The actual error rate provides an indication of the quality of programming and the effectiveness of the different stages of testing (user acceptance, system and module).

(iii) **Number of transactions processed**

The original software specification will indicate how many transactions should be processed. Comparing the specification with the actual number processed will provide information on the usefulness of the system (if the system is not useful then presumably it will be used less than expected). A small number of transactions being processed could also be indicative of poor programming or inadequate hardware specifications, so further analysis may be needed to determine which of these is relevant.

(iv)   Number of change requests

Users may request changes to the system, either where that system did not meet their original requirements, or where the system as implemented does not meet their expectations in some way. Changes requested due to initial specifications not being met provides some measure on the quality of the design and testing processes. Changes requested because the software is not meeting expectations may indicate weaknesses in this method of obtaining data for the initial specification.

(c)   **A procedure for recording, prioritising and implementing change requested for a live system are outlined below.**

- A means for the user to record and request a change to the system

- A method of collating these change requests

- A means of providing a impact analysis and business case for each change

- A process for reviewing each request with agreed criteria for accepting or rejecting a request

- A method of prioritising requests that have been accepted

- Provision of appropriate documentation to record each change request with analysis and design implications for the existing system

- A method of allocating amendments to programmers

- A process for reviewing the work of programmers and ensuring that the change meets the initial specification

- A process for testing the change within the whole program suite

- Procedures for informing users date and nature of the change

- Procedures for updating system and user documentation prior to the release of the change

- A process for releasing that change into the live software

Marking guide		Marks
6	(a) One mark for each valid point up to a maximum of four marks.	4
	(b) One mark for each valid point up to a maximum of three marks for each measure. Three measures required giving a total of nine marks.	3 3 3
		9
	(c) One mark for each valid point up to a maximum of seven marks.	7
		20

REVIEW FORM & FREE PRIZE DRAW

All original review forms from the entire BPP range, completed with genuine comments, will be entered into one of two draws 31 January 2002 and 31 July 2002. The names on the first four forms picked out on each occasion will be sent a cheque for £50.

Name: _____   **Address:** _____

_____

_____

How have you used this Kit?
(Tick one box only)

☐ Self study (book only)

☐ On a course: college (please state)_____

_____

☐ With 'correspondence' package

☐ Other _____

Why did you decide to purchase this Kit? *(Tick one box only)*

☐ Have used the complementary Study Text

☐ Have used other BPP products in the past

☐ Recommendation by friend/colleague

☐ Recommendation by a lecturer at college

☐ Saw advertising in journals

☐ Saw website

☐ Other _____

During the past six months do you recall seeing/receiving any of the following?
(Tick as many boxes as are relevant)

☐ Our advertisement in *Student Accountant*

☐ Our advertisement in *Pass*

☐ Our brochure with a letter through the post

☐ Our website

Which (if any) aspects of our advertising do you find useful?
(Tick as many boxes as are relevant)

☐ Prices and publication dates of new editions

☐ Information on product content

☐ Facility to order books off-the-page

☐ None of the above

When did you sit the exam? _____

Which of the following BPP products have you used for this paper?

☐ Study Text   ☐ MCQ Cards   ☑ Kit   ☐ Passcards   ☐ Success Tape   ☐ Breakthrough Video

Your ratings, comments and suggestions would be appreciated on the following areas of this Kit.

	Very useful	Useful	Not useful
'Question search tools'	☐	☐	☐
'The exam'	☐	☐	☐
'Background'	☐	☐	☐
Preparation questions	☐	☐	☐
Exam standard questions	☐	☐	☐
'Tutor's hints' section in answers	☐	☐	☐
Content and structure of answers	☐	☐	☐
Mock exams	☐	☐	☐
'Plan of attack'	☐	☐	☐
Mock exam answers	☐	☐	☐

	Excellent	Good	Adequate	Poor
Overall opinion of this Kit	☐	☐	☐	☐

Do you intend to continue using BPP products?   ☐ Yes   ☐ No

Please note any further comments and suggestions/errors on the reverse of this page. The BPP author of this edition can be e-mailed at: barrywalsh@bpp.com

Please return this form to: Katy Hibbert, ACCA range manager, BPP Publishing Ltd, FREEPOST, London, W12 8BR

REVIEW FORM & FREE PRIZE DRAW (continued)

Please note any further comments and suggestions/errors below.

FREE PRIZE DRAW RULES

1   Closing date for 31 July 2002 draw is 30 June 2002. Closing date for 31 January 2002 draw is 31 December 2001.

2   Restricted to entries with UK and Eire addresses only. BPP employees, their families and business associates are excluded.

3   No purchase necessary. Entry forms are available upon request from BPP Publishing. No more than one entry per title, per person. Draw restricted to persons aged 16 and over.

4   Winners will be notified by post and receive their cheques not later than 6 weeks after the relevant draw date.

5   The decision of the promoter in all matters is final and binding. No correspondence will be entered into.

See overleaf for information on other
BPP products and how to order

ACCA Order - New Syllabus

To BPP Publishing Ltd, Aldine Place, London W12 8AA
Tel: 020 8740 2211. Fax: 020 8740 1184
email: publishing@bpp.com
online: www.bpp.com

Mr/Mrs/Ms (Full name) _____
Daytime delivery address _____
Postcode _____
Date of exam (month/year) _____
Daytime Tel _____

	2/01 Texts	8/01 Kits	9/01 Passcards	MCQ cards	Tapes	Videos
PART 1						
1.1 Preparing Financial Statements	£19.95 ☐	£10.95 ☐	£5.95 ☐	£5.95 ☐	£12.95 ☐	£25.00 ☐
1.2 Financial Information for Management	£19.95 ☐	£10.95 ☐	£5.95 ☐	£5.95 ☐	£12.95 ☐	£25.00 ☐
1.3 Managing People	£19.95 ☐	£10.95 ☐	£5.95 ☐		£12.95 ☐	£25.00 ☐
PART 2						
2.1 Information Systems	£19.95 ☐	£10.95 ☐	£5.95 ☐		£12.95 ☐	£25.00 ☐
2.2 Corporate and Business Law (6/01)	£19.95 ☐	£10.95 ☐	£5.95 ☐		£12.95 ☐	£25.00 ☐
2.3 Business Taxation FA 2000 (for 12/01 exam)	£19.95 ☐	£10.95 ☐ (4/01)	£5.95 ☐ (4/01)		£12.95 ☐	£25.00 ☐
2.4 Financial Management and Control	£19.95 ☐	£10.95 ☐	£5.95 ☐		£12.95 ☐	£25.00 ☐
2.5 Financial Reporting (6/01)	£19.95 ☐	£10.95 ☐	£5.95 ☐		£12.95 ☐	£25.00 ☐
2.6 Audit and Internal Review (6/01)	£19.95 ☐	£10.95 ☐	£5.95 ☐		£12.95 ☐	£25.00 ☐
PART 3						
3.1 Audit and Assurance Services (6/01)	£20.95 ☐	£10.95 ☐	£5.95 ☐		£12.95 ☐	£25.00 ☐
3.2 Advanced Taxation FA 2000 (for 12/01 exam)	£20.95 ☐	£10.95 ☐ (4/01)	£5.95 ☐ (4/01)		£12.95 ☐	£25.00 ☐
3.3 Performance Management	£20.95 ☐	£10.95 ☐	£5.95 ☐		£12.95 ☐	£25.00 ☐
3.4 Business Information Management	£20.95 ☐	£10.95 ☐	£5.95 ☐		£12.95 ☐	£25.00 ☐
3.5 Strategic Business Planning and Development	£20.95 ☐	£10.95 ☐	£5.95 ☐		£12.95 ☐	£25.00 ☐
3.6 Advanced Corporate Reporting (6/01)	£20.95 ☐	£10.95 ☐	£5.95 ☐		£12.95 ☐	£25.00 ☐
3.7 Strategic Financial Management	£20.95 ☐	£10.95 ☐	£5.95 ☐		£12.95 ☐	£25.00 ☐
INTERNATIONAL STREAM						
1.1 Preparing Financial Statements	£19.95 ☐	£10.95 ☐	£5.95 ☐	£5.95 ☐	£12.95 ☐	£25.00 ☐
2.5 Financial Reporting (6/01)	£19.95 ☐	£10.95 ☐	£5.95 ☐		£12.95 ☐	£25.00 ☐
2.6 Audit and Internal Review (6/01)	£19.95 ☐	£10.95 ☐	£5.95 ☐		£12.95 ☐	£25.00 ☐
3.1 Audit and Assurance services (6/01)	£20.95 ☐	£10.95 ☐	£5.95 ☐		£12.95 ☐	£25.00 ☐
3.6 Advanced Corporate Reporting (6/01)	£20.95 ☐	£10.95 ☐	£5.95 ☐		£12.95 ☐	£25.00 ☐
SUCCESS IN YOUR RESEARCH AND ANALYSIS PROJECT						
Tutorial Text (9/00) (new edition 9/01)	£19.95 ☐					

SUBTOTAL £ _____

POSTAGE & PACKING

Study Texts

	First	Each extra	
UK	£3.00	£2.00	£ ____
Europe*	£5.00	£4.00	£ ____
Rest of world	£20.00	£10.00	£ ____

Kits/Passcards/Success Tapes/MCQ cards

	First	Each extra	
UK	£2.00	£1.00	£ ____
Europe*	£2.50	£1.00	£ ____
Rest of world	£15.00	£8.00	£ ____

Breakthrough Videos

	First	Each extra	
UK	£2.00	£2.00	£ ____
Europe*	£2.00	£2.00	£ ____
Rest of world	£20.00	£10.00	£ ____

Grand Total (Cheques to *BPP Publishing*) I enclose
a cheque for (incl. Postage) £ ☐
Or charge to Access/Visa/Switch
Card Number ☐☐☐☐☐☐☐☐☐☐☐☐
Expiry date _____ Start Date _____
Issue Number (Switch Only) _____
Signature _____

We aim to deliver to all UK addresses inside 5 working days; a signature will be required. Orders to all EU addresses should be delivered within 6 working days. All other orders to overseas addresses should be delivered within 8 working days. * Europe includes the Republic of Ireland and the Channel Islands.